W9-BVC-438

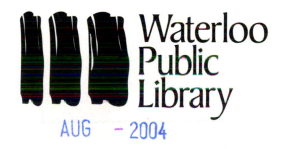

Waterloo
Public
Library

AUG - 2004

Reference Collection
Adult Department

How It Works®

Science and Technology

Third Edition

Marshall Cavendish
99 White Plains Road
Tarrytown, NY 10591

Website: www.marshallcavendish.com

© 2003 Marshall Cavendish Corporation
HOW IT WORKS is a registered trademark of Marshall Cavendish Corporation

Third edition updated by Brown Reference Group plc.

All rights reserved. No part of this book may be reproduced or utilized in
any form or by any means electronic or mechanical, including photocopying,
recording, or by any information storage and retrieval system, without
prior written permission from the publisher and copyright holder.

Library of Congress Cataloging-in-Publication Data
How it works: science and technology.—3rd ed.
p. cm.
Includes index.
ISBN 0-7614-7314-9 (set)   ISBN 0-7614-7327-0 (Vol. 13)
1. Technology—Encyclopedias. 2. Science—Encyclopedias.
[1. Technology—Encyclopedias. 2. Science—Encyclopedias.]
T9 .H738 2003
603—dc21   2001028771

Consultant: Donald R. Franceschetti, Ph.D., University of Memphis

Brown Reference Group
Editor: Wendy Horobin
Associate Editors: Paul Thompson, Martin Clowes, Lis Stedman
Managing Editor: Tim Cooke
Design: Alison Gardner
Picture Research: Becky Cox
Illustrations: Mark Walker, Darren Awuah

Marshall Cavendish
Project Editor: Peter Mavrikis
Production Manager: Alan Tsai
Editorial Director: Paul Bernabeo

Printed in Malaysia
Bound in the United States of America
08 07 06 05 04   6 5 4 3 2

Title picture: Reel-to-reel projector, see *Projector, Movie and Slide*

How It Works®

Science and Technology

Volume 13

Physiology

Pyramid

Marshall Cavendish

New York • London • Toronto • Sydney

WATERLOO PUBLIC LIBRARY

Contents

Volume 13

Physiology	1733	Polygraph	1807
Piano	1735	Polymer and Polymerization	1809
Pickup, Acoustic	1739	Polytetrafluoroethylene	
Picture Restoration	1741	(Teflon)	1814
Piezoelectric Material	1744	Population	1816
Pile Driver	1746	Potential Energy	1820
Pilotless Aircraft	1747	Potentiometer	1821
Pipe and Tube Manufacture	1749	Powder Coating	1823
Pipeline	1753	Power	1825
Planetarium Projector	1755	Power Plant	1827
Planetary Science	1757	Power Supply	1833
Plasma Physics	1762	Pressure	1839
Plastic Surgery	1764	Pressure Cooker	1841
Plastics	1768	Pressure Gauge	1842
Plastics Processing	1773	Printed Circuit	1844
Plate Tectonics	1777	Printing	1847
Platinum Metals	1781	Prism	1853
Plumbing	1784	Projector, Movie and Slide	1854
Pneumatic Tool	1788	Propeller	1858
Poison	1790	Protective Clothing	1860
Polarimeter	1793	Protein	1864
Polarization	1794	Psychiatry	1867
Pollution Monitoring		Pulley	1869
and Control	1797	Pyramid	1870
Polyamide	1804		

Physiology

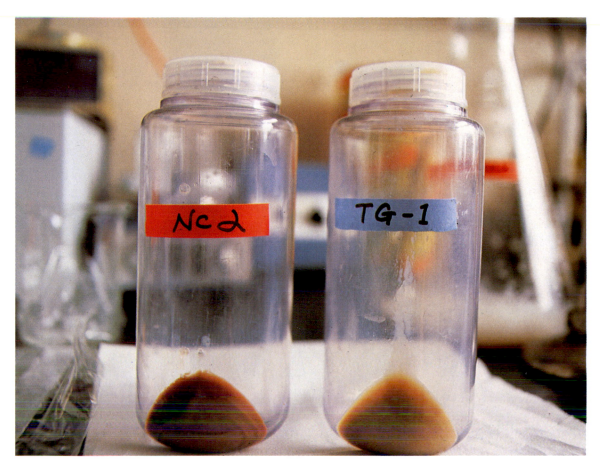

◀ Synthetic human hemoglobin, which can be used as a blood substitute. It was developed by American and British scientists using genetic-engineering techniques and the bacterium *E. coli*. The bottle on the left contains bacterial cells producing hemoglobin, which is red in color, while the one on the right consists of normal *E. coli,* which have no hemoglobin production.

Physiology is the study of the functions and activities of organisms and their tissues and cells. Physiology thus includes the traditional subjects of the movement, nutrition, metabolism, excretion, reproduction, and behavior of living things. Investigations into the physiology of microorganisms belong to microbiology; plant physiology is part of botany. As well as being a fundamental experimental science in itself, physiology has wide applications in human and veterinary medicine, in agriculture, in industry, and in environmental science.

Although the ancient Greeks were interested in physiology, modern experimental physiology is considered to have begun in 1616 with the discovery, by the British physician William Harvey, of the circulation of blood. Prior to this discovery, scientists thought that blood moved by a tidal ebb and flow. Other important discoveries followed, many of which were dependent on the development of microscopy by scientists, such as the Dutch amateur physiologist Anton van Leeuwenhoek. Leeuwenhoek made careful observations of a wide range of organisms and tissues and was the first to observe protozoa, bacteria, red blood cells, and spermatazoa. Physiology, however, remained closely tied to the study of medicine until the 19th century, when it began to develop into a distinct discipline involving aspects of physics, chemistry, and the study of anatomy.

In the 20th century, advances in physics and chemistry led to the development of a number of important scientific fields related to physiology, such as biophysics, biochemistry, and molecular biology. These fields of study have led to significant discoveries in areas such as genetics and cell biology as well as medical research.

Recent developments

Many physiologists study functions at the level of the molecule or of individual cells. These investigations have, for example, given us a new insight into how potassium and calcium pass through channels in the membranes of cells to cause the transmission of a nerve impulse or bring about a muscle contraction. Much research is carried out on cells grown in culture. For instance, mouse pituitary gland cells have been genetically altered to produce human insulin. In early 1992, physiologists at the University of Texas Southwestern Medical Center successfully demonstrated that such cells will secrete stored insulin when glucose seeps into them from the medium surrounding them. This discovery has raised the possibility of developing an artificial pancreas that could be implanted in diabetics. More recent research, however, has focused on the transplantation of insulin producing cells (islets of Langerhans cells) from a healthy pancreas into the liver of a person with diabetes, where they will secrete insulin directly into the circulatory system. Although this procedure is still considered experimental, the early results have been promising, and researchers expect the transplant of islets of Langerhans cells to become commonplace in the near future.

In 2001, another area of diabetes research led to the discovery that in mice with type 1 diabetes—where the diabetes is caused by the immune system attacking the islets of Langerhans —the immune system may be retrained to stop attacking these cells. The islets of Langerhans are then able to recover and produce insulin once more. Researchers hope that this discovery may lead to a similar treatment for humans.

Often it is necessary for physiologists to examine the whole animal, because a particular response may involve a number of tissues and organs. For example, motor neuron diseases result from the degeneration and death of nerve cells in the spinal cord and brain, leading to progressive muscle weakness. Frequently, the outcome is fatal because of respiratory paralysis. The first hope that a therapeutic strategy for these devastating diseases might be possible was reported in August 1992. Danish and German scientists influenced the course of the disease in affected mice with a growth-promoting factor that rescued the motor neurons from degeneration.

With the development of many new rejection-suppressing drugs, it is becoming possible to transplant animal organs (xenotransplants) into humans, thus overcoming the chronic shortage of donors. In June 1992, a baboon's liver was successfully transplanted into a 35-year-old man in Pennsylvania. Although he survived only two months, his death was due to infection, not rejection. Pig's livers have also been transplanted into humans as a temporary replacement until a human donor can be found. The next area of development in organ replacement, however, is in genetic engineering. Scientists are currently experimenting with techniques to insert human genes into animal organs so that the human immune system will not reject the organ as being foreign to the body.

Reproductive research

Few areas of physiological research have had as great an impact on human behavior as that which led to a revolution in birth control—the development of the contraceptive pill. During the 1950s,

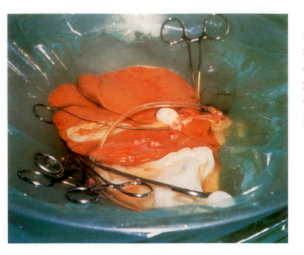
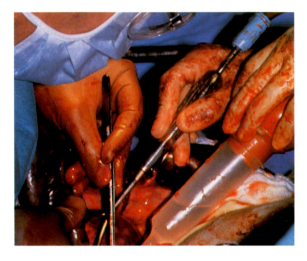
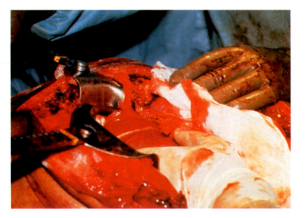

◄ These three photographs show surgeons at the University of Pittsburgh Medical School performing the first transplant of a baboon's liver into a human recipient.

doctors Pincus, Rock, and Change demonstrated at the Worcester Foundation in Massachusetts that ovulation could be suppressed with synthetic hormones. The contraceptive pill, licensed by the Food and Drug Administration in 1960, is currently used by over 60 million women worldwide. It has an extraordinarily low failure rate when used properly—less than two pregnancies per thousand users per year.

SEE ALSO: BIOCHEMISTRY • BIOPHYSICS • BIOTECHNOLOGY • CANCER TREATMENT • CELL BIOLOGY • ENZYME • HORMONE • SURGERY • TRANSPLANT

Piano

The complexity of the modern piano is second only to that of the organ. This complexity arises from the nature of its sound production compared with its ancestors, the clavichord and the harpsichord. These instruments share the fact that the strings are activated through the depression of a key, but the means of striking the strings is different in each.

Clavichord

The clavichord became prominent among instrumentalists in the 16th century and was obsolete by 1800. The right-hand (treble) end of the box-shaped case contains the soundboard, the bridge, and the tuning pins; the left-hand (bass) end contains the keyboard. The strings are stretched across horizontally. The action is a simple tangent action; that is, the key is pivoted in the middle and when it is depressed, a small brass blade called the tangent rises on the other end and strikes the string smartly. When the string is struck, it is divided into two parts between the hitch pin and the bridge. The right-hand part vibrates and the left-hand part is damped by a piece of felt.

The clavichord has a soft sound best suited for domestic music making, but it is unique among prepiano keyboard instruments in that dynamic range is possible.

Harpsichord

The harpsichord reached its peak of popularity in the 17th and 18th centuries. When a key is depressed, a jack carrying a plectrum and a damper rises past the string. The end of the plectrum is angled upward so that it plucks the string as it rises. The top of the jack is hinged and lightly spring-loaded with a bristle, and the string turns it aside as it falls. A felt damper just above the plectrum prevents the string from sounding.

A simple harpsichord, with one set of strings, was known as a spinet, or a virginal in Britain; more usually, the harpsichord has two, three, or

▲ Internal view of an upright piano in which the strings are mounted vertically. The upright design, of a size suitable for the ordinary home, became very popular in the 19th century.

four sets of strings, each with its own set of jacks. The sets of strings are tuned in unison and the player can select or stop out different sets by means of slides that move an entire set of jacks to hit or miss the strings. This procedure varies the tone as well as the volume of the instrument.

Piano

Early in the 18th century, instrument makers began trying to build an instrument with a more variable tone than that of the harpsichord. This led to the invention of the instrument that is the ancestor of the piano, which is generally credited to Italian harpsichord maker Bartolomeo Cristofori, a Paduan who was Keeper of Musical Instruments for a Medici prince. A letter written in 1711 praises "the piano and forte (soft and loud) in the theme and its answer, (and) the gradual lessening of the tone little by little, and then suddenly returning to the full power of the instrument." By 1731, music was being especially written for the new instrument.

Piano action

The essence of the piano's individuality is a felt-covered hammer that is thrown up at the string and rebounds immediately, regardless of the action of the player. Since the hammer is projected rather than carried, it is necessary for it to move faster than the key that sets it in motion. The intervening levers between the key and the hammer are called the action, though in common usage the action has come to mean all the parts.

For maximum control of the dynamic level created by the velocity of the hammer, a device called the backcheck is fitted that catches the hammer on its return and thus prevents the possibility of dampening caused by rebound. The escapement moves aside the jack or, in the case of a grand, a grand jack, which lifts the hammer so as to allow the hammer to fall back farther than it was lifted regardless of whether the key is kept depressed or not. Modern grand pianos have a repetition action, or double escapement, that stops the return of the hammer at an intermediate stage, allowing for rapid repetition of the same note.

The keys control not only hammers but also dampers, which rise with the depression of the key and return to damp the sound when the key is let loose. The dampers are also connected to rods at each end of their rank that are operated by another rod connected to the right pedal called the damper, or loud, pedal. This raises all the dampers at once, allowing, first, all the strings to vibrate whether struck or not, giving added resonance and tone quality, and, second, the player to move from one note or chord to another without a break in the sound caused by damping. The left

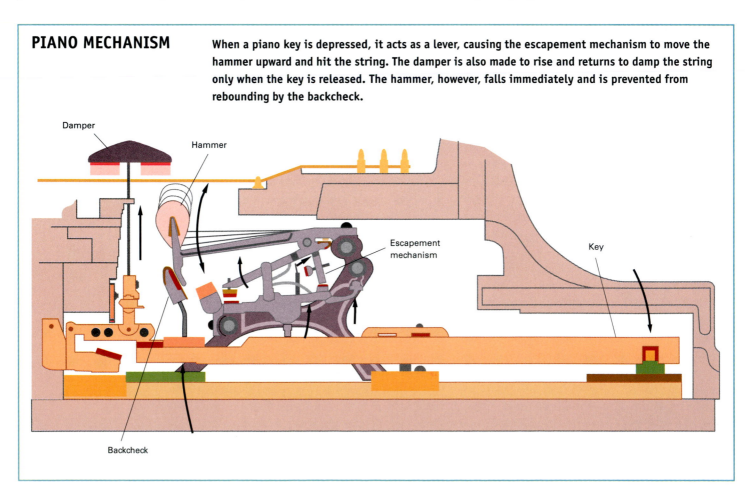

PIANO MECHANISM When a piano key is depressed, it acts as a lever, causing the escapement mechanism to move the hammer upward and hit the string. The damper is also made to rise and returns to damp the string only when the key is released. The hammer, however, falls immediately and is prevented from rebounding by the backcheck.

Damper

Hammer

Escapement mechanism

Key

Backcheck

pedal, called the una corda, or soft pedal, moves the whole mechanism to the right so that the hammer strikes only two (instead of all three) of the treble strings. This device produces a thin, softer tone that is used sparingly for a coloristic effect. Most concert grands today have a third pedal, called the sostenuto, or sustaining pedal, which holds off only those dampers connected to the keys being struck.

Strings

While Cristofori's first instrument used a new method of making the strings vibrate, at first the sound produced was not very different from that of the harpsichord. The harpsichord action was very efficient in terms of energy transference, because the strings were light and able to absorb all the energy from the plectrum. This lightness, however, meant that the ability to vary the speed (and therefore the force) with which the hammer struck the string was negated by the limited ability of the light string to absorb the new energy. Until 1834, the wire was made from iron or brass, producing a biting though relatively quiet tone. Steel wire was introduced by a piano maker from Birmingham, England; the firm of Webster and Horsfall vied throughout the 19th century with the Viennese firm of Muller. Steel has an extremely high tensile strength, and it is this feature that is responsible for the power of the modern grand piano.

The pitch of a vibrating string depends on three factors: its length, its mass per unit length, and the tension it is under. Reducing the string's length by half yields a note an octave higher. To produce bass notes without requiring unmanageably long strings, the bass strings are made thicker and have copper wire coiled around them. Piano strings are tuned by adjusting the tension applied to them; increased tension raises the pitch. Increases in thickness and tension of the strings meant that throughout the 19th century the frame of the developing instrument was constantly having to be strengthened.

Construction

The piece of wood (actually made from several pieces) above which the strings are strung is called the soundboard. As the soundboard controls the amplification of the small displacement of air caused by the vibration of the strings, it is an important element in the tone of the instrument. The chosen wood must transmit sound quickly and with little absorption; the best woods, such as Rumanian pine, Canadian Sitka spruce, Norway spruce, and silver fir, transmit sound at up to 14 times the speed through air. The position of the

◀ Balancing the checks, which catch the hammers on their return in order to prevent rebound.

strings relative to the soundboard also has an effect on the instrument's tone.

Early pianos were of wooden construction, like harpsichords. But as the piano developed, thicker strings and tighter stringing made stronger frames necessary, and metal bars were introduced into the piano cabinet. In 1820, a design was patented using a combination of metal bars and plates of different metals. Based on the principle of thermal expansion of different metals suggested by pendulums in clocks, this frame allowed the hitch pins holding the strings to move slightly according to their temperature. The first casting of an all-metal frame complete with hitch pin block was carried out in Boston in 1825. Three years later pianos were made with cross-stringing, so that the long bass strings passed over the others. This design is commonly used today and adds greater richness to the bass tone, as well as making possible a more compact cabinet design.

A German single-action design lasted through the 18th century, and many pianos had a hand stop for raising the dampers. The German piano maker Andreas Stein invented the escapement mechanism, and in England, in 1783, John Broadwood patented the damper pedal. John Isaac Hawkins, an Englishman who lived in the United States, developed the soft pedal, which, by grading the thickness of strips of cloth or leather from one edge to the other, enables the player to fake a diminuendo or a crescendo by gradually introducing or withdrawing the pedal. By the end of the 18th century, Broadwood became preeminent among English piano makers for the introduction of an up-striking grand action as well as for experiments with regard to the striking place of the hammers on the strings.

During the 19th century, America began to make an impact on the industry, with such firms as Chickering and Steinway showing their wares at international exhibitions. America also possessed the Merino sheep, whose wool was found to be best for compression into felt for hammers, although much work on hammers was also done by the British makers Whitehead and Naish.

The need for more compact pianos suitable for domestic settings led to the development in the 18th century of the upright piano. The first upright pianos were very tall, like grands on edge, and had strange-shaped cabinets. In 1800, Hawkins took the strings down to floor level, giving the low, square shape of the modern upright. The British piano maker Robert Wornum was another important designer of uprights, and by 1860, uprights had replaced other domestic pianos, such as square pianos, for home use.

Player piano

The first mechanical player piano was a device that was placed in front of an ordinary piano, and the piano played by means of hammers that struck the keys. Later the mechanism was installed inside an enlarged piano cabinet, and the instrument became known as a player piano.

The earliest players were operated mechanically by planchettes, small wooden boards studded with projecting pins that played the notes by means of a system of levers. Some instruments were operated by means of slotted and folded cards, like those used today in fairground organs.

The modern player piano, which reached its peak of popularity in the 1920s, is a pneumatic device that uses a roll of paper with perforations. The roll is 11.75 in. (30 cm) wide and the perforations are spaced nine per inch (2.5 cm). The spool box, with a tracker bar, is placed in front of the operator behind the keyboard; the drive mechanism is placed on the right-hand side. Directly underneath is the valve chest, and underneath the keyboard are the suction bellows, or exhausters, operated by pedals. The expression-controlling devices are also located here: the sustaining (loud) pedal and the half-blow (soft) pedal, together with any accentuating mechanisms. The pedals of the piano are operated by two large pneumatics activated by perforations in the margin of the roll.

Operation

The performer, having placed the roll in the spool box and hitched the leader to the take-up spool, starts pedaling. This action exhausts the main pneumatic chest, and the drive motor moves the roll forward. The speed is controlled by the tempo lever on the front of the keyboard. Usually the tempo is printed on the paper: 40 means 4 ft. (1.2 m) per minute, and so on. Underneath the right-hand end of the keyboard, a suction governor is connected in a tube from the motor to the exhausters. Moving the tempo lever also moves a

slide valve that, in conjunction with a pneumatic coupled to another slide valve in the governor, regulates the suction on the motor, controlling the speed independent of the pedaling.

As the first perforation opens a hole in the tracker bar, air passes in and lifts a soft leather diaphragm, which in turn lifts a poppet valve that opens a port to the small note pneumatic connecting it to the suction chest. This pneumatic closes quickly and operates the piano hammer in the same manner as if the key were struck. When the perforation has gone past, air is cut off from the diaphragm, which returns to its original position. The poppet valve drops, cutting off suction from the pneumatic, which opens, allowing the hammer to fall back and the note to be damped. Equalization of air pressure takes place through a tiny hole by-passing the diaphragm.

The degree of suction determines the loudness of the music. Expression is achieved mainly by pedaling lightly or heavily, but many player pianos have alternative means, making it possible to accentuate chords or single notes; it is in these devices that the various makes of player pianos differ. In the case of the Pianola (trade name of the Aeolian Company), the pneumatics are divided into 44 notes in each half. The loudness of each can be subdued with respect to the other by means of levers operating sliding valves connected to section governors in an arrangement similar to that controlling the speed of the driving motor. Therefore, it is possible, for example, for the melody (right-hand piano part) to be played more loudly than the accompaniment (left-hand, or bass, part).

▲ The music room in the house of Ludwig van Beethoven's brother, Johann. Beethoven would have played a piano like this when staying there.

 SEE ALSO: Jukebox • Organ, musical • Phonography

Pickup, Acoustic

Pickup is a general term for a transducer that converts signals—usually associated with music and musical instruments—into an electric form. In record players and the transcription units of hi-fi systems, the pickup converts the mechanical vibrations of the stylus moving in the record groove into an electric signal for amplification. Such devices are more commonly known as cartridges and may be either ceramic, capacitive, or magnetic, depending on the method of conversion. The term pickup is usually reserved for electric guitars and related stringed instruments.

Guitar pickup

Guitar devices pick up the vibrations of the strings by the principle of induced magnetism. The strings must consequently be of steel or some other magnetic material. A steel string, when placed in a magnetic field, will distort that field. The reason for this phenomenon is that the magnetic flux will take the path of least reluctance—that is, least resistance to the flow of flux—and steel has a lower reluctance than air. A coil of wire is placed in the vicinity of the strings. When the string moves the magnetic field, the flux pattern will change, thus inducing a voltage in the coil. By connecting the coil terminals to an amplifier, a manageable signal can be obtained.

In practice, a small permanent magnet is placed under each string—or a bar magnet is placed underneath all the strings—six in all for a guitar and four for a bass guitar. Around these is placed a coil consisting of many turns of light-gauge insulated copper wire. The coil terminals are taken to a socket on the instrument for connection to amplifier and speakers.

This is the simplest arrangement possible and in principle the best. There is, however, one major drawback with this system. Given the environment of the electric guitarist, usually situated among a mass of electronic equipment, the pickup will respond to any stray magnetic fields, and hum will thus become a problem.

Eliminating hum

As it is not possible to eliminate the stray magnetic fields emanating from electric cables at source, they must be eliminated at the pickup. This goal is achieved by an arrangement of two coils such that the hum in one of the coils cancels out that in the other, while the signals in each coil combine to produce a stronger signal.

In this arrangement, rather than having 12 separate permanent magnets (six for each coil), one long and slender bar magnet is used. It is arranged so that the poles are along the two long narrow faces of the bar, which is mounted flat under the strings with its long axis across them. Along the pole faces, mounted vertically, are 12 soft-iron pole pieces, which concentrate the field

▼ The guitar pickup. A magnet is placed near a steel string and a concentration of magnetic flux lines appears around the string. The string vibrates, and the vibrating flux pattern induces a similarly oscillating voltage in the pickup. Hum is eliminated by two coils wound in opposite directions.

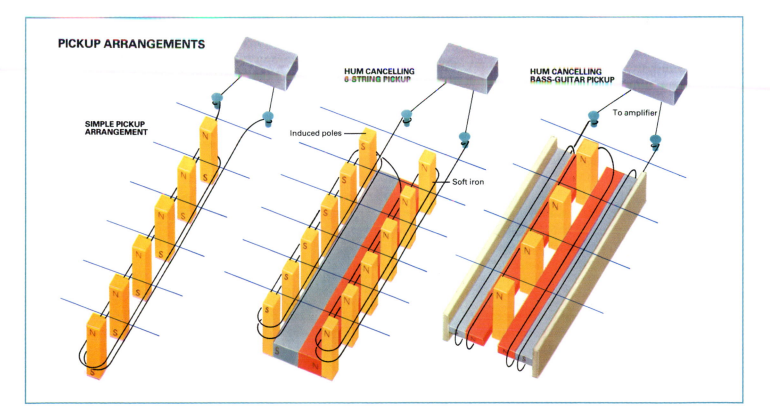

PICKUP ARRANGEMENTS

SIMPLE PICKUP ARRANGEMENT

HUM CANCELLING 6-STRING PICKUP

Induced poles

Soft iron

HUM CANCELLING BASS-GUITAR PICKUP

To amplifier

 A Yamaha semiacoustic guitar with two pickups. Electric guitars are significantly louder than acoustic guitars and produce a different sound.

in the vicinity of the strings. The north pole pieces form one line and the south poles a second line so that there is one north and one south pole to each string. The coils around the two sets of poles are wound in opposite directions and connected together in series.

The net signal is the sum of the signals in the two coils, because although they are wound in opposite directions, the poles associated with each are likewise opposites. With stray external magnetic fields, however, the winding arrangement causes cancellation of any hum.

A similar arrangement is made for the four-string bass guitar pickup, but it is usually of a sturdier construction so that low-frequency vibrations do not create a fuzzy signal. Two bar magnets are used instead of one, placed side by side in a south-north-south configuration with two coils (again wound in opposite directions) lengthwise around the two bars. The flat soft-iron pole pieces are attached to the outer south poles and four vertical pole pieces, concentrating the field near the strings, positioned along the central north pole.

Design

One of the advantages of using pickups on guitars is the increased volume levels that are possible. Electric guitars also produce sounds that are quite distinct from acoustic guitars. Placing the pickup near the bridge, for example, produces a more jangly sound, while placing the pickup near the

neck results in a richer and deeper tone. One problem, however, is that—particularly with pickups on bass guitars—vibrations in the pickup and between it and the guitar body lead to a low-quality signal. In such a situation, pickups are mounted firmly on a solid brass plate that is attached to the instrument. With bass guitars, this plate is usually placed in a recess in the wooden body of the instrument.

Because the coil has an associated inductance, this, coupled with any stray capacitance in the system, leads to a characteristic resonant frequency determined by the values of capacitance and inductance. This means that the circuit offers less resistance to an oscillating current at one frequency than at any other. If this resonant frequency occurs somewhere in the instrument's range of notes, then one note will be louder. Consequently, the pole pieces can be adjusted to obtain a fairly uniform signal at all frequencies. With the double-coil arrangement, one set of poles is adjustable while the others are fixed.

Other instruments have also been adapted for use with pickups. They include the Wurlitzer piano, where electrostatic pickups convert the movement of reeds into electrical signals; the Hammond organ, where the pickups are on tone wheels; and the Hohner Clavinet, where the pickups are on strings.

▶ A six-string electric guitar pickup. It has two coils of wire so arranged that any stray magnetic fields from electric currents cancel each other out.

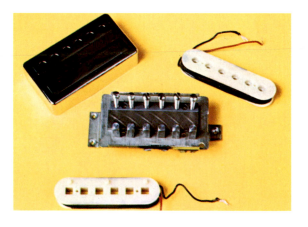

▶ A single-coil pickup. The coil forms a complete circuit, and the frequency response is corrected by adjusting the pole heights.

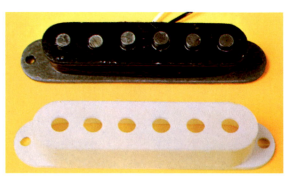

SEE ALSO: AMPLIFIER • INDUCTION • MAGNETISM • PHONOGRAPHY • STRINGED INSTRUMENT • TRANSDUCER AND SENSOR

Picture Restoration

Picture restorers and conservators are increasingly guided by the methods of analytical science. A well-known example is the use of X rays to detect forgeries, overpainted pictures, or changes of composition by the artist. Simple color photography for recording all stages of treatment is also important as well as infrared photography for showing underdrawings and ultraviolet fluorescent photography for observing changes on the surface of a painting.

As well as microscopes, conservators also use an X-ray macroprobe, a fine-focus fluorescent spectrograph, to help in the analysis of paint and varnish. This device enables picture restorers to accurately restore damaged areas of paintings.

Although picture restoration is probably the better-known term, emphasis is placed more today on conservation—that is, maintaining a painting in a stable state by correct storage and treatment and thus delaying the rate of decay and the necessity for restoration. Restoring a picture to its original appearance is only one aspect of the conservation of paintings.

Structure of paintings

Paint consists of a colored material in powder form (the pigment) mixed with a liquid that sets to a hard film (the medium). The main structural layer of a painting is known as the support.

When they are dry, oil paintings are usually varnished to improve their appearance and to protect the surface from damage. In the past, varnishing was done with a natural resin dissolved in an organic liquid. Natural resins, such as dammar and copal, discolor badly with time; discoloration is one of the main reasons why paintings have to be cleaned and revarnished.

Easel paintings

Conservation and restoration of easel paintings fall into two main categories: treatment of the support and treatment of the painted surface. In most cases, the support layers must be made secure before work is done on the front of a painting.

Wood panels used for painting have a problem in common with all wooden objects in that they expand and contract widthwise across the grain as

▲ The restored *Last Supper* by Leonardo da Vinci. This controversial restoration took 22 years to complete—almost two decades longer than it took Leonardo to paint it.

◄ The painstaking restoration of Leonardo's *Last Supper* began in 1977 and was not completed until 1999.

the humidity of the air changes. This movement can lead to warping, cracking, and loosening of the original joints in the panel. However, more damage is done in trying physically to prevent the movement than in allowing it to proceed under controlled atmospheric conditions. In the past, bars of wood and complicated slotted wooden grids were glued to the back of panels to prevent them from warping. When the panel tried to move, it strained against the restriction, and splits and corrugations developed at the weakest points. Today restorers favor removal of all such restrictions, and the panels are flattened under their own weight in conditions of high humidity. The moisture content is then made stable by sealing the back of the panel with a water-impervious layer known as a moisture barrier. Various methods have also been devised for joining splits and strengthening or supporting weak panels without restricting their movement.

Canvas supports are less susceptible to atmospheric changes than wood, but they have the disadvantage of being easily torn or dented. Also their flexibility can cause brittle paint to flake, curl, or crack. Weak or torn canvases and loose paint are often treated by lining the painting: gluing a new piece of canvas to the back of the original canvas using a suitable adhesive. In cases where the paint is loose, the adhesive is made to penetrate both canvases to fix the paint in place.

When the support is secure, the paint layers may be treated. The cleaning of a painting means the removal not only of dirt but also of discolored varnish layers and retouchings put on in the past to cover older damage. Suitable solvents or solvent mixtures—usually alcohol based—are applied to the painting on small swabs of cotton wool that absorb the old varnish and retouchings as they dissolve.

After cleaning, damaged areas of the painting are retouched using pigments ground in a clear synthetic resin as the medium. The painting is then revarnished, but because varnishes made of natural resins, such as mastic, copal, and dammar,

◄ One of the restorers with a special photograph that pinpoints cracks and bulges in the wall on which Leonardo painted the *Last Supper*.

tend to become yellow and brittle with age, conservationists today prefer to replace these resins with synthetic varnishes. Varnishes such as polycyclohexanones and acrylic copolymers are commonly used; they are more chemically stable and are also easier to remove than natural resins.

In some cases, a restoration technique called inpainting is employed where the restorer fills damaged areas with colors chosen to match the colors surrounding the damaged area. With this technique, great care is taken not to obscure any of the original surrounding paint. Inpainting is carried out only after the painting has been varnished, thus providing a protective layer between the old paint and any new paint that may be accidently applied outside of the damaged area. It also enables the easy removal of the new paint by future conservationists.

Watercolors

A common problem of watercolors on paper is that they are easily stained by contact with materials such as animal glues and inferior types of backing boards. Often watercolors have been mounted on cards with glues that are breeding grounds for molds and small insects, and the first task of the restorer will usually be to remove everything from the reverse of the paper. Stains are then removed by local or overall treatment with very mild bleach solutions, followed by extremely thorough washing with pure water to remove all traces of the bleach.

After treatment, the watercolor painting is lightly attached to best-quality card with hinges of thin paper before framing. Watercolors must never be exposed to strong light, as the delicate colors will often fade.

Wall paintings

Murals, or wall paintings, pose unique problems for the conservator, because treatments almost always have to be carried out where the paintings stand, without the aid of the restorer's studio.

The main enemy of wall paintings and frescoes is damp, soaking down from the roof of the building or upward from the earth bringing with it salts that crystallize within and on the surface of the painting. The colored surface may then swell and fall off, revealing large pockets of powdery calcium sulfate. To solve this particular problem, the fresco is treated with solutions that precipitate barium sulfate throughout the plaster layer—it is insoluble, inert, and forms a hard, strong network protecting and reinforcing the plaster.

Sometimes the only way of saving a fresco is to remove it from the wall and mount it on a stronger support—a process known as transfer.

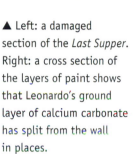

▲ Left: a damaged section of the *Last Supper*. Right: a cross section of the layers of paint shows that Leonardo's ground layer of calcium carbonate has split from the wall in places.

The technique is simply described but requires great skill to carry it out without damaging the painting: two layers of cloth are carefully glued to the face of the fresco, left to dry, and then pulled away from the wall, bringing the fresco with them. There are different degrees of transfer called strappo and stacco, depending on whether only the color layers are removed or the outer layer of plaster as well. In the case of strappo, once the fresco has been removed, synthetic resins are used to apply it to a rigid board, while in stacco, the back surface of plaster is made smooth before it is applied to a board. A bonus of stacco transfer is that the preliminary drawings for frescoes are often revealed: they are named sinopie after the red pigment used and are sometimes very beautiful works of art themselves.

▶ A low-power upright binocular microscope was used to view the painting when minute sections were being repainted.

SEE ALSO: Chemistry, analytical • Lacquer and varnish • Microscope, optical • Paint • X-ray imaging

Piezoelectric Material

Piezo derives from the Greek verb *piezein*—"to press"—and piezoelectricity is a separation of charge that occurs when pressure is applied to a piezoelectric material. The piezoelectric effect occurs only in certain crystalline electrical insulators, and the charge separation is manifested by an electrical potential difference between opposite faces of a crystal. A converse effect to piezoelectricity also exists: when an electrical field is applied to a piezoelectric crystal, the crystal becomes distorted as long as the field is present.

Most piezoelectric materials are ionic salts, which consist of positively charged cations and negatively charged anions. In the solid state, these ions form a regular lattice that is described by a unit cell—the smallest group of ions that represents the whole structure of the cell—and a crystal can be thought of as a three-dimensional array of unit cells. A few piezoelectric materials are highly polar crystalline polymers, such as polyvinylidene chloride (a polymer of 1,1-dichloroethene, CH_2CHCl_2).

Any unit cell has a center of positive charge and a center of negative charge; these are the average positions of the positive and negative charge respectively. If the two charge centers coincide, the unit cell has no electrical dipole. If they do not coincide, the unit cell has a dipole proportional to the magnitude of the charges and the distance between the centers of positive and negative charges in the unit cell.

Whether or not a crystalline material exhibits piezoelectricity depends on whether the unit cell has a center of symmetry, that is a point about which the atoms are symmetrically arranged. Pressure distorts any type of unit cell, but the centers continue to coincide in a cell with a center of symmetry under compression. In the case of an asymmetrical cell, pressure can cause distortions that change the distance between the centers of positive and negative charges, thereby altering the electrical dipole. When such a distortion happens in a single crystal, the tiny dipoles of all the unit cells combine to form a powerful electrical field. Of the 32 standard unit cells, 20 have the asymmetry necessary for piezoelectric properties.

Constants of piezoelectricity

The piezoelectric constant, *d*, is defined as the ratio of strain (deformation per unit length) to applied electrical field. Its standard unit of measurement is the meter per volt (m/V). The piezoelectric constant applies both to the deformation caused by an applied electrical field and to the

electrical field caused by deformation. Quartz has a piezoelectric constant of 3×10^{-12} m/V. Thus, the thickness of an appropriately cut slice of quartz will change by 3 nm for every kilovolt of potential difference applied across its two faces. This dimensional change is largely independent of the original thickness of the slice.

Another measure of the piezoelectric effect is the electromechanical coupling constant, *K*. This constant is the fraction of the electrical energy converted into mechanical energy by the piezoelectric effect, or vice versa. It is therefore an indication of how well a material can perform in transducers, which are energy-converting devices.

Piezoelectric materials

One of the most widely used piezoelectric materials is quartz, a crystalline form of silicon dioxide (SiO_2). Quartz is useful because of its chemical stability and because of the strong mechanical resonance that occurs when stimulated by an alternating voltage whose frequency coincides with the resonant frequency of the crystal. This resonant frequency is determined by the dimensions of the crystal and is the basis of the use of quartz crystals in electronic timing circuits.

Other crystalline piezoelectric materials include ammonium dihydrogenphosphate (ADP, $NH_4H_2PO_4$) and potassium sodium tartrate (Rochelle salt, $KNaC_4H_4O_6 \cdot 4H_2O$). These materials have stronger piezoelectric responses than quartz, and they are used in many low-cost devices. Because they are mechanically weak relative to quartz, it is difficult to cut their crystals to

▲ Rochelle salt, viewed under polarized light. This salt—potassium sodium tartrate tetrahydrate ($KNaC_4H_4O_6 \cdot 4H_2O$)—was one of the compounds in which the piezoelectric effect was first observed.

precise dimensions. They also decompose at moderate temperatures and absorb water, so they must be protected from heat and moisture.

Many piezoelectric materials are ceramic mixed-metal oxides, which are cheaper than quartz and can be made in any size or shape. Suitable ceramics consist of asymmetrical microcrystals that can change their orientation above a threshold temperature, called the Curie point. Piezoelectric ceramics are made by fusing such a substance and then allowing it to cool through the Curie point in a strong electrical field. Above that temperature, the microcrystals tend to align themselves with the field—an effect called poling. Below the Curie point, the orientations of the microcrystals remain frozen in the material, which continues to exhibit the piezoelectric effect unless it is heated beyond its Curie point in the absence of an electrical field.

Piezoelectric ceramics include barium titanate ($BaTiO_3$) and lead zirconate titanate (PZT, approximately $PbZr_{0.5}Ti_{0.5}O_2$). These materials form the basis for two families of materials whose exact properties depend on chemical composition and the conditions of preparation. For example, chemical composition can be modified until the Curie point is above the intended working temperature range of the material.

Applications as transducers

Piezoelectric materials find uses in applications where mechanical and electric energy must be interconverted. The mechanical displacements and movements of electrical charge tend to be of limited magnitudes in these applications.

Piezoelectrics are used in microphones and ultrasound detectors, where they convert the oscillations of a diaphragm, caused by incident pressure waves, into a varying electrical signal. A related use is in record-player pickups, where the force from the stylus varies between 0.01 and 0.05 N and the resulting output signal varies from 0.1 to 0.5 volts. Ceramics are used in both cases.

Piezoelectric ceramics are also used in ignition devices. Pressures of around 7,000 psi (50 MPa) can produce potential differences in the range of 13,000 to 39,000 volts per in. (around 5,000–15,000 V/cm), so a small chip of piezoelectric can produce sparking voltages at easily manageable pressures. Such devices are used in "electronic" lighters and ignition systems for gas stoves and heating appliances.

Resonant applications

Solid objects often have natural frequencies at which they vibrate elastically when stimulated by a physical blow or some other energy input. Near their resonant frequencies, the efficiency with which piezoelectrics interconvert mechanical and electrical energy increases dramatically. This effect is used in ultrasound devices, whose resonant frequencies typically lie between 20 kHz and 100 kHz. In ultrasound sources, stimulation by an electrical signal at or near the resonant frequency produces intense ultrasonic vibrations. These can cause an effect called cavitation in liquids, whereby voids form and collapse as pressure waves pass through the liquid. Such physical disturbance is used to dislodge dirt from objects in ultrasonic cleaning baths and as a means of increasing the rates of chemical reactions.

Piezoelectric ultrasound sensors resonate in the frequency range that they are designed to detect. They produce an oscillating electrical signal when struck by ultrasonic waves, and this property makes them useful in detecting ultrasound echoes to probe the depth and extent of underwater reflectors, such as submarine craft and wrecks and shoals of fish. The same principle is used in ultrasound body scanning to form images of fetuses and internal organs.

The resonant frequencies of quartz crystals are particularly well defined when compared with those of ceramic piezoelectrics. This makes quartz the material of choice in frequency benchmarks for electronic circuits. In contrast, ceramic piezoelectrics are useful as ultrasound sources and detectors, since they respond well over a broad range of near-resonant frequencies.

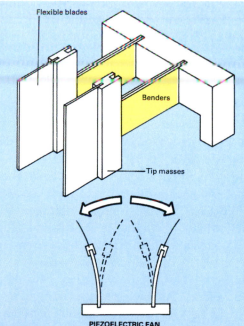

PIEZOELECTRIC FAN

Flexible blades

Benders

Tip masses

◄ A bilayer of metal and piezoelectric material can be used to drive a fan. The metal layer acts as one electrode, while a thin film of metal on the opposite face of the piezoelectric acts as the other electrode. A voltage applied across the electrodes changes the size of the piezoelectric material, while the metal maintains its dimensions, thus forcing the sandwich to bend; an alternating voltage causes the blade of the fan to oscillate.

SEE ALSO: ELECTRICITY • INSULATOR, ELECTRIC • ION AND IONIZATION • MICROPHONE • PRESSURE • TRANSDUCER AND SENSOR

Pile Driver

A pile driver is a machine used to install piles, which are columns or sheets of steel, wood, or reinforced concrete driven into the ground to act as vertical supports or to resist lateral forces.

Piles fall into two main categories. Sheet piling is used to withstand horizontal forces, generally having material (earth) on one side and an excavation such as a dock or a road cutting on the other. Bearing piles are used to support buildings in soft or unstable ground or where the loads involved—as in skyscraper foundations—are too great for the soil.

Types of pile drivers

The drop hammer uses a heavy weight that is dropped onto the pile to drive it into the ground. These hammers are normally made of cast iron with weights of ½ ton up to 5 tons (0.4–4.5 tonnes). The hammers slide up and down in vertical guides to ensure that driving blows are central on the pile, and a driving cap is often used to take the impact and protect the head of the pile.

There are two main types of air hammer, single acting and double acting. The single-acting driver is similar in action to a drop hammer, but the heavy falling ram is raised by air or steam pressure instead of by a crane.

When the desired stroke (height) has been reached, the pressure is released, letting the ram fall and knock the pile into the ground. The rams vary in weight between 2.5 and 15 tons (2.3–13.6 tonnes), and the single-acting driver is more efficient than the drop hammer. Single-acting hammers are used to install bearing piles.

The double-acting air hammer is a lighter tool used to install sheet piling. It normally operates on compressed air and has a light ram rather like a piston that moves up and down within a cylinder, the bottom end of which is the anvil that rests on the top of the pile. Air is admitted to the cylinder to lift the ram, which on its upward journey actuates a valve arrangement that cuts off the air supply to the lower part of the cylinder and transfers it to the upper part above the ram. This action forces the ram back down the cylinder to strike the anvil, which in turn strikes the pile.

Unlike the air and steam hammers, which require an auxiliary source of power (compressor or steam generators), the diesel hammer is a self-contained unit. Like the double-acting air hammer, the ram is in the form of a piston moving within a cylinder. The hammer is started by lifting the ram with a crane and releasing it at the required height. When the ram strikes the anvil

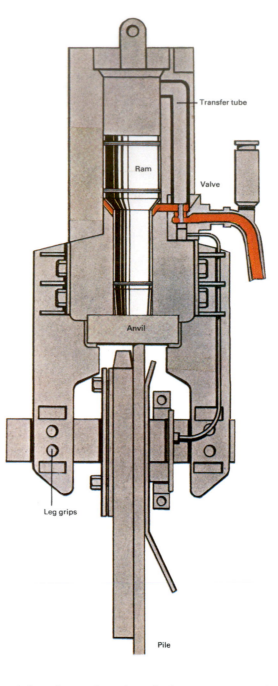

◄ This double-acting air hammer is raised by air or steam. The air or steam is then redirected behind the hammer to give it extra power when dropping.

Transfer tube

Ram

Valve

Anvil

Leg grips

Pile

and thus drives the pile, a fuel-air mixture in the cylinder ignites, and the resulting explosion drives the ram upward to start the cycle again.

The force needed to drive a pile can be reduced by injecting water down the center of the pile to act as a lubricant at the driving point. A similar effect can be achieved in some soils by the use of a vibratory driver that transmits high-frequency vibrations along the pile and shakes the pile through the soil to give a rapid sinking rate. Piles can also be formed in situ by boring or driving a suitable hole into the soil, inserting reinforcement, and then filling it with concrete (casting) to make the pile.

SEE ALSO: Building techniques • Jackhammer • Pneumatic tool

Pilotless Aircraft

A pilotless aircraft, like a guided missile, is a self-propelled airborne vehicle whose flight may be guided either by remote control or by preset onboard equipment. Unlike guided missiles, most pilotless aircraft are designed to be recovered after a mission and used again.

One of the first aircraft to be flown "hands off" was a Curtiss flying boat of the U.S. Navy, which was tested in 1913 with a gyroscopic stabilizer designed by the U.S. inventor Elmer Sperry. This device formed the basis for the first practical autopilot. Pilotless aircraft have always been used chiefly as targets for fighter aircraft and antiaircraft weapons. A few pilotless aircraft are otherwise-standard full-sized craft converted for remotely controlled flight, but they are outnumbered by specially built small-scale target drones.

A class of more sophisticated pilotless aircraft is formed by remotely piloted vehicles, or RPVs. The main impetus for the development of RPVs has been their usefulness in military reconnaissance, where their small size and maneuverability make them less vulnerable than conventional aircraft, and their low cost compared with a conventional aircraft and trained pilot makes them more expendable in hazardous circumstances.

The basic components of a pilotless aircraft are its airframe; motor; and onboard control, command, and guidance systems. In operation, they are supported by launch, remote control, and (usually) retrieval systems. Target drones also feature target augmentation systems that give them the radar signatures of full-sized aircraft and scoring systems that report strike accuracy.

Airframe and motor

Almost without exception, the airframe designs and construction of pilotless aircraft are similar to those of conventional aircraft or air-breathing missiles. Standard control surfaces—wings, ailerons, elevators, and rudder—are fitted, and the motor may be a piston, turbojet, turboprop, or rocket engine. Piloted aircraft converted for drone use normally retain the cockpit—often with provision for a human pilot to monitor the instruments—and the wheeled undercarriage.

Guidance systems

Of the two main types of guidance systems—preprogrammed and radio remote control—the simpler is preprogrammed guidance. Aircraft that use this system follow flight instructions programmed before launch. The instructions define the course and maneuvers that the craft undergoes after

launch, and onboard systems adjust the power and control surfaces, often with compensation for prevailing weather conditions. After the preset series of maneuvers, the flight is completed and the aircraft recovered. In many cases, the final stage of the flight is a parachute-assisted drop.

In the case of remote-control guidance, radio command signals are transmitted from a land-based or seaborne ground station to be detected by the aircraft's control antenna. An onboard receiver decodes these signals and responds to them by sending commands to the appropriate subsystems for flight control and for activating reconnaissance equipment, for example. In some cases, an onboard transmitter sends signals to the ground station that confirm responses to command signals or to report failures to respond. Some pilotless aircraft transmit video signals from onboard cameras to assist the remote operator.

Launch system

Target drones and RPVs (other than conversions from piloted aircraft) are launched either from a ground or ship launcher, or from an aircraft in flight. Typical surface launchers are fixed or mobile short, rail-type structures from which the drone is launched at an upward angle. In some cases, a JATO (jet-assisted takeoff) bottle fires for a few seconds to supplement the aircraft's own power plant and then drops away once its fuel is expended. For an air launch, a drone, or RPV, is suspended from pylons under the wings of a carrier aircraft. The engine is started via umbilical connections, which are retracted before launch.

▲ The experimental Vindicator RPV pilotless autogyro, which can be controlled by a simple line-of-sight radio-control system. Because of its small payload and size, the Vindicator is best suited for surveillance work; on trials, it carried forward-looking infrared linescan and high-resolution cameras. The information is either recorded onboard or relayed back to a base.

Then, the drone drops away from the pylon, and the remote controller assumes command. Drones converted from piloted aircraft, and some larger RPVs, have conventional undercarriages for normal runway takeoff and landing.

Retrieval system

Pilotless aircraft without undercarriage usually have some form of parachute recovery system, actuated automatically or by remote control. In one type of retrieval, a drogue (small parachute) opens first to pull out a large main parachute that decelerates the drone and controls its descent to the ground or water for pickup. A safety device activates the recovery parachutes automatically if the command signal is lost or becomes interrupted for longer than a specified period.

In another system, called the helicopter midair recovery system (MARS), a load line attached to the drone extends upward above the main parachute to a smaller engagement parachute. A hook

lowered from a helicopter then snares this third parachute. Once the helicopter is safely supporting the drone's weight, the main parachute disconnects automatically. The helicopter then returns to base with the drone hanging below it.

In a third recovery system, the pilotless aircraft approaches ground at the lowest speed possible without stalling. It then flies into a truck-mounted net that catches it.

Target augmentation

Target drones and decoys have to represent aircraft that are much larger than themselves, and this is made possible by target-augmentation techniques. Augmentation may range from a simple smoke-dispensing system, which makes a drone more visible in combat training, to more sophisticated systems that make it appear larger to detector instruments. A decoy for heat-seeking missiles might carry a heat source that enlarges its infrared signature and draws such missiles away from the aircraft it defends. Alternatively, an onboard microwave transmitter can transmit a signal when an antenna detects a pulse from a tracking radar. The microwave emission matches the frequency and timing of the pulse, so the drone appears much larger on radar.

Scoring system

In most missile-firing situations, the target drone is outside the interceptor's visual range. Hence, it must carry equipment that measures the accuracy of weapons fired against it. Typical systems use Doppler radar or a series of separate transmitters in the drone, the interceptor, and the missile—all feeding data to a computer at the control center.

RPVs

Remotely piloted vehicles have a number of potential and actual applications in both military and civilian fields. Their attraction lies in their small size, which helps them avoid detection; low cost compared with large aircraft; real-time flight control rather than preset instructions; and capacity for strenuous maneuvers that would be too physically taxing for an onboard pilot.

RPVs have been used for photographic and electronic reconnaissance, radar intelligence-gathering, electronic countermeasures, sensor dropping, and weapons delivery. Their potential civilian uses include the observation and measurement of weather conditions over oceans and monitoring traffic on busy highways.

FACT FILE

- The British ML Aviation Sprite is an unpiloted mini helicopter, powered by a 7 horsepower two-stroke engine, with counter-rotating rotors of 5 ft. 3 in. (1.6 m) diameter. The Sprite is designed for battlefield surveillance and weighs 53 lbs. (24 kg) empty.

- With a level speed of 100 mph (161 km/h) and a ceiling of 10,000 ft. (3,050 m), the Flogger-D aerial target is designed to look like a Soviet Mikoyan MiG 27 ground-attack aircraft. Catapult launched, it can perform a typical MiG flight sequence.

- The X-43A pilotless aircraft are the test vehicles of NASA's Hyper-X hypersonic flight development program. Measuring around 12 ft. (4 m) in length, these vehicles are designed to be carried to an altitude of 20,000 ft. (6,100 m) under a B-52 bomber, then taken to 100,000 ft. (30,500 m) and Mach 7 or Mach 10 on a Pegasus booster rocket. Once at this altitude and speed, the X-43A will fly under the power of its own hydrogen-fueled, air-breathing scramjet (supersonic-combustion ramjet). The craft will follow a set of preprogrammed flight instructions, terminating in descent and speed-reducing maneuvers before recovery.

SEE ALSO: AIRCRAFT DESIGN • MISSILE • RADAR • STEALTH TECHNOLOGIES

Pipe and Tube Manufacture

◀ A steel pipe 3 ft. (90 cm) in diameter being examined with an ultrasonic instrument to check that there are no flaws in the material.

Most pipes used for the transmission and distribution of liquids and gases under pressure are made of ferrous, cementitious, or plastic materials. Other materials of more limited and specialized application include stoneware, used for sewerage and drainage by gravity; aluminum, used because of its light weight for surface irrigation and emergency water supplies; and copper and lead, used for small-diameter service pipes to feed individual properties.

Ferrous pipes

One relatively recent advance in iron pipe technology is the replacement of brittle gray iron with ductile iron, a material with a ductility and strength similar to that of steel. It is made by converting the small carbon content of iron (about 3 percent) from flake to spheroidal form by adding small quantities of magnesium ferrosilicon alloy to the molten iron prior to casting.

Steel, because of its weldability and its high tensile strength—about 35,000 psi (2,500 kg/cm^2) for mild steel and up to 60,000 psi (4,200 kg/cm^2) and more for high-tensile steel—is the most versatile of all pipe materials. Pipes are made by a number of processes. In diameters up to 12 in. (30 cm), seamless pipes are produced either by extrusion under pressure or by hot rotary piercing. In the latter process, a heated cylindrical steel billet is passed between two rolls whose axes are set at an angle and pierced by a pointed mandrel.

For large diameters, up to about 60 in. (150 cm), the pipe is usually manufactured from steel plate of the required thickness; the length—usually about 40 ft. (12 m)—is that of the finished pipe and the width is the pipe's circumference. The plate edges are trimmed for welding, and the circular shape is cold-formed in presses. The edges are welded longitudinally either by electric-resistance welding or by submerged-arc welding.

Very large diameter pipes—up to 100 in. (250 cm) and more—require two or more longitudinal welds, or they can be made by spiral or helical welding. In the latter, pipes are fabricated from steel plate in rolled form, and the weld spirals around the pipe at an angle that is dependent on the relationship between pipe diameter and plate width. Spirally-welded pipes can be made in very long lengths, but the practical limit imposed by transportation constraints is about 80 ft. (24 m).

Galvanized mild steel (GMS) pipes are small-diameter steel pipes that are usually made using a seamless process. They are protected against corrosion by being dipped into a bath of molten zinc, a process that is known as galvanizing. These pipes are rarely used in diameters above 4 in. (10 cm).

Cementitious pipes

Reinforced concrete cracks under tension, so pipes made of reinforced concrete are mainly used in nonpressure sewers and drains, though they are used for low-pressure duties up to about 75 psi (5 kg/cm²). They are made by placing a steel reinforcing cage inside a steel cylinder and introducing high-quality concrete into the cylinder while it is spun in a near-horizontal position. When the concrete has set, the pipe is withdrawn and is either steam- or water-cured.

Prestressed concrete pipes are designed to resist moderate internal pressures of up to about 220 psi (15 kg/cm²) and are used primarily for large-diameter water transmission. Diameters range from 24 in. (60 cm) to more than 160 in. (400 cm). There are two types of prestressed concrete pipe: cylinder and noncylinder.

Cylinder pipes have a thin-wall steel cylinder core, made in the same way as normal steel pipes. A thick lining of concrete is spun centrifugally into the steel cylinder and allowed to cure. High-tensile steel wire is wound helically around the full length of the cylinder at a predetermined pitch and tension. Dense cement mortar is finally sprayed into the revolving pipe to provide a protective coating (gunite) at least 1 in. (2.5 cm) thick. For higher pressures, a second layer of prestressing wire and mortar coating is applied.

Noncylinder pipes have no steel core. Longitudinal high-tensile steel wires are placed into a cylindrical steel mold and tensioned. The mold is transferred to a spinning machine and concrete fed in as the mold rotates. After a curing period, the mold is removed, and high-tensile steel wire is wound around the pipe helically in the same way as it is for cylinder pipes. Finally, a dense protective cement mortar coating is applied.

Asbestos cement pipes, like prestressed concrete, are made to resist moderate pressures of up to about 220 psi (15 kg/cm²). Pressure pipes do not usually exceed 40 in. (1 m) in diameter, but nonpressure pipes are often made in much larger sizes. Pipes are manufactured from ordinary cement reinforced with about 15 percent by volume of asbestos fibers. A slurry of cement, asbestos fibers, and water is fed into a tank from which a revolving cylindrical sieve picks up a thin film of material. The film is transferred onto a polished steel mandrel by a felt conveyor belt, and the pipe is gradually built up to the required thickness. Rollers apply pressure over the full length of the mandrel to ensure cohesion between successive layers and to produce a dense pipe. The pipe is removed from the mandrel, and a split wooden former is introduced to prevent deformation before initial hardening occurs. The former

◀ Clay waste pipes are glazed and fired in underground furnaces to make them watertight.

is removed after about 24 hours, and the pipes are cured either by immersion in water for 7 to 14 days or by high-pressure steam curing.

Glass-reinforced concrete has so far only been used for nonpressure purposes. These pipes are centrifugally spun and reinforced on both inner and outer faces with alkali-resistant glass fiber.

Plastic pipes

Plastic pipes, though developed before World War II, did not come into general use until the 1950s. They are of two types—thermoplastic and thermosetting. Thermoplastic materials soften on heating and stiffen and return to their former state on cooling. Thermosetting materials, while they initially soften with heat to allow molding, harden by the application of continued heat and cannot be reprocessed once they have set.

The principal thermoplastic pipes in general use are made from unplasticized polyvinyl chloride (uPVC), molecularly oriented PVC (moPVC) and polyethylene (PE), which comes in low, medium, and high density varieties. Thermosetting pipes are made from either epoxy or polyester resins reinforced with glass fibers and are known as glass-reinforced plastic pipes (GRP).

Thermoplastic pipes are generally produced by continuous extrusion. Material in powdered or pellet form is fed through a hopper into a barrel, where it is heated, and the hot material is forced through a tube-forming die. The pipe tube is cooled and cut into the required lengths.

GRP pipes are made from either epoxy or polyester resins (mostly from polyester) and glass fiber in the form of cloths, rovings, chopped strands, or chopped-strand mats. Pipes made from these materials can resist moderate pressures even if they have extremely thin walls, so inert fillers such as sand are often added to provide increased thickness, making the pipe more rigid and easier to handle.

GRP pipes are made in diameters beyond 80 in. (2 m) and are used for both pressure and nonpressure duties. Pressure pipes resist pressures up to about 220 psi (15 kg/cm^2).

Other materials

Stoneware pipes have been used since antiquity, and because of their excellent resistance to corrosive action, they are still widely used for nonpressure drainage purposes in diameters up to 40 in. (1 m). Clay is ground to a powder and brought to a plastic state with water and other additives. It is then passed through a vacuum chamber to remove trapped air and fed into extruders in which the pipe is formed. The extruded pipes are trimmed and dried and then passed into kilns in which the temperature is raised to about 2000°F (1100°C) to cause fusion of the clay particles, or vitrification. Salt is sometimes added at this stage to produce glazed surfaces.

Aluminum pipes are either extruded or fusion welded, either longitudinally or spirally. Copper pipes are usually extruded, though various other seamless production processes (as for steel) are used for larger diameters. Lead pipes, which are obsolete and being replaced, used to be extruded.

Tube manufacture

Tubes and tubing are made from many kinds of materials, including metal, plastic, and glass. The choice of material depends on the product's application, and the choice of manufacturing process (which can be rolling, extrusion, or drawing, among others) depends on both the material and the application. Tubing is used for conveying liquids, slurries, powders, and gases and for chemical processing. It is used in medical practice and biological research—for example, the injection of drugs, vaccines, and saline solutions—and in the inspection of internal passages and cavities. In instrumentation, measurement, and control precision tubing is an integral element of many components. Tubing is also used as a structural building material in aircraft, oil rigs, communication masts, table legs, umbrella stands, coat racks, and many other objects. Tubes are usually thought of as long hollow cylinders, but they can be square, oval, or almost any shape. Often a large tube is called a pipe and a small pipe a tube.

The drawbench

Although similar in many respects to wire drawing, tube drawing is a more complex process. Because tubing cannot be bent around a capstan unless it is very small, tube drawing is generally carried out on a drawbench, which comprises a loop of chain driven by sprockets into which a dog can be engaged. The dog grips one end of the tube, which has been swaged (reduced in cross-section) to pass through the ring die. Often, several tubes are drawn simultaneously through a bank of dies to make the most effective use of the

◄ The Mannesmann process, in which steel pipes are rolled and bored simultaneously.

drawbench. Tube drawing is usually carried out cold to harden the material and produce a high surface finish. The extent to which cold drawing can be performed before annealing becomes necessary depends among other things on the ductility required in the end product.

The three tube-drawing processes are tube sinking, plug drawing, and rod drawing. In tube sinking, the tube is drawn through a die of the type used in wire drawing. No attempt is made to control the inside diameter. In the other two methods of manufacture, however, either a short plug or a long rod is drawn with the tube to control the inside diameter.

The stationary plug or mandrel used in plug drawing may be allowed to find its own position within the throat of the die, or it may be supported on the end of a long rod. The cylindrical piece of steel from which the tube is drawn may be turned and bored out of a solid bar, pierced from a solid billet, or rolled by the Mannesmann roll-piercing process.

Tubes can also be produced by extrusion. With the extrusion presses and tool steels available, the direct production of fine tubes down to about 0.06 in. (1.8 mm) wall thickness is possible.

Precision extruded tubing is offered in a range of bore diameters from 0.8 in. (2 cm) to 5.7 in. (14.5 cm) in steel and from 0.8 in. (2 cm) to 10 in. (25 cm) in aluminum, with a maximum wall thickness of 0.03 in. (0.8 mm) and a maximum length of 59 in. (150 cm). The best quality has diameter tolerances of about 0.1 percent with a total eccentricity of 5 percent of the wall thickness and a straightness tolerance of 1 in 1,200.

A type of precision tubing called hollow bar is used widely in the engineering industry. When hollow bar is used as a starting material, much less stock has to be removed, and some operations

▲ Manufacturing aluminum-alloy seamless tubes on a drawbench. The tube is being drawn by the dog, which grips one end of the tube to pull it through the die; the dog itself is attached by a length of continuous chain driven by sprockets.

may be eliminated. Hot-rolled hollow bar can be made to outside-diameter tolerances of about ±0.7 percent and straightness tolerances of 1 in 1,000. The corresponding tolerances for cold-reduced bar are ±0.25 percent and 1 in 1,500. The range of sizes is from 0.6 to 8 in. (1.5–20 cm) outside diameter with a range of outside-diameter-to-wall thickness ratios from 3.5:1 to 10.5:1.

The standard range of tubes for hypodermic needles is made from stainless steel varying from 0.13 in. (3.30 mm), or 10 SWG (standard wire gauge), to 0.011 in. (0.28 mm), or 31 SWG in outside diameter—and from 0.015 in. (0.38 mm) to 0.0028 in. (0.07 mm) in wall thickness. Tubes of 1 mm and less are manufactured from drawn, welded material, but seamless stock is used for larger sizes. This type of tube was originally intended exclusively for medical purposes, but because of the range of sizes, it is being used for an increasing number of applications in instrumentation—including thermocouples, torque devices, Bourdon linkages (a type of pressure gauge), fire-detection bellows, and gas chromatography.

A capillary tube with an integral bulb on one end can be made in lengths of up to 6.5 ft. (2 m). Tubular bulb capillaries are used as refrigerant metering devices—and to sense, measure, and control variations of temperature in cold stores, refrigerated trucks, air conditioning, and fire alarms. The capillary is filled with a small amount of liquid with a low boiling point. When the ambient temperature rises, the liquid starts to boil and fills the capillary with vapor whose pressure tends to uncoil the tubing. A fall in ambient temperature results in a drop in the capillary vapor, allowing the tubing to coil up. The coiling and uncoiling can be made to actuate electric relays to control an action, dependent on temperature.

Plastic

The plastic material known as PTFE (polytetrafluoroethylene, or Teflon) can be extruded in the form of precision tubing with a range of bore sizes. As a virgin polymer, it can be supplied in the form of thin-wall tubing for the handling of corrosives for lightweight components.

Peristaltic pumps use the squeezing action of rollers on flexible tubing to transfer liquids or gases. This tubing is made from a Teflon inner tube covered by an outer sheath of silicone rubber. It is suitable for solvents, acids, and alkaline and sterile solutions from –26 to 203°F (–32 to 95°C).

SEE ALSO: CEMENT MANUFACTURE • GLASS FIBER • IRON AND STEEL • METALWORKING • PIPELINE • PLASTICS • PLASTICS PROCESSING • POLYTETRAFLUOROETHYLENE (TEFLON)

Pipeline

The transportation of fluids by pipeline has been done since early civilization. The Chinese are believed to have used pipes made from bamboo or clay about 5000 B.C.E. Evidence can still be seen in Italy of the large aqueducts and the lead pipes constructed by the Romans about 2,000 years ago to bring fresh water to the cities. Until the 19th century, pipes made from wood or lead were mainly used for this purpose, laid sloping so that the water could flow under the force of gravity. Today cast iron or cement pipes are used joined with spigot and socket joints, enabling water flow under pressure.

Oil pipelines

With the development of commercial crude oil production, which commenced more than 100 years ago in the United States, pipelines became necessary. The first, 6 miles (10 km) long and of wood, was soon superseded by cast-iron pipes. Steel pipes were later introduced, and mechanical joints were used until recent years, when the all-welded system was adopted. Steel pipes are not, however, well suited to carrying water, because corrosion can occur on the inside of the pipe. Where steel is used, it is given an internal anticorrosion coating. The most famous pipelines carry oil or natural gas. The Trans-Alaska Pipeline,

which extends about 800 miles (1,300 km), carries oil from northern to southern Alaska.

In 1981, the Trans-Mediterranean Pipeline was completed, its 1,500 miles (2,400 km) running from Hassi R'Mel in the central Sahara to Minerbio in northern Italy. On its trip from the Tunisian coast to the toe of Italy, the pipeline submerges twice as it passes across the deep trough that separates Africa from Europe.

In Europe, steel pipeline systems were slower to develop, because most of the demand for petroleum products was met by the import of crude oil from the Middle East, there being little indigenous crude production. Refineries were usually located near to the coast and close to major areas of consumption, and product transportation was via road or waterway. The last 40 years have, however, seen a considerable growth of pipeline networks in Europe for moving crude oil or oil products and natural or manufactured gas. This increase has been brought about partly by the increasing size of tankers used for crude shipment, which in many cases can only berth at terminals that have water depths in excess of 60 ft. (18 m). The extraction of crude oil and natural gas from the large deposits found off the shores of Europe has also led to the demand for transportation systems both inland and offshore.

▲ The Trans-Alaska Pipeline stretches for 800 miles (1,300 km) linking oil fields at Prudhoe Bay on the Arctic Ocean with oil terminals at Valdez in southern Alaska.

◀ A welder at work on an oil pipeline. Systems for the distribution of oil and gas are most often constructed of durable high-quality steel pipes with welded joints. The pipes may run above or below ground or be submerged underwater.

Materials and production

Pipes can be made from a number of materials, including steel, cast iron, asbestos cement, aluminum, plastic, and even prestressed concrete. Mechanical joints are normally used for most of these materials but steel and aluminum pipes can be welded together. Distribution systems for the handling of crude oil products or gas are invariably constructed from high-quality steel pipes with welded end joints.

Early steel pipes were produced by rolling from plate and joined by electric resistance welding; later a solid, drawn system without a seam was adopted. For a long line, it may be necessary to install a number of pumping stations at intervals to provide the overall pressure requirements. Flow conditions for gas lines are more complicated because of the compressibility of gas; compressors are used to force the flow. On average, over flat terrain, pumping stations are 20 to 30 miles (32–48 km) apart.

The choice of drivers partly depends upon local conditions and the availability of fuel. They can be electric motors, steam turbines, gas engines, larger diesel engines, or gas turbines. Electric motors usually prove to be the most acceptable. Some petroleum pumping stations' engines also run on crude from the pipeline.

Control systems

Complicated pipeline systems are normally designed for failsafe, fully automatic operation. Control of a system, including all the principal equipment, can be done from one central room. All essential operating data are transmitted back to the control center continuously so that the controller is always fully informed of the operating conditions of the pipeline. Communication is usually by microwave radio or direct cable, although public utility circuits are sometimes used.

Many pipeline systems make use of computers to assist in batching schedules, that is, the predetermined cycle of liquid products. Some of the latest systems are designed so that the control of all operations can be linked directly to a computer.

Corrosion control and testing

Buried steel pipelines are protected externally by a wrapped coating on the outer pipe, and it is usual for a cathodic protection system to be applied by means of an impressed current or sacrificial zinc anodes. Should a fault develop in the coating, corrosive action is diverted away from the pipe.

All cross-country steel pipelines are tested for tightness and resistance to pressure before they are put into operation. The testing medium is usually water, and the test pressure is always higher than the actual maximum operating pressure. Before putting a pipeline into operation, it is also usual to pass a go devil, or pig, through its entire length, pushed through the pipe by air or water. A go devil consists of a short rod with circular steel plates attached at both ends, the front plate being made just a little smaller in diameter than the inside of the pipe. When passed through the whole line it clears the pipe of any obstructions and demonstrates that the pipe has been laid without damage.

SEE ALSO: CORROSION PREVENTION • IRON AND STEEL • OIL REFINING • PIPE AND TUBE MANUFACTURE

Planetarium Projector

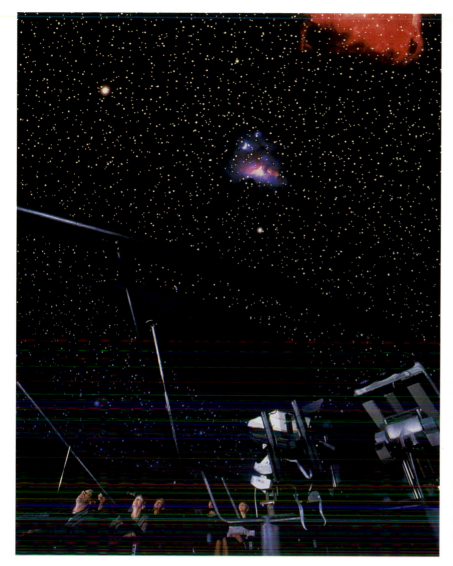

▲ The London Planetarium uses the Digistar II projector manufactured by Evans & Sutherland. Digital projectors use computer technology to generate the projected images.

A planetarium projector is a device capable of projecting onto the inside reflecting surface of a hemispherical dome a realistic view of the night sky as seen from any place on the surface of Earth. It is also able to demonstrate all the major movements associated with the sky, including the daily (diurnal) motion of the sky, the monthly motion of the Moon (including its phases), the annual motion of the Sun and planets against the background of the stars, and the precessional motion of Earth's axis. There are separate projectors for the stellar background, the Sun, the Moon, and the planets.

One of the simplest ways of obtaining the stellar background is by means of a sphere with many small holes drilled into its surface. The size of the holes is related to the brightness of the stars, and they are positioned so as to represent the stars in their correct relative positions. At the center of this sphere is a point source of light, giving sharp images without lenses, mounted in gimbals. A hemispherical cup cuts out light for stars that lie below the horizon, no matter which way the projector is pointing. Light from the point source passes through the holes in the sphere and causes spots of light to fall on the inside of the dome. Because the holes for the bigger stars must be large, lenses are used to focus the light to prevent these stars from appearing as blurred disks rather than points. This type of system is used in the Spitz projector, which uses a mercury–xenon arc light source.

The Zeiss projector uses a different system. This projector has a dumbbell shape. Each end of the dumbbell has 16 small projectors, and each has its own optical system. These projectors are so grouped around a central 1,000-watt bulb that together they can project a complete picture of the stellar background over the whole surface of the dome. Inside each projector, there is a photo-engraved plate of part of the sky. Mechanical blinkers swing over the projection lenses like artificial eyelids, thus preventing star images that are below the horizon from flashing across the eyes of the spectators.

Most projectors are able to move about three independent axes, to allow for the fact that the observer can be at any latitude, at any time of day, and at any era in time. Earth's axis moves slowly, like that of a spinning top or gyroscope—a movement called precession, which has to be allowed for to make an accurate projection.

Planets

Two different methods can be used to simulate the motions of the Sun, the Moon and the planets, which move along different paths in the sky at varying rates. In one system, the projectors themselves do the movement, while in the other, the light from the projectors reaches the screen via a system of movable mirrors. The movements of the Sun and Moon present little difficulty. The inclination of their orbits to the celestial equator (the projection of the terrestrial equator onto the sky) is achieved by means of cylindrical wedges. The Moon projector has an automatic shutter that simulates the phases of the Moon.

The movements of the planets are simulated by means of analogs, mechanical versions of the Solar System that contain the Sun, Earth, and one of the planets. Earth and the planet move around the Sun at the correct relative speeds and at the appropriate distances. The planet and Earth are connected to the same rod by means of sliding contacts. This rod represents the line of sight

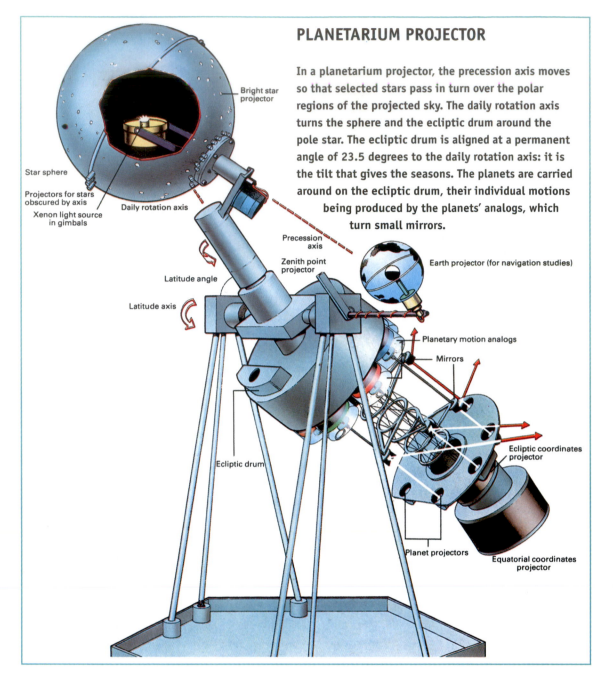

PLANETARIUM PROJECTOR

In a planetarium projector, the precession axis moves so that selected stars pass in turn over the polar regions of the projected sky. The daily rotation axis turns the sphere and the ecliptic drum around the pole star. The ecliptic drum is aligned at a permanent angle of 23.5 degrees to the daily rotation axis: it is the tilt that gives the seasons. The planets are carried around on the ecliptic drum, their individual motions being produced by the planets' analogs, which turn small mirrors.

Bright star projector

Star sphere

Projectors for stars obscured by axis

Xenon light source in gimbals

Daily rotation axis

Precession axis

Zenith point projector

Latitude angle

Latitude axis

Earth projector (for navigation studies)

Planetary motion analogs

Mirrors

Ecliptic drum

Ecliptic coordinates projector

Planet projectors

Equatorial coordinates projector

from Earth to the planet. In the first system, this rod carries the projector, and in the second system, the rod controls the movement of a mirror.

Auxiliary projectors can project onto the dome such things as coordinate systems, the meridian, the ecliptic (or the apparent pathway of the Sun against the background stars), and a view of the continents as seen from the center of the transparent Earth for navigation instruction. Some planetariums also have projection orreries (representations of the Solar System) that project onto the dome a view of the Solar System, including Earth, as seen from deep in space.

Digital projectors

Recent developments in the design of planetarium projectors include a complete departure from the kinds of projectors formerly used. New projectors are often made using technology derived from virtual reality simulation systems. Many planetariums now use the Digistar digital projectors made by Evans & Sutherland. Using computer-generated images, these systems offer more features than the traditional projectors, such as seamless projection of 360 degrees field of view and the ability to give the impression of actually travelling through space. The images themselves are extremely bright and are produced at high resolution (8,000 x 8,000 pixels) with a capacity to project over 9,000 stars. Together these features give the audience the impression of being immersed in the computer-generated environment.

SEE ALSO: FLIGHT SIMULATOR • PROJECTOR, MOVIE AND SLIDE • SPACE PHOTOGRAPHY • TELESCOPE, SPACE • VIRTUAL REALITY

Planetary Science

Earth is one of nine planets orbiting the Sun in nearly circular paths. While astronomers have predicted that there must be planets circling other stars in the Universe, it is only since the mid-1990s that the existence of such planetary systems has been confirmed. It is too early to say what fraction of the observable stars will turn out to have stable planetary systems. Most astronomers consider the probability of discovering Earth-like planets in these systems to be rather small.

An order emerges from the arrangement of the planets that scientists believe provides an important clue to the origin of the Solar System. The first four planets out from the Sun—Mercury, Venus, Earth, and Mars—are solid bodies composed of rock and silicates, with radioactive elements decaying and producing heat deep in their cores. They are called the terrestrial planets because they are similar to Earth in form and composition.

Beyond Mars and past the asteroid belt (a ring of small rocky bodies), four giant, gaseous planets reside at ever-increasing distances. Only Pluto breaks the pattern; lying in a distant orbit as the outermost known planet, Pluto is about the size of the Moon. The four giants—Jupiter, Saturn, Uranus, and Neptune—are much larger than the terrestrial planets and are composed of gases pulled in by gravitational forces.

The separation between the terrestrial and the gaseous planets is so orderly that it seems to obey some physical law—an important starting point for any theory. Another observation is that about 99 percent of all the material making up the Solar System is contained within the Sun. In sharp contrast, the planets and their satellites contain 99 percent of the Solar System's angular momentum. The amount of angular momentum in the planets could explain their orderly separation into different masses at different distances. It indicates a movement of energy from the Sun to the outer reaches of the Solar System at some time early in the latter's evolution.

For centuries, literal interpretation of the Bible prejudiced scientific opinion about the age and formation of Earth and its neighboring planets. In the 17th century, Archbishop Ussher of Ireland calculated that God created Earth, the Sun, all the planets and stars in a six-day period commencing 9 A.M., October 26, 4004 B.C.E. Not before the 20th century could science begin to fit the pieces of scant information into a sound theory. Even when astronomers joined the debate with theories on the formation of the Solar

▲ Jupiter is the largest planet in the Solar System. The search for planets orbiting other stars has revealed a number of bodies with even larger masses than Jupiter's that are providing interesting insights on the formation of planetary systems.

System that appeared to fit the facts, they were hampered because the facts themselves were too imprecise to aid them in reaching any accurate conclusions.

Geological record

The facts that the theorists so badly needed started to emerge. Considerable information was gathered in dating the Sun to fit Earth's geological record. This showed many millions of years of gradual evolution—some scientists saying as many as 75 million years. A great stumbling block was that at this time nothing could explain how the Sun could ever have maintained its tremendous heat output for more than 20 million years. Then the technique of dating by measuring radioactive decay completely astounded the scientific world by suggesting an even older Earth—several billion years.

The discovery in the 1930s that a nuclear reaction was responsible for the Sun's astonishingly large energy output appeared to explain the enigma. Today, aided by radioisotopic dating of

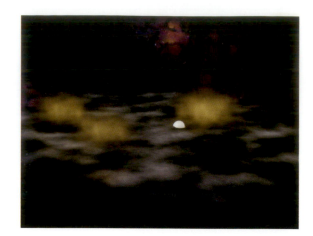

◀ When interstellar gas clouds collapse under gravity, they begin to spin, flattening the cloud into a disk with a star forming at its center. As the star grows, lumps form in the cloud that will eventually become planets. ▶

meteorites and lunar rock samples, scientists have dated the Solar System at about 4.7 billion years. This discovery was undoubtedly a significant breakthrough in knowledge, but in fact, the fundamental idea for the accepted model of how the Solar System formed fits in closely with a theory dating back two centuries.

This original concept was that the Sun and planets formed from a contracting and rotating cloud of gas and dust. The cloud collapsed into a disk, and the Sun and planets coalesced from the disk. This idea of planetary accretion (the coming together of many parts) persisted and forms the core for today's theories.

Planetary formation

Although there is wide agreement on the broad concept of planetary formation, the details of the process evade explanation. Scientists know that the Sun formed from a contracting nebula of gas and dust, which was drawn down upon its center with increasing rotational speed as it shrank. Because the gases were being compressed more and more tightly, they heated up and produced a system in which outer regions were comparatively cool, whereas the inner parts became progressively hotter. At the same time, increased spinning at the nebula's center tended to drive material out into a flattened disk, squeezed along the central region of the huge, contracting gas cloud.

Most of the material remained at the center, but a small amount was bled out into the disk, and it is from these grains that the planets could have formed. Particles of dust colliding at low speeds began to aggregate into granules that themselves joined together to make larger clumps called planetesimals. As the dust was swept up by the inner planets, a hole began to form between the Sun and the still-coalescing outer planets. Eventually the dust cleared leaving the Solar System as it is today.

If stripped of their gases, the giant, outer planets—Jupiter, Saturn, Uranus, and Neptune—are believed to consist of rocky bodies that may have accreted from granules and dust to a size similar to that of the inner, terrestrial planets.

Although the giant planets now support large gaseous envelopes, which their concealed cores might have drawn in, some explanation must be found for the fact that huge gas atmospheres have been stripped away from the inner planets.

As with the Sun, all new stars reach a point during contraction where the pressures and temperatures at the center are so great that nuclear fusion begins. By this process, the agitated atomic nuclei, predominantly hydrogen, fuse into larger helium nuclei. Enormous quantities of energy are liberated, and the star can reach a balance between the gravitational forces trying to pull it in and the thermal forces trying to push it apart.

At this stage, the cloud becomes a nuclear furnace that might cause the stripping of gases from planets close to the center of the nebula, the place where the star bursts forth with incandescent light. Scientists have calculated the amount of material needed to compress a cloud of gas down to the necessary pressures and temperatures for fusion to start. They find only 10 percent of the necessary mass in the Solar System today.

So the Sun has lost at least 90 percent of the original cloud that collapsed down. Where has it gone? Perhaps in the successive shells of matter seen elsewhere in the Universe to be blown away from a youthful star when its nuclear fusion becomes stable.

Known as T-Tauri stars, these youthful forerunners of the type of solar system we now populate provide evidence that great, forceful solar winds blew across the inner Solar System and carried away gases from the terrestrial planets that have been left around Jupiter, Saturn, Uranus, and Neptune. The cooler, outer regions of the gaseous giants aided the collection of the ices and liquids that are believed to surround the rocky cores, in turn attracting the hydrogen envelopes that now hide the interior.

◀ As material becomes incorporated into the star and protoplanets, the disk begins to thin. A hole forms where the inner planets have swept up the debris, though other planets are still forming farther out. The dust clears completely when all the planets have grown to their full size. ▶

The question of how the terrestrial planets and the cores of the giant planets actually formed remains. Several theories have been proposed, but only one is supported by the facts now known about the Solar System. This theory holds that the planets accrued in three stages.

The microscopic dust and ice grains within the disk surrounding the forming Sun often collided. Sometimes they stuck together and accumulated into loose, lightweight, fluffy balls of dust and ice. When small, the fluffy ice balls would have had little gravitational effect. Once they had grown to a few inches across, however, they began to feel each other's gravity, thus starting the second stage of accretion.

Calculations show that at this stage whole regions of these balls would have grouped together quickly to make up solid bodies a few miles across called planetesimals. Near the forming Sun, the temperature would have been so high that the planetesimals would have been composed of pure rock. In the outer regions of the disk, however, ice would have condensed out too, and the planetesimals would probably have consisted primarily of ice with only smaller amounts of rocky dirt.

The third stage in planet formation was the coming together of the ten billion or so planetesimals dispersed randomly in orbits. If the orbits were such that the planetesimals met slowly, mutual gravitational pull would have held them together, forming larger planetesimals. Computer simulations have shown that the largest planetesimals would have gradually swept up the smaller ones in their vicinity. In this way, the nine largest planetesimals could have accumulated from the others to become the planets known today.

The process of accretion did not stop when the Sun became stable and the planets reached their present sizes. Whatever mechanism started the accretion lasted only a brief few tens of millions of years about 4.7 billion years ago.

However, the Solar System contained much material that failed to hit the planets the first time, and the orbiting worlds became celestial vacuum cleaners, sweeping up the dust and rocks that continued to move around the Sun.

Chaotic bombardment

For more than 700 million years, asteroid-size boulders slammed into the planets and pulverized their surface. Today, the moons of the giant planets show the results of this chaotic bombardment. Even so, all the material falling on the gaseous envelopes would have contributed little to the composition of those huge bodies, so large was their initial bulk. The Moon has provided a useful reference for the early period of the Solar System—unlike Earth, which is changing continuously and has lost all evidence of the first third of its history. Since about 3.9 billion years ago, when the major phase of accretion ended, a steady trickle of material has continued to crater the surfaces of bodies in the Solar System. However, few large rocks remain outside the asteroid belts and only once every few million years will a dramatic impact of major size occur.

Extrasolar planetary systems

The search for planets around other stars has revealed more than 80 potential candidates. When the newly repaired Hubble telescope was pointed at stars in the Orion nebula in 1992, a number of dust disks were found. These protoplanetary disks, or proplyds, as they were termed, showed new stars at the center of disks containing enough material to form Earth-like planets. As yet, these stars, less than one million years old, are still contracting out of primordial gases, but in each case, the dust contains enough spin to resist being drawn into the star and has flattened out into a disk around the star's equator. The presence of such a large number of proplyds implies that planetary systems might be common throughout the Universe. However, observations

of these proplyds in 2001 has shown that fledgling planets have to form very quickly to avoid being blowtorched away by radiation from the nebula's largest star. Astronomers estimate that 90 percent of the proplyds are destroyed, but the remaining 10 percent have a good chance of developing into solar systems if shielded from radiation. However, the planets formed in such a hostile environment are most likely to be rocky planets like Earth—gas giants like Jupiter would have to condense out of the disk and grow quickly to avoid having their icy gases blasted into space.

Other observations of the Orion nebula have indicated that there may be free-floating planets that do not orbit any star. Spectral analysis of 13 faint objects has revealed the presence of water vapor, which is indicative of low-mass bodies several times the size of Jupiter. Their low temperatures are too cool to be distant stars, yet these objects are not massive enough to engender nuclear fusion reactions. Astronomers are puzzled by these "planetars" and how they might have formed. One possibility is that these planets have been thrown out of their solar systems by gravitational forces. Alternatively, they may have condensed out of a gas cloud in the same way as a star.

Growth of the gas giants

Most of the planets found orbiting other stars are large Jupiter-like planets—rocky planets like Earth are much too small and faint to be observed

with the instruments currently available. Prevailing theories of how our own Solar System formed suggest that the temperature of the disk material decreased with increasing distance from the Sun. Models of how the giant planets developed are based on a rocky core 10 times bigger than Earth, which gravitationally attracted hydrogen and helium gas from the protoplanetary disk. Compared with the inner planets, the gas giants are thought to have formed relatively quickly, within a few million years, while a substantial amount of gas remained in the disk. However, studies of protoplanetary disks around stars between 8 and 30 million years old suggest that there might be sufficient gas left to form at least one planet with Jupiter's mass. If giant planets are capable of forming on timescales of 10 to 20 million years, then it is probable that there are many orbiting isolated stars like our Sun.

What is causing astronomers to revise their theories of planet formation is the discovery that some of these giant planets are occupying much closer or eccentric orbits around their stars than expected. Models predict that giant planets cannot form too close to a star because there is not enough disk material and it would be too hot to coalesce. Yet four of the so-called 51 Pegasi-type extrasolar planets have orbits less than one-third the distance of Mercury from the Sun. One explanation put forward by researchers at the universities of California and Washington is that young

▲ Saturn's rings are composed of innumerable small rocky and icy particles orbiting in independent orbits. Complex tidal resonances operate between the rings and the so-called shepherd moons, which keep the rings in place. The origin of the ring systems around the gas giants is not known, but they are thought to have been formed when the planets were created.

protoplanets carve a groove in the disk. The inner edge of the groove dissipates energy through dynamical friction, causing the disk material and the protoplanet to spiral inward toward the star. What saves the planet from being engulfed is the gravitational effect it has on the star. Because the star is spinning faster than the planet is orbiting, the star begins to bulge and tugs the planet forward, propelling it into a larger orbit where it eventually becomes stabilized.

The discovery of planets with highly elliptical orbits has also prompted a rethink on planetary development. Most of the planets in the Solar System have almost circular orbits consistent with a spinning disk of material, with the exceptions of Mercury and Pluto, which have a slight oval eccentricity of 0.2. Two of the new planets have eccentricities of 0.68 and 0.4 by comparison. One theory put forward by NASA scientists and based on calculations of the gravitational forces exerted by protoplanets on the disk suggests that alternating spiral "density waves" are set up in the dust that eventually force the protoplanets out of a circular orbit. Another theory arises from the possibility of a number of superplanets forming. The gravitational interactions between such large planets would push some inward and fling others out of the system, leaving the remainder with highly eccentric orbits. It is lucky for our Solar System that Jupiter has a stable circular orbit—Earth might have been flung out beyond Pluto if it had not.

Planetary migration

Evidence that planets can change orbit during their formation exists within our Solar System. Pluto does not fit easily in the conventional theory of planetary evolution. It is a small and rocky planet lying in an elliptical orbit whose plane is at an angle to that of the other planets. For 20 years of its 248-year orbit it lies closer to the Sun than Neptune. Other objects that cross Neptune's path either collide with it or are ejected from the Solar System. Yet Pluto has managed to sustain its orbit by a phenomenon called resonance, in that it makes two revolutions around the Sun to Neptune's three, giving a 3:2 resonance. The relative motions of the two planets ensure that Pluto crosses Neptune's orbit at a safe distance.

A new theory speculates that Pluto's peculiar orbit may have arisen if the giant gas planets, particularly Saturn, Uranus, and Neptune, had migrated outward to their present orbits. Pluto would have been in a circular orbit in the same plane as the other planets, but as Neptune moved out, Pluto was pushed into its new orbit by resonant gravitational torque. Evidence that this theory may be correct is being collected by observing objects in the Kuiper Belt, a large collection of planetesimals occupying eccentric orbits far beyond Pluto. Little tracking has been done of the orbits of most of these objects, but some have been found to orbit in 3:2 resonances like Pluto. Further proof will occur if objects with even more eccentric orbits are found at a 2:1 resonances, indicating that planetary migration did indeed occur. The small number of objects at closer 5:3 and 4:3 resonances is indicative of Neptune's sweeping effect.

Calculations show that Neptune may have increased its original orbital distance by as much as 30 percent. The displacement was less for Jupiter, Saturn, and Uranus at approximately 2, 10, and 15 percent, respectively. It is thought that migration occurred over a period of about 100 million years, early in the evolution of the Solar System but after the planets had formed.

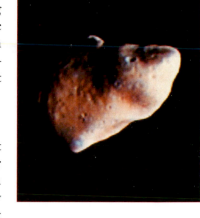

▲ Asteroids are rocky objects that orbit between Mars and Jupiter. They are believed to be the remains of a number of protoplanets that failed to coalesce into a planet during the formation of the Solar System because of the influence of Jupiter's gravity.

FACT FILE

■ Evidence that stars cannibalize their own planets may have been found in traces of lithium-6 detected in the atmosphere of the star HD 82934. This star is known to have a planetary system, but lithium-6 would not have survived the early evolutionary process of the star and must have been added later. The most likely hypothesis is that the star has swallowed one of its own planets.

■ The water in our oceans may have been provided by icy asteroids flung at Earth by Jupiter's gravity while it was still growing. The ratio of deuterium to hydrogen in Earth's seawater is about five times that found in the Sun but only one-third that of comets, indicating that local planetesimals were the probable source of water.

■ Location is the key to a habitable planet—too close to the Sun, any water would boil away; too far, it would freeze. Scientists are carrying out a census of nearby stars with planets to find out how many might lie within this "comfort zone."

SEE ALSO: ASTROPHYSICS • EARTH • GRAVITY • ORBIT • RESONANCE • SOLAR SYSTEM

Plasma Physics

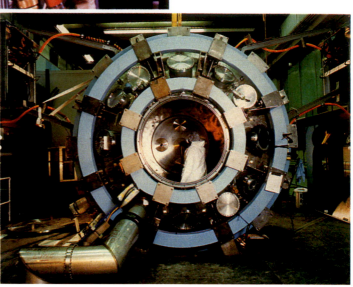

◄ A view through the inspection window of a magnetic containment nuclear fusion device. The blue haze is a hydrogen isotope that is superheated until it splits into nuclei and electrons, creating plasma. If this plasma can be further heated, nuclear fusion occurs.

A plasma is essentially a gas consisting not of complete molecules but of equal numbers of negative electrons, positive ions, and possibly some neutral atoms and molecules. It is considered the fourth state of matter, after solid, liquid, and gaseous states. Plasmas constitute most of the matter in the Universe, such as that in stars and interstellar matter. Artificial plasmas occur in gas discharge tubes and in plasma arcs. Plasmas occur naturally on Earth in lightning bolts, the aurora borealis, and in that portion of Earth's upper atmosphere known as the ionosphere. The freely moving electrons in the crystals of a metal have some of the characteristics of a plasma as well.

Matter changes state as it is exposed to heat. At high temperatures, a gas becomes ionized—the electrons acquire enough energy to free themselves from the attractive forces of the nucleus and so are able to move independently. The resulting state is called a plasma, which contains charged particles such as electrons and the positively charged nucleus ions. Because of these charged particles, a plasma can support an electric current and react to electric and magnetic fields applied to it. Plasma cannot be described as an ordinary gas that is electrically conducting; there is a fundamental difference between a gas and a plasma, resulting from the very different nature of the interparticle forces. The dynamics of a gas are dominated by two-body, billiard ball-like collisions, where the forces are strong but of short range. The forces between particles in a plasma, however, are comparatively weak and occur over a longer range.

Ionization energy

To achieve ionization, very high energies are needed. In the center of stars, the energy occurs as heat resulting from nuclear fusion, but in a star's corona, heating occurs through rapidly moving waves that emanate from the star's surface. In addition, plasmas may be created where the ionization energy is supplied by high-energy photons, such as in Earth's ionosphere, where X rays and ultraviolet rays produced by the Sun provide the necessary energy. In laboratories, powerful lasers have also been used to create plasmas.

Interest in plasma and its properties stems from its importance in astrophysics and in the development of controlled nuclear fusion. In the core of the Sun, at temperatures of 18 to 27 million°F (10–15 million°C), hydrogen is converted into helium by nuclear fusion, resulting in the release of energy. To use fusion to produce energy on Earth, the most suitable fusion reaction is the

▲ The spheromak S-1 nuclear fusion experiment at Princeton, New Jersey. The spheromak is designed to study the magnetic containment of fusion reactions.

one between the nuclei of the two heavy isotopes of hydrogen, namely deuterium and tritium. However, a temperature of over 180 million°F (100 million°C) is needed, at which temperature the isotopes are in the plasma state.

Aiming for breakeven

Today, scientists are mainly concerned with development of methods for the containment and control of such high-temperature plasmas, to get more energy out of the system than is put in—what is called energy breakeven. Two main schemes have emerged as candidates for future power reactors using fusion energy: inertial confinement and magnetic confinement. In a magnetic field the charged particles readily spiral along the field lines but diffuse only very slowly across them. The particles behave as if they were tied to the magnetic field. The most promising magnetic confinement systems are toroidal (doughnut shaped), and of these, the most advanced is the tokamak, which confines the plasma better than previous devices. In a tokamak, plasma is heated in a toroidal vessel isolated from the walls by magnetic fields. In the early 1990s, important experiments were made using the world's largest tokamaks, the Tokamak Fusion Test Reactor in the United States and the Joint European Torus in England. In these fusion demonstration experiments, scientists confined a deuterium–tritium plasma hotter than 180 million°F (100 million°C) to produce more than a megawatt of fusion power.

In inertial confinement fusion, a small pellet of deuterium–tritium fuel is irradiated by high-energy laser or particle beams to create an implosion, producing the high density and temperatures needed for fusion. This process is what happens inside hydrogen bombs, where the required energy to implode the pellet comes from a fission explosion. Less violent power production requires small millimeter-sized pellets to be ignited every second. Scientists at Lawrence Livermore National Laboratory in the United

◄ A plasma polymerization unit, which coats microprocessor chips to improve their electrical conductivity.

▶ A transmission gear undergoing a hardening process in a plasma chamber. Ions from the plasma dissolve onto the steel, forming a new, harder alloy on the surface. This photograph, taken through the inspection window of the chamber, shows the transmission gear fluorescing as the excited plasma ions recombine with electrons in the steel and give off energy.

States are planning to use pulses of 1.8 megajoules in energy to produce nuclear fusion.

Scientists are finding that plasmas can solve many technological problems, including plasma-etching processes in the semiconductor industry. Ion beams, produced in pulsing plasma discharges, etch silicon chips. Plasma deposition is commonly used to coat materials; for example, diamond coating can be achieved using high temperature hydrocarbon plasma discharges to produce very hard scratch-resistant surfaces.

Surfing particles

Scientists working at the University of California at Los Angeles have been able to produce an accelerating electric field of 700 million volts per meter, known as the plasma beat-wave accelerator. In this accelerator, two laser beams of slightly different frequencies are injected into a plasma. The interaction between the lasers and the plasma produces a space-charge wave, or plasma wave, capable of trapping and accelerating the plasma particles, which "surf" on the wave at velocities near the speed of light.

Conventional accelerator technology, used, for example, in accelerators at Fermilab near Chicago, produce very-high-energy particles, but these accelerators have to be very large—the Tevatron at Fermilab is 4 miles (6.4 km) long.

Research into plasma accelerators may one day produce much smaller accelerators with many applications from producing radioactive isotopes and X rays to tunable electromagnetic sources.

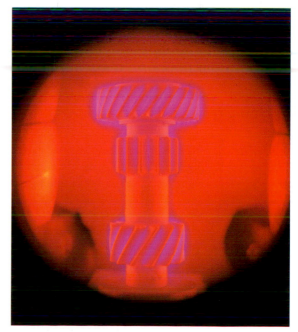

SEE ALSO: DISCHARGE TUBE • ELECTRICITY • FUSION • ION AND IONIZATION • MATTER, PROPERTIES OF • PARTICLE ACCELERATOR

Plastic Surgery

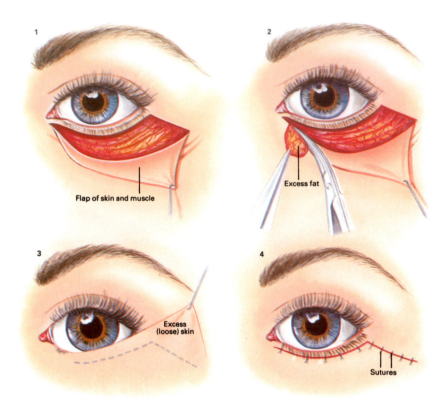

1

2

Flap of skin and muscle

Excess fat

3

4

Excess (loose) skin

Sutures

Plastic surgery is the surgical management of a wide variety of conditions of the skin and connective tissue. These conditions may be present from birth or result from injury, burns, age, or cancer.

Plastic surgeons, with their techniques and skills, can produce more pleasing cosmetic results (which are of more value to a patient) than can ordinary surgeons performing the same operation. They act as members of a clinical management team in the treatment of particularly difficult cases, such as patients with cleft lip and palate, head and neck cancer, and gross deformities of the head and face; victims of multiple injury; and people requesting sex-change operations.

▲ The stages in an operation to remove bags from under the eyes. An incision is made under the eyelid to pull down a flap of skin and muscle (1). Any excess fat is removed (2). The skin and muscle from the flap are then pulled up at the corner of the eye, and the excess tissue is removed (3). The incisions are then sutured (4).

History

The origins of plastic surgery can be traced back to around 600 B.C.E. in India, when Susruta described 16 different methods of repairing earlobes; to ancient Greece and Egypt, where Hippocrates and others over a number of centuries described ways of dealing with scars and correcting deformities of eyelids and hands; and to the Chinese T'ang dynasty of 618–907 C.E., where Fang Kan repaired cleft lips and palates. Advances in modern plastic surgery have taken place through the ingenuity of military surgeons in wartime over the past 400 years.

In the 16th century, Ambroise Paré described new methods of cleaning wounds and dressing

burns and designed a large variety of hand and face prostheses for French soldiers who were hideously deformed in war. At the same time, Gasparo Tagliacozzi devised a method of making a nose from a flap of tissue raised from the patient's upper arm. He was abused by his contemporaries and the clergy, who accused him of meddling with human destiny and God's handiwork.

Further development was delayed until around the Napoleonic Wars and the American Civil War, when surgeons became concerned not just with increasing the chance of survival for the injured but with improving the quality of the survivors' lives. However, it was only during and after World War I that this style of surgery received universal recognition as a special surgical art under the heading of plastic and reconstructive surgery. The Society of Plastic and Reconstructive Surgery was formed in the United States soon after the war and was followed by the formation of similar societies in Europe.

Since World War II, plastic surgery has become an established and respected surgical specialty with its own subspecialties.

Cosmetic surgery

Plastic surgery is often thought of as the surgery of face lifts, invisible scars, and the body beautiful. Interestingly enough, it is often the most attractive who request treatment, alongside those who suffer gross abnormalities.

More and more people in the United States and Europe are having their face lifted and wrinkles and crow feet removed, as they believe it makes them feel and look good and improves their performance at work. In some countries, however, debate continues as to whether this sort of surgery is a luxury and whether it should be available as a public health service.

The commonest cosmetic operation is nose reduction or reshaping—one of the most satisfying operations carried out by a plastic surgeon, since its effect is immediate. The result depends not only on the surgeon's technique but also on the way in which the patient's tissues heal.

Breast operations, in which breasts are enlarged by the insertion of silicone or saline-filled implants, are also common. Unfortunately, in about 10 to 20 percent of these operations the scar tissue around the implant becomes hard, making the breast tender, and surgery may be needed to remove and replace the implant. Simple breast massage can sometimes prevent this distressing side effect. There are also operations for reducing breast size and for firming up drooping breasts. Reconstruction is also a commonly used technique for women who have had a breast removed because of cancer. With modern medical techniques and devices, it is possible for surgeons to create a breast that is close in form and appearance to a natural breast.

Most of the sex-change operations performed change men into women. The most radical procedure is amputating the male genitalia and using the skin of the penis to line a newly created vagina. Other surgical sex-change procedures include increasing the size of breasts, changing the shape of the face, and using electrolysis to remove facial hair. The surgical change of a woman into a man has been much less successful, however, mainly because of the difficulty in constructing a satisfactory penis.

Microvascular surgery

Microvascular surgery allows plastic surgeons to join together very small blood vessels. It has revolutionized limb reattachment, organ transplantation, and skin grafting.

The reattachment of amputated limbs is a relatively new phenomenon in humans. It was only in the mid-1960s and early 1970s that successful human reattachments were being reported in China, Japan, Britain, and the United States. Now it is fairly common for patients who have had an accidental amputation of all or part of a limb to be considered for reattachment. The success of the operation, however, depends on a number of factors. For instance, the younger the patient, the better the result; a crushed body part injury makes reattachment far less satisfactory than does a cleanly sliced injury; and a severed finger is not as important as a thumb, which represents about 50 percent of hand function. In general, the best results are with fingers and thumbs, with 75 percent of patients obtaining

SKIN GRAFTS

Four different thicknesses of skin graft are used in plastic surgery. Split-skin grafts include only part of the dermis, but a full-thickness graft involves removal of the full depth of the skin. The thinner the layer of skin removed, the sooner the donor site heals by forming a new epidermis.

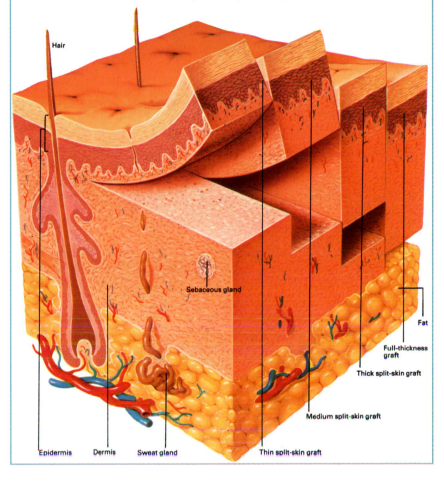

excellent results and returning to work and 60 percent of hand-reattachment cases achieving reasonable function. In the case of an arm, however, cosmetic appearance is usually excellent, but hand sensation and muscle power are poor. Therefore, a patient cannot return to work if he or she needs

▼ Rhinoplasty to alter the shape of the nose is one of the most common plastic surgery operations and is carried out from inside the nose to avoid scarring.

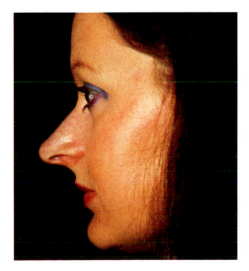

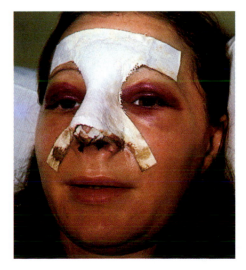

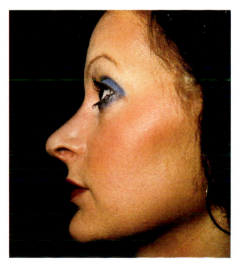

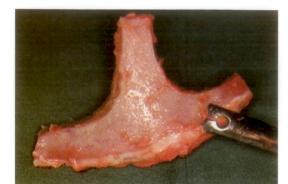

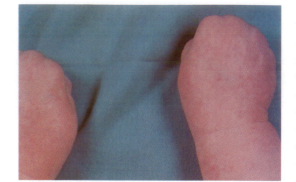

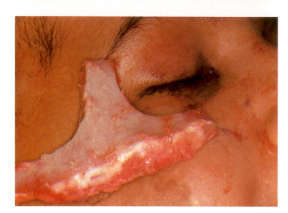

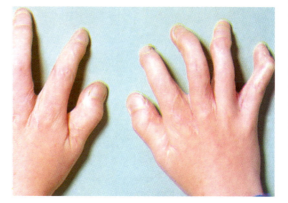

◄ Plastic surgery can involve the grafting of pieces of bone. Here, a section of bone from the pelvis (top left) is grafted onto a patient's cheekbone, which had been left with a depression after an injury (bottom left). After skin grafting and healing, the injury will not be apparent. In complete syndactyly (top right), a congenital abnormality of the hand, a baby's fingers are fused together. Plastic surgery with the bones and skin produces excellent results (bottom right).

two-handed coordination. Other amputated body parts that may be reattached are the scalp, the lip, the nose, the ears, the legs, and the penis.

Microvascular surgery has also been used for tissue transfer on organs such as testes, bowels, joints and nerves, as well as for skin grafting. For instance, a part of the bowel can be used to replace part of the gullet.

Another important advance from microsurgery is the use of free flaps for skin cover, that is, the transfer of skin to distant areas of the body that do not have suitable local flaps. In this procedure, the graft is removed from its normal blood supply, and the blood vessels are then joined to an undamaged artery and vein near the area of skin loss. This procedure is particularly valuable in the treatment of burns and other skin-loss conditions, such as deep bed sores or chronic ulcers.

Although microvascular procedures can take a very long time, reconstructions can be done in one stage, and therefore, patients usually have only one operation. Improvements in the technique have resulted in quicker transfers, and success rates compare favorably with other methods of reconstruction. Some plastic surgeons believe that, if the issue of tissue rejection is solved, the possibilities of tissue transfer could be limitless.

Examples of plastic surgery

Plastic surgeons are able to treat various types of abnormality or conditions. Cleft lip and palate is the most common congenital abnormality of the head and neck. At its worst (cleft lip and palate),

children are born with a large gap in the middle of their face with no upper lip, absence or deviation of the lower part of the nose, and a hole inside the mouth leading into the nose. At its best (cleft lip), there is a separation of the upper mouth. Unless treated, these children have an unfortunate appearance, difficulty in eating, speaking, and breathing, and in a considerable number, hearing difficulties. Cleft lip occurs in about 1 in 750 live births and is more common in boys, whereas cleft palate, with an incidence of 1 in 2,000 live births, is more common in girls. About 50 percent of cases have both conditions.

Patients with cleft lip and palate require medical supervision from birth through to adult life, and the attention of many different specialists, including plastic surgeons, orthodontists, oral surgeons, ear, nose, and throat surgeons, pediatricians, speech therapists, and child psychiatrists. It has become apparent that these patients benefit when managed by a combined team of specialists. Self-help organizations, run by parents of children with these abnormalities, are able to counsel other parents in the difficult period just after birth by visiting them at the hospital and at home and by advising them about such problems as feeding. In the repair of cleft lip, modern techniques appreciate that the deformity affects not only the skin but also muscles in the face, the upper jawbone and the nose. The emphasis is to correct as many of these deformities as possible at the initial operation, which usually takes place when the child is about ten weeks old.

Some plastic surgeons will do simple lip repairs within 48 hours of birth, usually as a psychological support to the parents, but final closure is required later on. In the repair of cleft palate, the soft palate is closed around six months to a year before speech develops, and it is becoming more common for the surgeon to delay closure of the hard palate so that scarring can be avoided and the upper jawbone can grow normally.

Head and neck cancers are generally treated by a clinical team; the plastic surgeon's role is to reconstruct those tissues and organs that have been removed by using techniques such as microvascular surgery to obtain a good cosmetic result. Sometimes, despite the techniques available, the use of a simple prosthesis, such as an artificial nose or eye attached to eyeglass frames, can be much better camouflage than plastic surgery.

Another innovative development, called craniofacial surgery, tackles the treatment of problems such as hideous facial deformities caused at birth or by accident. At present, this type of surgery is mainly available in specialist centers.

Computers and lasers

Magnetic resonance imaging, computerized tomography, and similar computer-imaging techniques have revolutionized the field of plastic surgery, making significant improvements in surgeons' abilities to analyze deformities and plan complex procedures.

Likewise, lasers have also brought plastic surgery forward by leaps and bounds. Surgeons use the laser as a "light scalpel," with the laser enabling tissue to be altered without making an incision. The laser allows an extremely controlled vaporization of tissue; therefore, surgeons can treat birthmarks and damaged blood vessels, shrink facial spider veins, and remove tattoos or port-wine stains, all without major surgery. Lasers can also be used to reduce fine wrinkles around the lips, eyes, or whole face.

Resurfacing and sculpting

Chemical peels and dermabrasion are used to alter the texture of the skin. Known technically as skin resurfacing, this treatment can reduce the pitting caused by acne scars and the effects of sun damage. For such a procedure, skin condition is of paramount importance—if the patient has a history of poor scarring, has dark skin, is prone to cold sores, or has previous burns or allergies, the case will need careful evaluation.

The mildest peel used is glycolic acid. Trichloroacetic acid (TCA) can be used in different strengths for longer-lasting effects. The deepest peel effect, however, is achieved with phenol.

The skin remains sensitive to sunlight for some time, so sun blocks are a necessary precaution in the aftermath of such treatment. Dermabrasion enables some deeper scars and wrinkles to be smoothed. The surgeon uses a high-speed rotating brush to remove the top layer of skin until the scar or wrinkle is smoothed away.

Liposuction is used to sculpt the body by removing unwanted fat from specific areas, including the abdomen, hips, buttocks, thighs, knees, upper arms, chin, cheeks, and neck. A narrow tube, or cannula, is inserted and used to suck out the fat layer deep beneath the skin. Several new techniques, including ultrasound-assisted lipoplasty, are now providing excellent results.

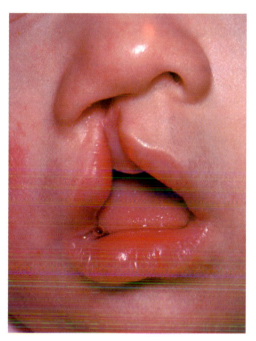

◄ A child born with a hare, or cleft, lip (a common condition) shows remarkable improvement after plastic surgery (below).

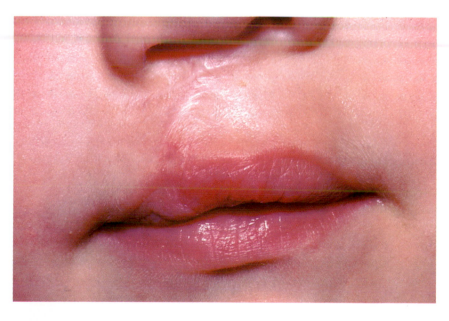

 SEE ALSO: MICROSURGERY • MUSCLE • OTOLARYNGOLOGY • SKIN • SURGERY • TRANSPLANT

Plastics

The word *plastic* comes from the Greek word *plastikos*, meaning "capable of being molded." The chief property of plastics is that they are deformable and easily made into almost any shape by processes such as molding or extrusion. Plastics consist of high-molecular-weight organic molecules, called polymers, made up of repeating units—monomers—chemically linked together in the form of a chain or network. Many plastics formulations also include substances, such as inert fillers, stabilizers, colorants, and plasticizers, that improve flexibility.

Cellulosic plastics

The first manufactured plastics were derived from cellulose—a polymer present in natural substances, such as cotton and wood. These plastics classify as semisynthetic, since their polymer backbones are already present in the natural source material, but chemical manipulation is required to free the polymers from impurities and produce them in useful forms.

Cellulose is a natural condensation polymer of the carbohydrate glucose ($C_6H_{12}O_6$). Ether linkages of formula $-CH_2-O-CH_2-$ link the glucose units together, and each glucose unit forms a six-membered ring from which three hydroxyl (–OH) groups hang. Those hydroxyl groups are responsible for the insolubility of cellulose, since they form strong hydrogen bonds between adjacent cellulose chains. All processes for making cellulose-derived plastics therefore start by converting hydroxyl groups into other groups that are incapable of hydrogen bonding, so the solubility of the polymer increases.

Cellulose nitrate. The first processes for making plastics from cellulose used nitration to convert hydroxyl groups into nitrate groups in a reaction similar to that used to make guncotton:

$$R-OH + HNO_3 \rightarrow R-O-NO_2 + H_2O$$

where R denotes the rest of the glucose unit. Whereas guncotton has practically all its hydroxyl groups nitrated and is explosive, cellulose nitrates for plastics have around 80 to 90 percent of their hydroxyl groups nitrated and are highly flammable—a major disadvantage of these materials.

The first nitrated-cellulose plastic was made in 1862 by the British chemist Alexander Parkes. He used a mixture of nitric and sulfuric acids to prepare a nitrated cellulose, which he dissolved in a solvent distilled from wood. The resulting substance—Parkesine—was readily molded but proved impossible to make on a large scale.

A colleague of Parkes improved the properties of cellulose nitrate by mixing it with castor oil and a little camphor—both of which are natural plasticizers—but the greatest development was that of the U.S. chemist John W. Hyatt, who in 1870 prepared Celluloid—the first commercially successful plastic. Like Parkesine, Celluloid was based on cellulose nitrate, but it contained only camphor as its plasticizer. The new material was used to make a wide range of products, including eyeglass frames, combs, billiard balls, knife handles, and photographic film. Nitrocellulose continued to be used as the basis for high-gloss automotive lacquers until the late 20th century, when it was superseded by acrylic coatings.

Cellulose nitrate fibers were made as early as 1846, when the German chemist Christian Schönbein treated cotton with nitric acid.

▲ The domes of the Eden Project, a giant flora conservancy scheme in Cornwall, Britain, are made of three layers of polycarbonate plastic. The polymer allows light into the greenhouses and traps heat, enabling tropical environments to be sustained. The lightness of the material is ideal for building large structures such as these.

Unfortunately, the combination of flammability and large surface area per unit volume made such fibers too hazardous for use in textiles. This situation changed in the late 1880s, when a process was developed for making cellulose nitrate fibers safe by converting them back into cellulose.

Cellulose acetates. The flammability problems of cellulose nitrate were addressed in the late-19th century by the conversion of cellulose into ethanoate (acetate) esters rather than nitrate esters. A combination of ethanoic anhydride and sulfuric acid causes the following change:

$$R–OH + (CH_3CO)_2O \rightarrow$$
$$R–O–COCH_3 + CH_3COOH$$

and the initial product is the triethanoate—the polymer in which all three hydroxyl groups on each glucose unit are esterified.

Cellulose triethanoate is soluble in trichloromethane (chloroform, $CHCl_3$), and such solutions can can be spun into warm air to produce fibers for making easy-care fabrics sold under the trade names Arnel and Tricel. Since the 1960s, such fibers have been largely replaced by cheaper and more heat-resistant polyesters.

In the early days of cellulose acetate development, trichloromethane was a relatively expensive solvent, so its requirement for the cellulose triethanoate process limited the commercial viability of that polymer. In 1905, however, the British chemist George Miles discovered that hydrolyzing one in every three ethanoate groups back to a hydroxyl group yielded a polymer that is soluble in cheap solvents, such as propanone (acetone, CH_3COCH_3). This product, called cellulose diacetate, could be spun from propanone solutions and extruded as film. Cellulose diethanoate and its solutions were used for coating and strengthening the fabric skins of World War I aircraft wings and to make safety film—a low-flammability replacement for nitrocellulose cinematographic film. Later, with the invention of injection molding, cellulose diacetate was used to make shatterproof transparent panels for safety goggles and instrument gauges.

Regenerated cellulose. Cellulose can be turned into textiles that have a more natural feel by converting it first into a soluble form for spinning, then restoring it to its original composition. In the cuprammonium process, a solution of copper hydroxide and ammonia in water dissolves cellulose from wood pulp. When the solution is sprayed into an acid bath through a spinneret—a perforated cap—solid fibers of cellulose form.

In the viscose process, wood pulp or cotton waste is first digested with a concentrated solution of sodium hydroxide (NaOH), forming unstable sodium salts of the hydroxyl groups of the glucose units. These salts then react with carbon disulfide to form sodium xanthates:

$$R–O^-Na^+ + CS_2 \rightarrow R–O–CS–S^-Na^+$$

The xanthate solution, which is viscous—hence the process name *viscose*—can then be forced through a spinneret into a bath of concentrated sulfuric acid. The acid converts the xanthates back into cellulose, which forms as fibers of viscose rayon. Alternatively, viscose can be extruded through a slit to form sheets of cellophane.

Toward the end of the 20th century, the viscose process was modified to produce Tencel—a regenerated cellulose fiber that accepts dyes better than viscose rayon and forms superior blends with natural fibers. At the same time, process modifications helped ensure that all the toxic carbon disulfide used in the first stage is reused rather than discharged to the environment.

Synthetic plastics

Most modern plastics are totally synthetic, that is, they are made by reacting simple compounds obtained directly from oil refining, such as ethene (ethylene, $CH_2{=}CH_2$), or by reacting their derivatives, such as polytetrafluoroethene ($CF_2{=}CF_2$).

In many cases, such polymers were made many years—decades even—before their first industrial manufacture. For example, the French chemist Henri Regnault noted as early as 1838 that sunlight turned chloroethene (vinyl chloride, CH_2CHCl) into a resinous substance (now known as PVC, polyvinyl chloride), but he had no idea of the significance of his observation. PVC was deliberately made for the first time in 1872, and its synthesis was patented in 1913.

▼ Plastic engineering components such as these can be made from nylon, polypropene, or even polytetrafluoroethene. They are much lighter than the equivalent metal parts, can often be molded in one piece, and run more smoothly than metal parts.

PVC came to be considered useful only after 1926, when Waldo Semon—then a new recruit at the research department of the B. F. Goodrich Company at Akron, Ohio—accidentally invented plasticized polyvinyl chloride.

Semon was boiling PVC in a high-boiling solvent in an attempt to eliminate hydrogen chloride from the polymer and make an adhesive for bonding rubber and metal. The result was solid PVC made flexible by its solvent content. In this form—rather than as pure polymer, which is brittle—PVC rapidly became a commercially successful product.

The histories of other polymer discoveries are similarly protracted. For example, the polymerization of phenylethene (styrene) was first reported in 1839 by the German chemist Eduard Simon. Styrene monomer is difficult to obtain pure, however, and impurities make its polymer brittle. It was only in 1937 that scientists at the Dow Chemical Company successfully polymerized pure phenylethene, and full-scale production of polystyrene started in 1938.

In the case of the condensation between phenol (C_6H_5OH) and methanal (formaldehyde, HCHO), the development of appropriate technology was the crucial factor in making useful polymers. The polymerization reaction had been reported as early as 1872, by the German chemist Adolf von Bayer, but it was the Belgian Leo Baekeland who is credited with the first synthesis of useful phenol-methanal resins, in 1909.

Baekeland's success was largely due to his invention and use of the Bakeliser: a chemical reactor vessel that allowed him to control the conditions of temperature and pressure in order to steer the reaction to produce the required materials. Using this equipment, Baekeland produced the resins that—when mixed with fillers and heated in molds—produced the hard, brown-to-black thermosets that he called Bakelite. They were the first fully synthetic plastics, and they were used to make casings for electrical goods.

The polymer of methyl 2-methylpropenoate (methyl methacrylate, $CH_2=C(CH_3)COOCH_3$) was first made in 1877 by the German chemists Fittig and Paul. Polymethylmethacrylate went into full-scale production only 50 years later, in 1927, and it would form the basis of the tough, transparent plastic sheeting sold under proprietary names such as Plexiglas and Perspex.

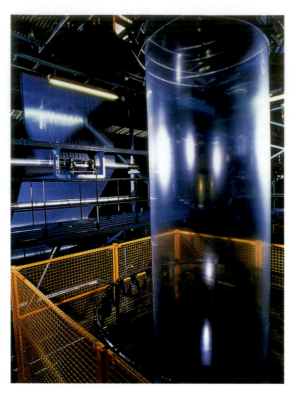

▲ Plastic bag production uses a molten film of polyethene that is extruded through a thin rectangular orifice. A current of film is passed through the film to expand it into a tube. It is then cut to size and heat sealed at one end to form bags.

Polyalkenes

In terms of chemical structure, the simplest polymers are the polyalkenes, also called polyolefins ("olefin" is an archaic name for an alkene—a hydrocarbon that contains a double bond). The raw materials for these polymers are usually obtained by cracking petroleum.

The simplest of the polyalkenes is polyethene, which consists of chains of $-CH_2-$ groups. The more detailed structure of the polymer depends on the conditions under which it is made and the catalysts used. Polymerization using a free-radical initiator at high pressure (around 1,000 atmospheres) and 390°F (200°C) produces highly branched low-density polyethene (LDPE), whereas lightly branched high-density polyethene (HDPE) is produced by polymerization at low pressure and near-ambient temperature using an organometallic Ziegler–Natta catalyst.

The extent of branching is directly related to density, since highly branched chains cannot pack together as closely as chains that have little or no branching. Branching also discourages the formation of regions of crystallinity, which harden the polymer. Hence, HDPE is stronger but less flexible than LDPE. The balance between flexibility and strength can be manipulated by copolymerizing ethene with other alkenes, such as but-1-ene ($C_2H_5CH=CH_2$), hex-1-ene ($C_4H_9CH=CH_2$), or oct-1-ene ($C_6H_{13}CH=CH_2$). The reaction is done under the mild conditions used with Ziegler–Natta catalysts to make HDPE, but the comonomers introduce side chains with two to six carbon atoms. The side chains reduce the density and improve the flexibility of the product, which is called linear low-density polyethene (LLDPE).

Polypropylene is the other major polyalkene. Its repeat unit is $-CH_2-CH(CH_3)-$. The polymerization is performed using mild conditions of temperature and pressure and organometallic Ziegler–Natta catalysts. The catalysts promote formation of isotactic polypropene—polymer in which all methyl ($-CH_3$) groups are on the same "side" of the chain. The methyl groups hinder free rotation at the carbon atoms of the chain, making the individual polymer chains stiffer and the polymer harder.

Low-density polyethylene is used to make plastic bags and flexible bottles, whereas high-density polyethene and polypropene are used to make more rigid bottles, bottle caps, and packaging films. Polypropene fibers are used to make ropes and cables that are flexible and waterproof and for nonwoven, heavy-duty, easy-care carpets.

PTFE

Polytetrafluoroethene (PTFE), made from tetrafluoroethene ($CF_2=CF_2$), is a fluorinated version of polyethene. The presence of fluorine instead of hydrogen makes it harder and more resistant to heat and chemicals than polyethene and also confers low surface friction. This combination of properties makes it a useful nonstick coating for cooking utensils, a useful powder lubricant, and a suitable material for making lubricant-free bearings, for example.

PVC and vinyl copolymers

Polychloroethene (polyvinyl chloride, PVC) has the repeat unit $-CH_2-CHCl-$. The presence of the chlorine atom inhibits free rotation in the carbon chain and makes pure PVC a much more rigid polymer than polypropene, for example.

Pure PVC decomposes before it reaches its softening temperature, and thus, it cannot be molded or extruded. Stabilized PVC contains compounds that inhibit thermal decomposition, so it can be molded hot and then cooled to form rigid objects, such as pipes and gutters.

Plasticized PVC contains up to 50 percent of an involatile solvent, typically diisooctyl phthalate (DOP). The plasticizing solvent makes the mixture flexible at room temperature, leading to its widespread use as a flexible packaging film for food. However, the suspected toxicity of DOP has greatly restricted this use in recent years.

PVC can also be made flexible by including plasticizing monomers, such as ethenyl ethanoate (vinyl acetate, $CH_3COOCH=CH_2$) or 1,1-dichloroethene (vinylidene chloride, $CH_2=CCl_2$). Copolymers with vinyl acetate are used to make the vinyl for records, while vinylidene chloride copolymerized with around 15 percent vinyl chloride is saran, the polymer used in food wrap.

Acrylics

Acrylic is a general term that describes polymers and copolymers of propenoic acid (acrylic acid, $CH_2=CHCOOH$) and acrylate esters, 2-methylpropenoic acid (methacrylic acid, $CH_2=C(CH_3)COOH$) and methacrylate esters, propenonitrile (acrylonitrile, $CH_2=CHCN$) and propenamide (acrylamide, $CH_2=CHCONH_2$). A wide variety of properties can be obtained using different monomer blends, and chemical functionality can be added by including function-bearing monomers, such as 2-hydroxyethyl propenoate (2-hydroxyethyl acrylate,

$CH_2=CHCOOCH_2CH_2OH$). The polymerization of such blends is usually done in solution and is initiated by free-radical sources, such as benzoyl peroxide ($(C_6H_5CO)_2O_2$).

The acrylic used in textiles is polyacrylonitrile (PAN, trade name Acrilan), whose fibers are also the starting point for making carbon fiber. Flame-resistant fabrics called modacrylics are made using a copolymer of around 35 percent vinyl chloride with acrylonitrile.

Copolymers of acrylic and methacrylic acids and esters are used in transparent "glasses" and surface coatings. In general, methacrylates are harder than acrylates, whereas esters of long-chain alcohols—2-ethylhexanol, for example—contribute flexibility by plasticizing the polymer. Hardness and water resistance can be improved by including some phenylethene (styrene, $C_6H_5CH=CH_2$) in the monomer blend.

Synthetic rubber

The structure of natural rubber corresponds to it having been produced by polymerizing isoprene (2-methylbuta-1,3-diene, C_5H_8):

$$xCH_2=C(CH_3)-CH=CH_2 \rightarrow$$
$$-(CH_2-C(CH_3)=CH-CH_2)_x$$

In fact, the natural process is much more complicated than this, and isoprene could not at first be made to polymerize synthetically. Hence, most synthetic rubber is based on buta-1,3-diene and its derivatives, although some polyisoprene is now made using Ziegler–Natta catalysts.

The first synthetic rubber was Buna (a modified contraction of *bu*ta-1,3-diene and *Na*, the symbol for sodium, which catalyzed the reaction). Buna is softer than natural rubber, and it is usually hardened by including comonomers, such as styrene (Buna-S) or acrylonitrile (Buna-N), or by adding fillers, such as carbon black, a form of soot.

Neoprene is produced by polymerizing 2-chlorobuta-1,3-diene. It has greater mechanical strength than Buna rubber and better resistance

▼ The hull of this boat has a Kevlar skin. Kevlar is a tough polyamide that has a strength-to-weight ratio five times greater than steel, so the boat is much lighter than if it had a metal hull. Kevlar also has the benefits of abrasion resistance and shock-absorbing properties.

to swelling caused by solvents and mineral oils. Neoprene can be made tougher by treatment with zinc oxide (ZnO), which creates cross-links.

Polystyrene

The repeat unit in polystyrene is $-CH_2-CHPh-$, where Ph represents the phenyl (C_6H_5-) group. Pure polystyrene is hard and brittle, limiting its usefulness. However, it can be foamed by treatment with isopentane to produce a tough low-density material that is widely used as an insulating material for food packaging and as shock-absorbing "beans" in packing cases.

Styrene is useful in blends with other monomers, since it imparts hardness to the copolymer. One example is in ABS (acrylonitrile–butadiene–styrene) rubber, a tough material used to make plastic fenders and instrument panels for vehicles. Another is SAN (styrene–acrylonitrile copolymer). Polystyrene-based plastics are used to make molded casings and the insulating parts of electrical components.

Polyamides

The first polyamide—Nylon-6,6—was prepared in 1934 by the U.S. chemist W. H. Carothers, and commercial production started in 1937. Polyamides have one of two types of repeat units:

$$-OC-R_1-CONH-R_2-NH- \text{ (Nylon-6,6 type)}$$
$$\text{and } -OC-R_1-NH- \text{ (Nylon-6 type)}$$

In Nylon-6,6, R_1 is C_4H_8 and R_2 is C_6H_{12}; in Nylon-6, R_1 is C_5H_{10}. These polymers are used to make molded components and can be drawn into fibers for making textiles.

The properties of nylons can be modified by changing the groups that form the chain. Aromatic (benzene-based) R groups produce aramids—stiff polyamides such as Kevlar.

Polyesters and polycarbonates

These plastics are made by reacting an organic acid that has at least two carboxylic acid ($-COOH$) groups with a compound that has at least two hydroxy ($-OH$) groups. Polyester molecules have the following repeat unit:

$$-OC-R_1-CO-O-R_2-O-$$

R_1 and R_2 are hydrocarbon groups that depend on the particular polyester. In polyethylene terephthalate (PET), R_1 is an aromatic ring with formula C_6H_4, and R_2 is a $-CH_2CH_2-$ group. This polymer is used to make synthetic fibers, such as Dacron, plastic films, and bottles.

A more flexible polyester has the same R_1 group as PET, but its R_2 group is $-C_4H_8-$. This substance is used for moldings and films.

Polycarbonates have a structural formula that corresponds to a polyester formed between a bisphenol (a compound with two hydroxy groups attached to different aromatic rings) and carbonic acid (HO–CO–OH). The most common polycarbonate is made by reacting bisphenol A, formula $HO-C_6H_4-C(CH_3)_2-C_6H_4-OH$ with phosgene ($COCl_2$). It has the following repeat unit:

$$-C_6H_4-C(CH_3)_2-C_6H_4-O(CO)O-$$

and it is an extremely tough transparent material that can be extruded and molded to make safety glass and protective helmets.

Epoxies

Epoxy resins are made by reacting a bisphenol, such as bisphenol A, with epichlorhydrin (CH_2OCHCH_2Cl), a compound that has a three membered C–O–C ring, called an oxirane or epoxy group. The repeat unit is as follows:

$$OC_6H_4-C(CH_3)_2-C_6H_4O-CH_2CH(OH)CH_2-$$

Each end of the chain has an oxirane group. Typical epoxy resins have 2 to 20 repeat units, and their oxirane end groups react with diamines to form tough cross-linked polymers. Epoxies are used in two-pack adhesives and surface coatings.

Polyurethanes

Polyurethanes (PUs) are made by reacting a compound that has at least two isocyanate (–NCO) groups with another that has at least two hydroxy (–OH) groups. The repeat unit is as follows:

$$-(OC)HN-R_1-NH(CO)-O-R_2-O$$

For Perlon U, a typical PU, R_1 is C_6H_{12} and R_2 is C_4H_8.

Polyurethanes are flexible, impact-resistant polymers and thus are useful for high-performance coating applications.

Flexible polyurethane foams are made by reacting a polyester that has two hydroxy end groups with toluene diisocyanate (TDI), so R_1 would be $-C_6H_3(CH_3)-$ in the above formula. Some water is included in the mixture, and it releases carbon dioxide by reacting with excess TDI as the polymerization occurs. The carbon dioxide forms as bubbles that become trapped in the solid polymer.

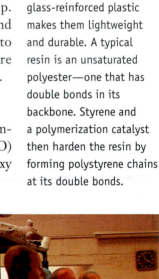

▼ These mannequins are made by curing a resin, reinforced with glass fiber, in a clay mold. The use of glass-reinforced plastic makes them lightweight and durable. A typical resin is an unsaturated polyester—one that has double bonds in its backbone. Styrene and a polymerization catalyst then harden the resin by forming polystyrene chains at its double bonds.

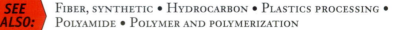

SEE ALSO: Fiber, synthetic • Hydrocarbon • Plastics processing • Polyamide • Polymer and polymerization

Plastics Processing

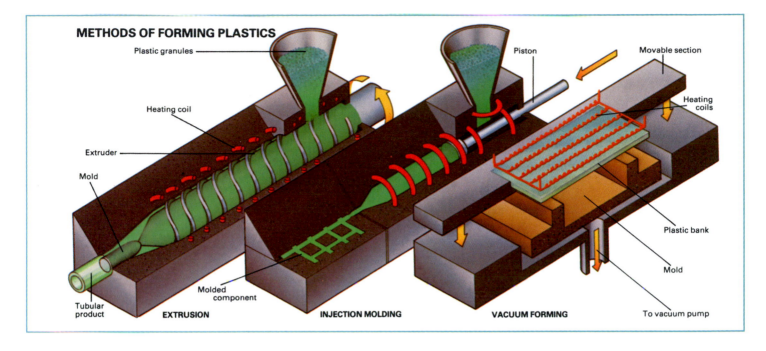

METHODS OF FORMING PLASTICS

Plastic granules · Piston · Movable section · Heating coil · Heating coils · Extruder · Mold · Plastic bank · Mold · Tubular product · Molded component · To vacuum pump

EXTRUSION   **INJECTION MOLDING**   **VACUUM FORMING**

Since the mid-20th century, the invention and developments of plastics have placed them in the same league as materials such as steel—the material that played a key role in the Industrial Revolution—and the materials that lent their names to the Stone Age, Bronze Age, and Iron Age. Now, plastics are the fourth most widely used materials after wood, concrete, and steel.

Plastics have many advantages over other materials. Components made from plastics tend to be much lighter than their counterparts made from other materials, so they are useful in making portable goods and fuel-efficient vehicles. Plastics do not corrode in moisture or pollution, although some can be degraded by the ultraviolet component of sunlight. This resistance to corrosion is not always a benefit, however, since it impedes the biodegradation that helpfully reduces the volumes of other types of waste in refuse landfill.

Plastics tend to be cheaper than materials such as steel and other alloys, since their raw materials are substances such as ethene, propene, and styrene—all low-cost products of the cracker and reformer units of oil refineries. They are also cheaper to process than steel and other alloys, because they require less energy to heat them to temperatures at which they become flexible.

The early plastics were not without limitations, however. Phenol-formaldehyde (phenolmethanal) polymers, such as Bakelite, were among the first synthetic polymers. They are thermosetting resins that become dark brown or black and extremely brittle when cured. Their excellent insulating properties suited them for making the casings for radio sets, telephones, and other electrical equipment, but their dark colors were impossible to disguise, and their brittleness made them liable to crack or chip on impact. Phenol-formaldehyde polymers were later superseded by melamine-formaldehyde polymers, which are tougher than phenol-formaldehyde polymers and practically colorless, so they can be colored to almost any shade.

Early thermoplastics included polyethene, which was at first only available in a waxy, low-density form. This material was used to make resealable food containers, for example. Low-density polyethene becomes whitened when subjected to stress, however, spoiling its appearance. Hence, stronger polymers—high-density polyethene and polypropene, for example—have superseded it in many applications.

The early problems with plastic—mainly caused by their being used in applications that exceeded their capabilities—led to their being associated with inferior goods. The reputation of plastics has since been greatly improved by the development of high-performance plastics, such as nylon engineering polymers; by product designers choosing materials whose properties are adequate for the intended use; and by advances in the formulation and processing of plastics.

Apart from one or more polymers, plastic formulations can include a plasticizer, a nonvolatile solventlike compound that softens the plastic; pigments and dyes that add color; antioxidants and stabilizers that inhibit degradation by air and ultraviolet light, respectively; lubricants that

▲ Extrusion and injection molding both start with granular plastic being melted and pressurized in a heated cylinder. In extrusion, an Archimedes' screw continuously forces the molten plastic through a die; in injection molding, a screw or ram forces the plastic into a mold that is then cooled and opened to release the formed object. In vacuum forming, a film or sheet of plastic is first softened by heating, then sucked into the mold by a partial vacuum.

improve the mold release, abrasion resistance, and slip characteristics of plastic goods; and inert solid fillers, such as talc, that provide hardness and bulk. Materials such as glass and carbon fibers can be added to contribute tensile strength.

Techniques for forming plastics include extrusion as sheets, rods, or tubes; injection molding; vacuum thermoforming; blow molding; and compression molding. The choice of technique depends on the shape of the finished object and the type of material used—thermoplastic, such as polyethene, or thermosetting, such as Bakelite.

Thermoplastics

Thermoplastics are polymer-based materials that soften reversibly on heating and whose properties do not change significantly after a cycle of heating and cooling. As its temperature increases, a thermoplastic first becomes flexible and elastic, like rubber, and then completely plastic, like a viscous liquid. The temperature to which a thermoplastic is heated for forming depends on the softening temperature of the plastic and the degree of softening that best suits the process.

Extrusion. Extrusion is a continuous or semi-continuous process used for making linear forms, such as sheets, rods, and tubes. An extruder consists of a heated, pressure-resistant barrel in which there is a helical screw, as in a domestic meat grinder. The screw forces granules of the plastic through a heated cylinder at a typical temperature of 392°F (200°C). The heat softens the thermoplastic and the screw pressurizes it to between 1,450 and 4,350 psi (10–30 MPa), forcing it through a die aperture as it exits the cylinder. A wide range of differently shaped products can be made by this method, depending on the shape of the die aperture. If the die is circular, rods or filaments are produced; if it is annular, pipes and tubes are formed; and if it is a slit, plastic sheeting or film will be produced. The continuous products emerging from the extruder die are cooled by air, water, cooled rollers, or contact with cooled metal surfaces that finish the shape of the extruded material. Flexible films are often drawn (stretched) at this point to improve their mechanical properties by "orienting" (aligning) the polymer chains. Extruded tubes of film, used to make plastic bags, can be pulled and inflated to draw the film along two perpendicular axes.

The finished product is then rolled up or cut into suitable lengths. Extrusion is used to make packaging films, plastic piping, and PVC cladding for window frames and many other products.

Injection molding. Injection molding can make objects whose shapes are more complex than those that can be achieved by extrusion. Like extrusion, the process starts with plastic being heated and pressurized as it is forced along a hot barrel by means of a screw. Instead of the screw forcing the softened plastic through a die, it forces it through a duct into a steel mold at temperatures of from about 355 to 570°F (180–300°C) and pressures of 14,500 psi (100 MPa) or more. After cooling, the mold opens and the article is removed. Inclusion of a mold-release agent—a type of lubricant—in the plastic formulation helps the finished object leave the mold.

Blow molding. Blow molding is used to make hollow articles with small openings, such as bottles, cans, drums, tanks and toys. In some cases, the process starts with a preform—a test-tube-shaped block of plastic. The hot preform is placed in the neck of a two-piece blow mold and inflated

▼ In pultrusion, layers of glass fiber matting are bonded with resin by drawing the resin-soaked sheets through rollers.

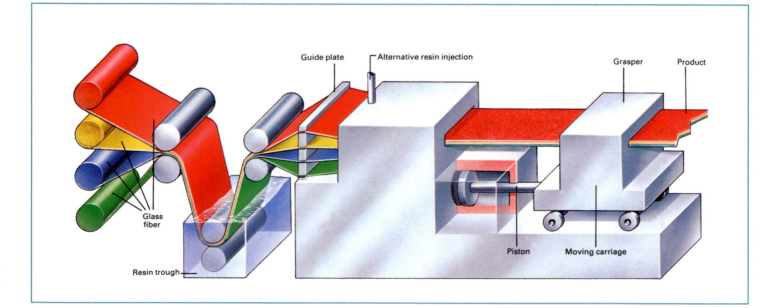

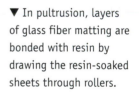

Guide plate | Alternative resin injection | Grasper | Product | Glass fiber | Resin trough | Piston | Moving carriage

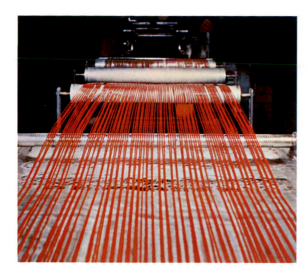

Examples of thermosetting resins include phenolic resins, which are based on condensation products formed by the reaction of methanal (formaldehyde, $H_2C=O$) with phenol (C_6H_5OH) and related compounds. The initial products are phenol molecules in which methylol groups ($-CH_2OH$) have replaced an average of at least two hydrogen atoms. Methylol groups can react together to form ether linkages ($-CH_2-O-CH_2-$) or methylene bridges ($-CH_2-$), either of which link molecules together. Heating the initial product increases molecular weight by starting the reaction between methylol groups.

Heating stops when the required molecular weight is reached, and the same reaction can then be resumed when the thermoset is in the mold. Short curing times are achieved by producing a high-molecular-weight resin in this first stage, but care must be taken to stop the reaction before the reaction goes too far, otherwise the product would be impossible to manipulate.

Thermosets are formulated as liquid, doughy, or solid substances by mixing thermosetting resins with other formulation components, such as fillers and catalysts. In compression molding, the mixture is then shaped by pushing it into a steel mold—sometimes with a reinforcing material, such as a glass-fiber mat. Heating elements in the mold then raise the temperature of its contents for a few minutes. The increase in temperature softens or melts the thermoset and triggers the curing reaction. In the alternative cold-curing process, a potent catalyst can be added just before molding, and the resin is then left to cure for a few hours at room temperature. After curing, the thermoset is removed from the mold. It can no longer be softened by heating.

Thermosetting resins can also be processed by injection molding. The thermoset is first heated gently to soften it in the barrel of an injection machine. Then, it is injected at high pressure into a hot mold, where curing takes place.

until it fills the mold. The mold then splits, and the formed object is removed. This technique is used to make plastic bottles for drinks.

In a slight variant on the preform process, a tube of plastic is extruded directly into the open blow mold. As the mold closes, it presses one end of the tubular section together to seal it. Compressed air is blown into the other end of the tube until it fills the cooled mold and solidifies.

Vacuum thermoforming. Thermoforming is a process for making shaped articles, such as bowls or beakers, from plastic sheeting or film. Infrared radiation heats the plastic to between 250 and 355°F (120–180°C), softening it. A vacuum then sucks the softened sheet against a single-section mold. When the sheet has cooled and solidified, the molded article is cut from the surrounding sheet and separated from the mold.

Rotational molding. In rotational molding, powdered or granular plastic is placed in a hot metal mold that rotates slowly about two perpendicular axes. The plastic melts and distributes itself evenly over the inner surface of the mold. After cooling, the mold is opened and the article removed. This technique is used to make heavy-duty hollow objects, such as polyethene drums.

Thermosets

In contrast to thermoplastics, thermosets are materials that harden when heated. Furthermore, they do not soften, and even become harder, on subsequent cooling. The hardening process, called curing, is the result of a heat-induced chemical reaction that forms a three-dimensional polymer network that is often extremely hard. Many curing reactions are catalyzed by acids or other trace compounds in the formulation. The principal components of thermosets are polymeric solids or viscous liquids called resins. They have moderate molecular weights and carry the reactive groups that take part in curing.

▶ This dye-dispensing machine automatically controls the dosage of colorants to be added to a plastic before extrusion.

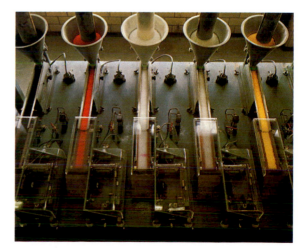

Foamed plastics

Plastics are foamed by generating a gas within a liquid or softened polymer. The use of polymers in foamed states not only reduces the amount of material used and makes for more lightweight goods but also brings other favorable properties. Foamed polymers are excellent thermal insulators, for example, since the gases trapped in their voids are unable to move and conduct heat. Foams also absorb sound and the energy of impacts, which crumple them.

Expanded polystyrene, whose trade name is Styrofoam, is perhaps the most familiar example of a foamed plastic. It is made by first infusing pellets of polystyrene with isopentane (C_5H_{12}), a volatile liquid hydrocarbon. Heating the infused pellets softens the polystyrene and causes the isopentane trapped within it to boil. The boiling hydrocarbon forms voids in the polymer, which expands and then sets as the evaporation of the solvent absorbs heat from the polymer. After the foaming process, the isopentane diffuses out of the voids in the foam, and its place is taken by air. The foaming process can be done in heated molds, or by hot extrusion to form sheets of expanded polystyrene that can then be molded by thermoforming. Expanded polystyrene is used to make egg cartons, insulated drinks cups, and shock-absorbing pellets for packaging.

Polyurethane foam is more elastic than polystyrene foam, making it useful in upholstering furniture. The gas that produces the foam is released by the reaction that forms the polymer—a condensation of polyfunctional isocyanate with a polyester prepolymer. In reaction injection molding (RIM), polyisocyanate, polyester prepolymer, and an organotin catalyst are premixed just before injection into a heated mold. The polymerization and foaming reaction ensues, filling the mold with polyurethane foam. This process is used to make shock-absorbing fenders that reduce injuries to pedestrians struck by cars, and that bounce back into shape after minor impacts during parking maneuvers, for example.

Recycling

One disadvantage of plastics is that they can seldom be recycled; steel, for example, can be melted down and reused after being scrapped from an earlier application. For this reason, plastics-processing technology is exploring methods for reusing the resources in scrapped plastics.

Polyesters are prime candidates for recycling, since they can be recovered by a process called methanolysis. Under appropriate conditions, methanol can break open the ester linkages that hold together polyester chains. The products are

◄ These molds are for making polyurethane shoe soles by reaction-injection molding. The dyes remain closed during the molding process and then open again to release the finished soles.

polyols and methyl esters of polyesters—exactly the materials used to make the polymer in the first place. These materials can be purified by distillation and repolymerized as required.

Another process that has potential for future use is pyrolysis—a thermal cracking process that breaks down polymers to make complex hydrocarbon mixtures that resemble petroleum and can be separated in the same way. For the present, however, recycled plastics are mainly shredded and used in low-grade applications, such as in the making of thermally molded floor tiles.

▼ Injection molding is used to make these tough and flexible inner and outer soles for shoes.

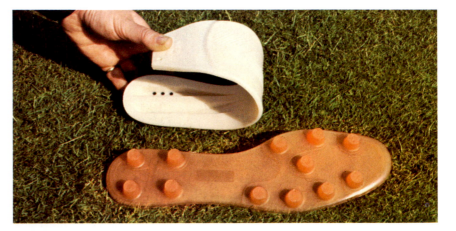

SEE ALSO: CATALYST • CHEMISTRY, ORGANIC • FIBER, SYNTHETIC • GLASS FIBER • POLYMER AND POLYMERIZATION • RECYCLING

Plate Tectonics

◄ The result of an earthquake in India clearly shows the effects of the release of elastic strain. Elastic strain builds up over time owing to the movement of opposing plates. Eventually, the pressure becomes too great for the rocks to withstand and the energy is released, resulting in an earthquake.

The concept of plate tectonics describes the outer rigid shell of Earth—the lithosphere—as consisting of six major plates and a number of smaller ones. These plates converge, move apart, and slide past each other over a partially molten layer of rock called the asthenosphere. It is these movements that explain the dynamics of earthquakes and volcanoes. The framework of plate tectonics encompasses the theories of continental drift and seafloor spreading, and through plate tectonics, scientists in a wide range of Earth-science disciplines have found their work to be interdependent.

In 1912, the German meteorologist and geophysicist Alfred Wegener proposed that the geological characteristics of opposing continents such as Africa and South America could be adequately explained only if they had once been joined. How continents actually moved, however, remained a stumbling block for the acceptance of this theory. Years later, suggestions that volcanic eruptions on the seafloor and intrusions in Earth's crust below it could push the continents apart (so-called seafloor spreading) were substantiated by studies of the magnetic properties of the oceanic crust. Earth's magnetic field periodically reverses polarity, and the magnetic minerals of erupting basalts record the ambient orientation of the field as they cool. They define a linear pattern of magnetic reversal stripes about the axis from which they were produced. Each ocean has such an axis, which takes the form of a linear (usually central) submarine mountain chain, or midocean ridge system.

In 1965, the Canadian geologist and geophysicist J. T. Wilson combined the concepts of continental drift and seafloor spreading into a global picture of rigid moving plates. Support for this idea spread rapidly in the late 1960s, when geophysicists presented further evidence for seafloor spreading and for the underthrusting, or subduction, of plates. This process, in which a plate capped by oceanic crust thrusts below either a plate capped by continental crust or another oceanic plate, explains why the spreading of the ocean floors around midocean ridges has not caused Earth to expand. It further accounts for both the distribution and compressional character of most major earthquakes.

Confirmation of theories

Since 1968, there have been many demonstrations of seafloor spreading, continental drift, and hence, plate tectonics. An early success, achieved at the outset of the international Deep Sea Drilling Project, was the use of magnetometers to date the ages of the magnetic anomalies over the ocean crust. A variety of techniques were used, such as drilling holes into the sediments resting on the oceanic basement and taking measurements within the hole. As expected, the farther the drill site was from the midocean ridge, the older was the basal sediment.

One of the principal ways in which plate margins are mapped is by plotting earthquake and volcanic activity, since the majority of these dynamic processes occur where plates are in the process of being created or destroyed.

Plate margins

Plates have three kinds of margin. At constructive margins, or spreading centers, new oceanic crust is created by continuous activity along mountain ranges in the middle of ocean basins. Geophysical surveys followed by dives with submersibles have been used to show that processes of ocean-plate construction have differed greatly between the Pacific—fast spreading at up to 4.3 in. (11 cm) per year—and Atlantic Oceans—slow spreading at about 0.4 in. (1 cm) per year. In the Pacific Ocean, hot springs were discovered on the spreading centers. Driven by the interaction of seawater with molten and hot rock below the volcanic zone, the spring waters vent at up to 662°F (350°C) and are often laden with particles of metal sulfides, which come to rest in large quantities on the ocean floor.

Plates are destroyed along their destructive (or active) margins by a process known as subduction. Plates capped by oceanic crust are thrust below plates capped either by continental crust (as in Japan and the Andean coast of South America) or by oceanic crust (as in the Mariana Islands) along deep depressions known as oceanic trenches. Stresses in the crust arising from subduction generate earthquakes along active margins, and melting about 60 miles (100 km) or more down in a subduction zone generates arcs of volcanoes on the overriding plate.

What happens between trenches and volcanic arcs (the fore-arc area) has important implications for the evolution of continents and for the understanding of earthquakes. International deep-sea drilling and related investigations have revealed a number of processes that occur in response to a subduction. Accretion occurs where sediments on the under-thrusting plate are thick: their upper layers are stripped off and folded and faulted against the front of the fore-arc, giving rise to net outward growth of the over-riding plate. Examples are the Pacific fore-arc of Mexico and the Barbados fore-arc. Sediment subduction is where sediments are carried below the fore-arc, perhaps to be recycled in the Earth's mantle, so that the over-riding plate is essentially unmodified by subduction (for example, in the Quaternary fore-arc of Guatemala). Tectonic erosion, a rather surprising discovery, occurs where the under-thrusting plate abrades the over-riding plate, causing a retreat of the outer margin of the fore-arc (such as in the Mariana fore-arc). A fourth process, underplating, is a type of accretion in which sediments on an under-thrusting plate move under a fore-arc and are plastered onto the over-riding plate from below.

As well as diverging and converging, plates also slide past each other at conservative, or strike-slip, margins. In terms of total length of each type of margin worldwide, these are the least important. However, some of the most destructive of all earthquakes occur along them—San Francisco, site of a huge earthquake in 1906, sits on a strike-slip margin of the North American and Pacific plates.

Small sedimentary basins arranged along the braiding fault zones that characterize some strike-slip margins can accumulate disproportionate thicknesses of sediments and have considerable significance in oil exploration.

Plate geography

A plate is made of crust (continental or oceanic) and the uppermost layer of Earth's mantle. Together the two components are called the lith-

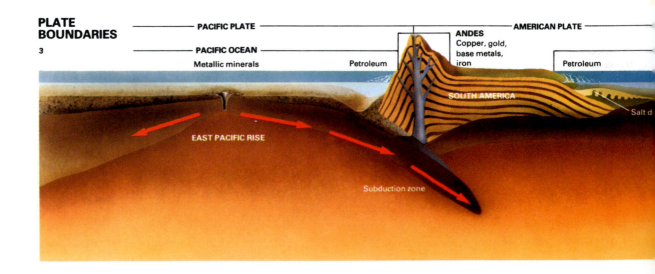

PLATE BOUNDARIES

3

PACIFIC PLATE

PACIFIC OCEAN

Metallic minerals

Petroleum

EAST PACIFIC RISE

Subduction zone

ANDES
Copper, gold, base metals, iron

AMERICAN PLATE

SOUTH AMERICA

Petroleum

Salt d

osphere. The lithosphere is around 93 miles (150 km) thick under the continents and around 43 miles (70 km) thick under the oceans. The crustal part of a plate can be composed entirely of oceanic crust or part oceanic and part continental crust.

The main plates are classified in this way as oceanic plates (Pacific, Nazca, Philippine, and Cocos) or composite plates (South American, North American, African, Indo-Australian, Eurasian, Antarctic, and Arabian).

A plate, by definition, must be bounded by a spreading center and a combination of convergent and conservative margins. The crust between these boundaries can be either oceanic or both oceanic and continental, but never completely continental.

The Indo-Australian plate, for example, is bounded by the Mid-Indian Ridge to the south. Australia, a large block of continental crust, sits on the plate and is bounded on almost all sides by a passive continental margin (also called a mid-plate margin, because it occurs between a spreading center and a subduction zone). To the north of Australia, continental crust of the Australian block is being pushed into a subduction zone, the Sundra Trench. In other words, an arc–continental collision is now occurring on this part of the plate boundary.

Further west along the Sundra Trench, the nature of the northern boundary of the Indo-Australian plate changes in character. West of Australia, oceanic crust is being subducted in a normal fashion below Java and Sumatra. Still further along the plate boundary is another collision zone: along the Himalayas, India has collided with continental crust of the Eurasian plate. This is an example of a continent–continent collision.

In some regions, deciding exactly where part of a plate boundary occurs is difficult. The South American plate is an example. It is clearly bounded by a spreading center in the east (Mid-Atlantic Ridge) and a subduction zone in the west (Peru–Chile Trench). In the south and north, however, the definition of boundaries is not as clear. In the south is a complex boundary linking the Peru Trench and the Scotia Arc. In the north is the problematic Caribbean plate, which may largely comprise ancient Pacific oceanic crust, trapped when subduction started along the Middle-America Trench.

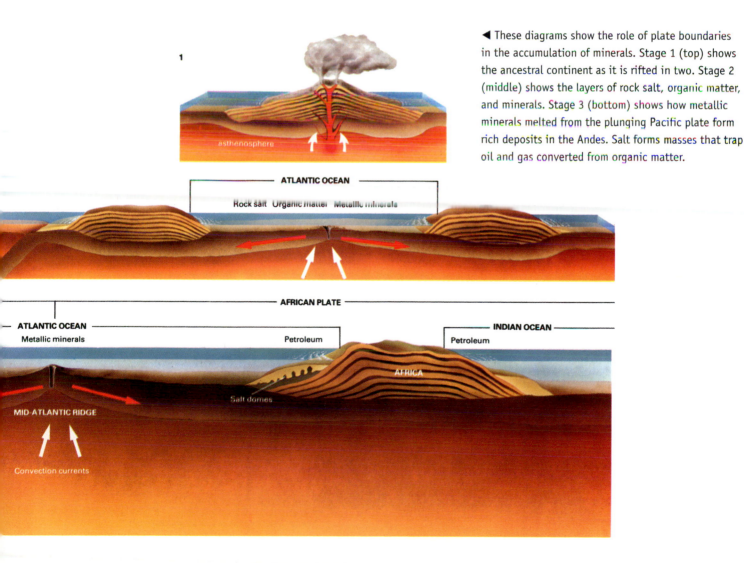

1

asthenosphere

ATLANTIC OCEAN

Rock salt   Organic matter   Metallic minerals

AFRICAN PLATE

ATLANTIC OCEAN
Metallic minerals

Petroleum

INDIAN OCEAN
Petroleum

AFRICA

Salt domes

MID-ATLANTIC RIDGE

Convection currents

◄ These diagrams show the role of plate boundaries in the accumulation of minerals. Stage 1 (top) shows the ancestral continent as it is rifted in two. Stage 2 (middle) shows the layers of rock salt, organic matter, and minerals. Stage 3 (bottom) shows how metallic minerals melted from the plunging Pacific plate form rich deposits in the Andes. Salt forms masses that trap oil and gas converted from organic matter.

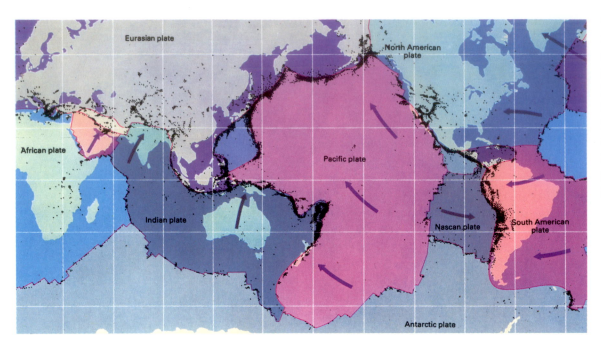

◄ The plates that make up Earth's outer shell. Most earthquakes occur near plate boundaries. It is the movement of these plates that has resulted in the positions of the continents today, but they are constantly moving toward and away from each other.

Because of complexities such as these, geologists now speak of plates (the major plates) and the microplates (smaller regions that are bounded by spreading centers, trenches, or transforms).

The relative motion of a plate (from its constructive boundary toward a destructive boundary, in most cases) is inevitably affected by the motion of adjoining plates. Relative motion for each plate can differ from spreading motion. J. T. Wilson was the first geologist to realize the significance of transform faults. He realized that they must be parallel to the direction of spreading and that they are inherited from irregular opening during the birth of the midocean ridge. They are the sites of active strike-slip movement between the ridge sediments. Their extensions beyond the offset ridge segments are known as fracture zones.

In 1968, the U.S. geologist W. Jason Morgan pointed out that, because Earth is spherical, the spreading rate must increase away from the pole about which a plate is rotating. The rotation pole is the point on Earth's surface about which the spreading direction (marked by the trend of transform faults, which are slightly curved on a surface view of the spherical Earth) forms a small circle. Thus, a line from the rotation pole to any transform is of equal length at the points along that transform. Accordingly, to accommodate such geometry, the amount of spreading must increase away from the rotation pole.

Unanswered questions

Key questions remain unanswered despite the alacrity with which scientists have greeted plate tectonics. Perhaps most important is the question of what forces drive the plate motion. Geophysicists believe it is a combination of thermal convection, gravity, and thermal plumes, but the exact way in which these three factors combine to influence plate movement is still not clear.

FACT FILE

- *Radar altimeters carried aboard satellites are used to map fluctuations in the actual height of the sea's surface. The sea bulges above an upswelling in Earth's mantle and seems to be depressed above regions where the mantle is moving downward beneath the ocean.*

- *Additional satellite methods for studying plate tectonics include the global positioning system (GPS). GPS enables geologists to make repeated measurements between specific points and thus accurately measure movement between plates and along fault lines.*

- *The piloted submersible* Cyana *has taken photographs of heated water billowing out from vents in the ocean floor crust. Known as black smokers, these dark plumes are rich in sulfides dissolved from the crustal rock. Plate motion creates the fissures and vents that suck in seawater and then expel it once it has heated up.*

SEE ALSO: EARTH • EARTHQUAKE • GEOCHEMISTRY • GEOLOGY • GEOPHYSICS • MAGNETOMETER • SEISMOLOGY

Platinum Metals

The platinum metals consist of a group of six closely related rare metals: rhodium (Rh), ruthenium (Ru), palladium (Pd), osmium (Os), iridium (Ir), and platinum (Pt), which is the most important member of the group. The first three occur at the end of the second series of transition elements in the periodic table, before silver. The second three, which occur at the end of the third transition series, precede gold and are among the densest known substances, having densities between 21.4 and 22.4 times that of water.

Platinum and palladium are the most abundant of the six metals. Platinum was the earliest known, discovered by the Spaniards in the South American silver mines about 1550. The Spanish called it *platina*—little silver. They recognized it as being different from true silver because it could not be melted—platinum has a melting point of 3225°F (1774°C). It also caused difficulties for the Spaniards, as its density was close to that of gold,

and when gold plated, it was virtually indistinguishable from the solid metal. The properties of platinum were first seriously studied in the mid-18th century, but it was not until 1803 that the British chemist W. H. Wollaston showed that all the platinum previously examined was in fact an alloy with similar metals. He managed to isolate two; one he named palladium for Pallas, a newly discovered minor planet, and the other rhodium from the Greek word *rhodon*, meaning "rose," because some of its compounds are rose-colored. One year later, the British chemist Smithson Tennant discovered two more of the platinum metals, naming them osmium from the Greek *osme*, meaning "a smell," because its oxide has an unpleasant odor, and iridium from *iris*, the Greek word for "rainbow." In 1845, the Russian chemist Karl Klaus discovered the sixth platinum metal, ruthenium, which he named for a province of Russia.

▲ Early in the refining process, ore is crushed and reduced by smelting to produce converter matte, containing copper, nickel, and cobalt, as well as the platinum group metals.

Occurrence and extraction

Platinum metals are found in their native state in alluvial deposits in Colombia and the Ural Mountains in Russia and in gold-bearing rock at Witwatersrand in South Africa. Platinum occurs as its sulfide, PtS (cooperite) and a mixed sulfide containing palladium, platinum, and nickel at Rustenburg in South Africa and is found as platinum diarsenide, $PtAs_2$ (sperrylite), in the huge copper and nickel sulfide deposits in Canada.

Where platinum metals are gathered in their native state, they are concentrated by methods similar to those employed in gold mines. Where, however, they are obtained as by-products in the large-scale extraction of copper and nickel from their sulfides, the concentration is effected by adding slightly less than sufficient sulfur at the matte-forming stage so as to preserve small regions of nickel or copper metal in which the platinum metals dissolve. These enriched alloys are removed by crushing and magnetic separation and further concentrated by heating with more sulfur and repeating the cycle. Electrorefining of the enriched concentrate leaves the platinum metals as insoluble anode slimes.

The separation and refining of the various members of the platinum family involves a series of complex chemical operations that may vary in detail but are basically similar. The first stage of the process is treatment with hot aqua regia (a mixture of nitric and hydrochloric acids), which dissolves only the platinum and palladium. These metals are precipitated separately from the solution as ammonium salts, which are reduced to the metal at high temperature. The fraction that is insoluble in aqua regia is reacted with molten sodium chloride at 1290°F (700°C) in the presence of chlorine to form double chlorides, which are water soluble. Osmium, which is not dissolved at any stage, is recovered from the final residue by forming its volatile oxide. Ruthenium and rhodium are precipitated from the double chloride solution as sulfides, which are subsequently separated by redissolution followed by individual precipitation. Iridium is finally removed from the double chloride solution as its oxide and reduced to pure metal by hydrogen.

Applications

Platinum is a useful catalyst for a wide range of chemical reactions, both organic and inorganic. For example, it is used as a catalyst in petroleum refining, and it catalyzes the oxidation of ammonia in the production of a nitric acid, its efficiency being increased by the addition of 10 percent rhodium. Both platinum and palladium catalysts are used extensively in the pharmaceutical industry, where they enable highly specific chemical reactions to be carried out in the building of particular molecules. In the manufacture of margarine, hydrogenation is brought about by a palladium catalyst. The metals are often most effective as catalysts when in the form of finely divided powders known as blacks.

The ability of platinum to initiate low-temperature oxidation reactions was first exploited by the German chemist Johann Wolfgang Döbereiner to produce a lighter before the invention of friction matches. The principle is used today in ignition devices for domestic gas stoves. Platinum metals are also used to catalyze both the oxidation of unburnt hydrocarbons and the reduction of nitrogen oxides in antipollution units incorporated in car exhaust systems. Such devices, known as catalytic converters, can therefore transform toxic exhaust gases into harmless water vapor and carbon dioxide.

An important property of platinum metals is their outstanding resistance to chemical attack. Platinum itself is used for analytical apparatus, such as crucibles, combustion boats, and grids for metal deposition in electrochemical techniques. Other industrial applications include spinnerets in the artificial fiber industry and crucibles for the manufacture of optical glass, where contamination from nonmetallic refractories must be avoided. Often platinum is alloyed with up to 20 percent rhodium to improve its strength. Palladium has a unique affinity for hydrogen, absorbing up to 850 times its own volume of hydrogen, and is employed as a diffusion medium for the purification of the gas. In this application, it is alloyed with silver to reduce the shape changes that would otherwise occur during thermal cycling.

The refractory properties of the platinum metals once made them candidates for electric light bulb filaments. Tungsten is now universally used,

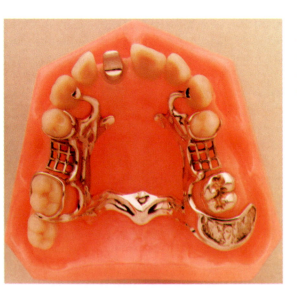

◄ Alloys of palladium and platinum are used in dentistry, mainly because of their strength and resistance to corrosion.

but formerly osmium was often used. The thermal expansion coefficient of platinum is very similar to that of glass, making it an ideal material for glass-to-metal seals, although a copper-coated nickel–iron alloy has been developed that is also suitable and much cheaper. Thermocouples made from platinum and a platinum–rhodium alloy operate reliably up to 3100°F (1700°C) and are widely used in the steel industry. For very accurate temperature measurement, the platinum resistance thermometer is a standard measuring instrument. The platinum metals are suitable materials for relay contacts that are required to switch reliably for many years without attention and for electrodes in spark plugs for high-performance internal combustion engines.

Medical uses for platinum include the drug cis-platinum $[PtCl_2(NH_3)_2]$, which is used as a treatment for certain form of cancer, such as testicular cancer and leukemia. Platinum is also used in implants such as heart pacemakers and replacement valves, and both platinum and palladium are used in dentistry.

Platinum and palladium are used extensively in the jewelry industry, palladium having the additional advantages that it is not under such heavy demand from the chemical industry and is about half the density of platinum. Like gold, both metals are seldom used in their pure state, as they are too soft. A thin layer of rhodium—the easiest of the group to electrodeposit—electroplated onto silver, prevents tarnishing through sulfide formation. The tips of fountain pen nibs are usually made from alloys of platinum, osmium, and iridium, where the combination of hardness and resistance to corrosion by ink is especially valuable.

▲ Welding the edge of a gauze pad made of a platinum–rhodium alloy. Such gauzes are used as catalysts in the oxidation of ammonia to nitric oxide in the preparation of nitric acid.

SEE ALSO: ALLOY • CATALYST • CORROSION PREVENTION • ELEMENTS, ORIGINS OF • METAL • PERIODIC TABLE • TRANSITION ELEMENT

Plumbing

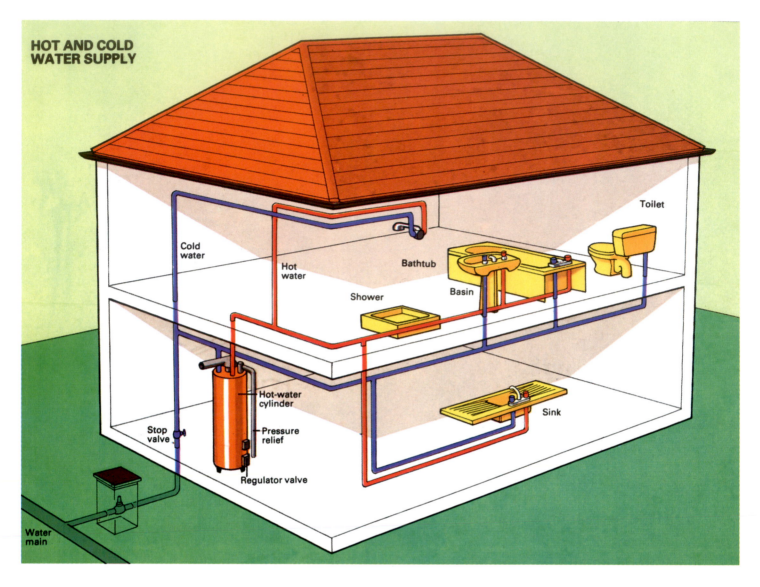

Cold water

Hot water

Bathtub

Toilet

Basin

Shower

Hot-water cylinder

Pressure relief

Stop valve

Regulator valve

Sink

Water main

The craft of plumbing originated in medieval times, when the roofs of the great cathedrals throughout Europe were being covered in sheet lead, which had been cast on a bed of sand. Later, when the water supply industry was developing, pipes and cisterns were similarly made from cast-lead sheet, although hundreds of years before that the Romans had made water pipes of lead to feed their fountains and baths.

Today the modern plumber embraces many skills and materials: cold and hot water supply, sanitation, and the installation of pipelines in all types of buildings for carrying both liquids and gases. The plumber has to be able to work in lead, copper, aluminum, cast iron, steel, and plastics.

Cold-water supply

It is the task of the water industry to supply pure potable water in sufficient quantity wherever it is needed; it is then the job of the plumber to ensure that the water is conveyed to all parts of the build-ing where it is required and to preserve its purity up to the point of use. Since careful design and choice of materials are necessary to prevent the water from becoming polluted, there are regulations and laws that must be adhered to.

Because of geographical and physical differences, cold water installations vary from country to country, but in the United States, one system is most common. Clean fresh water is directed around the community by a system of water pipes buried under the roads. The water running through the pipes is under pressure and is taken into each building by a service pipe. The service pipe is connected directly to the water meter, which registers the amount of water used in each installation for the purpose of billing by the water utility. Just beyond the water meter is a main valve that is used to halt the flow of water through the building in an emergency. The cold water is supplied under pressure, usually between 40 and 50 psi (2.8–3.35 kg/cm^2). It is directed to all the cold-

▲ A typical arrangement of a home hot-water system. The cylinder takes the form of a hot-water storage tank and water heater combined. The water heater may be fueled by gas, oil, or electric immersion heaters— all thermostatically controlled. The system is pressurized from the water main.

water faucets and the other fixtures by a network of branch pipes of varying dimensions. The largest is usually 0.75 in. (19 mm) in diameter, and the smallest—used in the flexible tubing that is used to connect a toilet faucet—is 0.375 in. (9.5 mm) in diameter. There are usually shutoff valves fitted near each fixture and faucet to allow them to be isolated for individual repairs.

Hot-water supply

One branch leading off the cold-water main is directed to the hot-water storage tank. Like other fixtures, the inlet pipe is fitted with a shutoff valve to isolate it if necessary. The tank itself is also fitted with a drain valve, so it can be emptied for repairs or cleaning out any sediment that may accumulate in the bottom. The water held in the tank is heated by electric elements or a gas flame.

Because the water enters the hot-water tank under the same pressure as the rest of the cold-water system, it also leaves the tank under the same pressure. It is directed throughout the house to all the hot-water faucets and fixtures through a network of pipes similar to the cold-water system. The hot-water tank is equipped with a thermostat that regulates the temperature of the water in the tank. In case the thermostat is faulty, each hot-water tank also has an emergency relief valve that automatically opens to release overheated water before it can boil and explode the tank. The overheated water is run harmlessly into a drain and out to the sewer.

Drain-waste-vent system

Once the clean water has been used, it must be directed back to the sewer system efficiently and hygienically. Although water is supplied and reaches fixtures under pressure, the flow for drainage is entirely dependent upon gravity. Therefore the pipes involved are of a much greater diameter than the supply pipes and must run downward at a slight angle, usually about 0.25 in. (6 mm) for every foot of pipe length, in order to assist the flow of water.

The pipe that serves the toilet is called the soil pipe and is 3 to 4 in. (7.5–10 cm) in diameter. Other drainpipes for household fixtures are 1.5 to 2 in. (3.8–5 cm) in diameter. The connection to each fixture must have a trap, which is a special U-shaped or P-shaped fitting that allows an easy flow of water but retains a small amount in the bend to prevent noxious sewer gases from seeping up through the drains into the atmosphere in the house. The only exception is toilets; they are all manufactured with their own internal trap.

From the trap, the drain flows to the main stack, a vertical pipe leading to the main branch

of the sewer line connected to the house. At the point where the soil stack connects with the main drain is a branch fitted with a screw-in plug that can be opened to allow access in the event of a blockage in the main drain. The main stack itself continues up through the roof of the building to provide the vent for the system. This vent allows noxious sewer gases to escape into the atmosphere and the free movement of air throughout the drainage system. Each branch of the drainage system must be connected to the main vent stack or have a separate vent to allow air to escape. If air is trapped in the drainage system, a gurgling sound occurs as the water drains away. Trapped

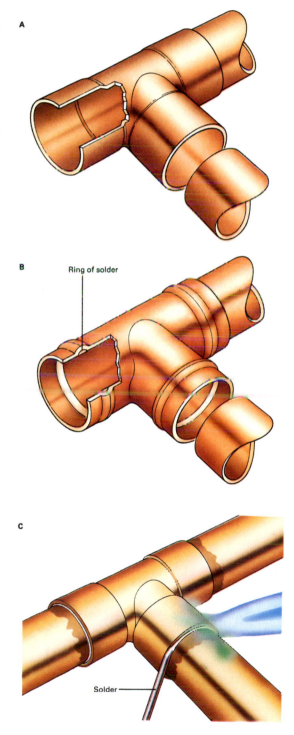

A

B   Ring of solder

C   Solder

◀ Solder is melted onto the mating surfaces of an end-feed joint (A), which is then assembled. A presoldered joint (B) is assembled and then heated to melt a ring of solder. After assembly, additional solder can be applied (C).

▶ Blow torches are used by plumbers to solder and anneal pipes. Annealing involves heating the pipe to soften it and make it much easier to work than the cold metal.

air can also cause water to be siphoned out of the traps, allowing sewer gas to seep into the house through the now-absent water seal.

Independent systems

If the home is not connected to a community water and sewerage system, as is the case with some 15 million American homes, an independent system must be set up. In such cases, fresh water is generally supplied from a well that feeds water to a pressurized holding tank. The water under pressure in the tank is then fed through a conventional system throughout the house.

The internal arrangement of the drain-waste-vent system is also similar to that of a conventional system, except that the main drain is usually connected to a septic tank. In some instances, a grease trap is fitted between the house and the septic tank to reduce the load on the septic tank itself. Inside the septic tank, the sewage is broken

down by bacterial action, resulting in a sludge that settles at the bottom of the tank and a relatively clear liquid that rises to the top. This liquid flows out of the septic tank to a distribution box that directs it through a series of underground pipes in a seepage field, where it is dispersed harmlessly into the soil over a fairly large area. The sludge from the septic tank is pumped out occasionally by professionals in order to prevent excessive sludge buildup, which might affect the performance and safety of the system.

Impurities

The water supply, although tested for safety, is not perfectly pure and does vary considerably from region to region owing to the minerals and other particles dissolved or suspended in the water supply. Most impurities are removed by the local water treatment plant. However, if the water supply is taken directly from a well or borehole, it may be necessary to install treatment equipment to make it safe to drink.

Cloudy water is usually the result of silt or algae suspended in the water. These impurities can be removed by passing the water through a filter: a sand filter for silt and algae and a charcoal filter to adsorb chemical residues such as pesticides and fertilizers. A reddish brown color indicates the presence of iron in the water supply, which can be treated in mild cases with an ordinary water softener. Carbonic acid can result when substantial amounts of carbon dioxide are present and can corrode plumbing fittings. In some cases, it can be treated with an alkaline solution introduced through a chemical feeder.

Hard water, which is a problem in almost 80 percent of North America, is caused by calcium and magnesium compounds dissolved in the

▶ Two forms of compression joints for joining pipework; the nonmanipulative joints are above the manipulative joints. The parts are named as follows: (a) capnut, (b) coupler, (c) gland sleeve, or olive, (d) brass cone insert.

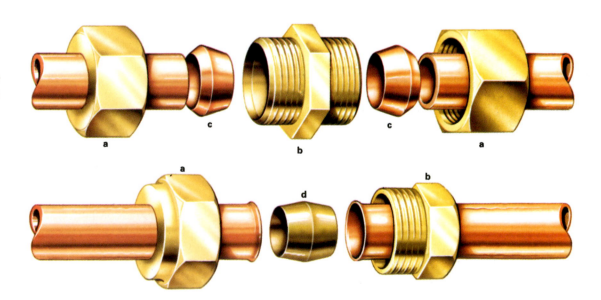

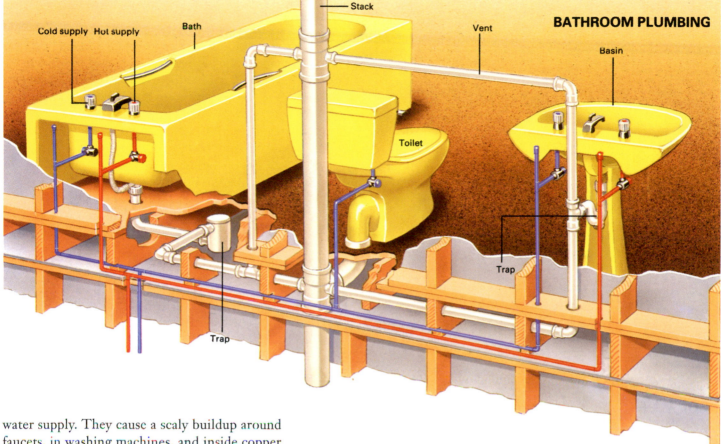

BATHROOM PLUMBING

Stack · Vent · Basin · Cold supply · Hot supply · Bath · Toilet · Trap · Trap

water supply. They cause a scaly buildup around faucets, in washing machines, and inside copper pipes. The rate at which the scale forms is accelerated by an increase in water temperature and consequently can cause considerable problems in hot-water storage tanks. Hard water will also reduce the effectiveness of many soaps and some detergents. It is possible to alleviate the problem by fitting domestic water softeners, which generally work by a process of chemical exchange. The water flows through a tank in which the calcium and magnesium compounds are removed and replaced with sodium. When all the sodium has been removed from the ion-exchange resin, the tank must be flushed out and recharged with more sodium solution. Water treated in such a way should never be drunk, particularly by babies, young children, or people on a low-sodium diet because of heart or kidney disorders. Where water softeners are used, a separate tap is often plumbed in specifically for drinking water.

In places where the water is extremely hard, scale may build up and coat the insides of copper pipes. The flow of water would be so restricted that another type of pipe has to be used. Similarly, in areas of very soft water, copper pipe is affected by acids in the water supply. In both cases, galvanized steel or plastic pipe should be used instead. Lead pipes are also affected by soft water, allowing lead to enter the household water supply. This problem is usually combated either by adding orthophosphate to the water supply at the water

treatment works, by flushing water pipes after periods when they have not been in use, or by replacing the pipes with a more inert material.

Plastic pipe has been used for some time for drainage of both rain and domestic water. The development of new types of plastic tubing has allowed plastic pipe to be used for both hot- and cold-water supply. The standard method of joining lengths of plastic tubing is by solvent welding, but there are also compatible plastic compression joints that tighten together to provide a secure seal. The most recent development in the use of plastic for plumbing purposes is push-fit compression joints. These connectors simply push onto a length of pipe and are held in place by an internal gripping ring.

Composite joints are also now available to enable metal pipes to be jointed to plastic pipes in older houses where a mixed system might exist. Other recent introductions include nonreturn valves for use with external taps. These valves are used to ensure that water in any garden equipment such as hoses or sprinkler systems cannot back up through the external tap and pollute the household water supply system.

▲ A typical plumbing layout for a bathroom with a single-stack drainage system, in which all wastes are discharged through a single downpipe to an internal duct.

SEE ALSO: DRAINAGE • PIPE AND TUBE MANUFACTURE • TOILET • WASTEWATER TREATMENT • WATER SUPPLY

Pneumatic Tool

▲ This pneumatic drill is powerful enough to break through asphalt. Air-driven tools, such as this drill, are often reliable, low in maintenance costs, and easy to use.

A pneumatic, or air, tool is driven by various types of air motors or pistons; the power is provided by compressed air from a compressor system.

The air motor has many advantages for use in tools, especially hand-operated ones. The motor is small and light for the high torque and power it delivers, and it does not overheat—even when stalled for long periods, since the flow of air has a cooling effect. It cannot be damaged by overloading. In addition, pneumatic air tools can be instantly reversed without causing any damage to the mechanism. Another advantage is that the motor starts almost instantaneously, and there is no overrun when the air supply is cut, except in high-speed motors where no gearing is used. The fact that the driving air passes into the tool from a clean supply and is exhausted to the atmosphere means that abrasive or clogging dust can be excluded from the mechanism, making it suitable for use in severe conditions. Many pneumatic tools are basically similar to power tools driven by electric motors, the main difference being the use of air motors instead of electric ones.

For operation, air tools need a supply of compressed air. The normal working pressure is in the range 80 to 100 psi (5.5–7 bar), though lower pressures can also be used. Normally the air is supplied by a fixed or portable compressor system. In factories, fixed systems are generally used, and the compressed air is distributed around the factory by air lines. Outlets are provided for connecting the pneumatic tools; flexible hoses allow free movement of the tools in use. Automatic connectors that cut off the air flow when disconnected are often used, or alternatively, a hand-operated valve is fitted to the outlet.

Since vapor compressed with the air can condense and cause damage to tools, water traps are fitted and filters are provided to prevent foreign matter damaging or clogging the tool. Lubrication of the working parts is often achieved by the use of oil-fog lubricators fitted in the air line and supplying a finely atomized oil mist to the motor.

Air motors

The main types of air motors are the vane, piston, and turbine designs. Turbines are used where high speed and little torque are required, for instance, in some of the small grinders or in a dentist's drill. Heavier work, where massive power and good starting torque are required at fairly low speeds, generally involves the use of piston motors. Piston motors generally have pistons in a radial arrangement around a central crankshaft, but in-line and V-shape configurations are also used.

The most common design is positive-displacement motors of the vane type, used in power tools. With this type, one can get the most power into a small space. It is a flexible power unit with a high-speed rotor that, when coupled to suitable gearing, is capable of producing high torque at the final drive.

Positive-displacement motors have multiple longitudinal vanes fitted into radial slots in a rotor that is mounted eccentrically in a cylinder, similar to the rotor of a rotary vane compressor. The compressed air enters the side of the cylinder at one end and leaves through an exhaust port halfway along the cylinder and further around it, turning the rotor as it goes.

Reciprocating pistons

Another type of air drive, used in tools such as road breakers, riveting hammers, and stapling machines, is the reciprocating piston. This type of piston is driven up and down inside the working cylinder by expansion of the compressed air. A system of valves or ports is used to direct the compressed air to each end of the piston in turn, giving a rapid oscillating motion. In most designs the piston movement is transmitted by allowing the piston to strike against the working head, which then transmits the blows to the workpiece.

Hand tools

For many applications, the pneumatic motor or reciprocating piston is incorporated in a hand tool for direct use by an operator. When such tools are used for assembly-line work, they are often mounted overhead on counterbalanced suspension systems that allow them to be pulled down for use and released to return to the storage position until required again. Another common use of air motors on assembly and machining lines is in hoist systems, where the fine control that can be achieved is of particular value in positioning parts.

Specialized tooling

Standard pneumatic tools are also used in the construction of special-purpose tooling arrangements where their relatively small overall diameter allows for close grouping of the working elements for machining and assembly. A typical assembly application involves a machine used for securing the cap of a bottled gas regulator by eight cheesehead screws. As a manual operation this requires two full-time operators, but the application of a pneumatic system allows the work to be performed by one. The system has eight pneumatic screwdrivers carried on a tool head that is lowered to the working position and subsequently raised by double-acting pneumatic cylinders. The air supply to the screwdrivers is routed through an air valve that distributes air through a channeled mounting plate to the air inlets of the tools. When the air control to the pneumatic cylinder is opened and the tools are lowered, their screwdriving bits engage in the slots in the screws, and as the pressure increases, the drive from the motors is taken up by the spring-loaded clutches. The whole operation is essentially an individual process. Each tool drives its associated screw independently of the other tools and ceases driving as soon as the torque loading of its clutch is overcome. Thus, every screw is tightened to the same pressure or, if the clutch torque settings differ, to the various pressures at which the different clutches disengage.

To cover fully the multiple tooling requirements of industry, two systems of torque control are available. The first is the minimum torque indication (MTI) system, where the normal stalled torque motors are used in the conventional manner but with a visual indication to the operator that the minimum torque value required has been achieved.

The second is a torque-controlled motor system with visual indication (ITC). This system uses standard motors, each fitted with a control top. The torque reaction through the motor body is used to initiate an air signal that passes to the control top and shuts off the air to the motor. The movement of the control top shuttle valve actuates a relay that switches on an indicator light.

▲ This multitool pneumatic drilling machine requires only one person to operate it.

◀ A pneumatic wrench used for tightening the nuts on automobile wheels. It is fast and easy to use and tightens each nut to the right torque.

SEE ALSO: Compressor and pump • Jackhammer • Pile driver

Poison

A poison is any substance that, when taken into the body, impairs health or causes death. The broad definition reflects the number of substances that can be classified as poisons. Aside from obvious poisons such as arsenic and snake venom, even water taken in sufficient quantities can cause death. The deciding factor in whether or not a substance is poisonous is often simply the concentration in the body.

Poisons may be introduced into the body by mouth, inhalation, injection, or skin absorption. The medical profession often divides poisons into different categories—pharmaceutical, industrial, chemical, and agrochemical; plant and mushroom; snake venom; and marine animal.

An approximate idea of the acute toxicity of a particular substance is given by its oral LD (lethal dose) 50, that is, the amount of the substance that would need to be ingested, for a given body weight, to prove fatal in 50 percent of cases. For humans, LD50s can be estimated only very approximately. They vary from about 1.6 oz. per lb. (100 g/kg) for the least toxic substances, such as water, down to about 0.0000000016 oz. per lb. (0.0001 mg/kg) for the most potent poisons, such as plutonium-239.

▲ All parts of the flowering plant, deadly nightshade, *Atropa belladonna*, are highly poisonous, but chemicals extracted from this plant have medicinal properties. One alkaloid taken from the leaves and roots, for example, is used to dilate the pupils in eye examinations.

APPROXIMATE ACUTE LD50s* OF VARIOUS SUBSTANCES

(orally ingested unless otherwise stated)	mg/kg
Alcohol	10,000
Sodium chloride	4,000
Ferrous sulfate	1,500
Aspirin	300
DDT insecticide	100
Sulfuric acid	100
Paraquat weed killer	50
Amylobarbitone	25
Lead acetate	15
Cocaine	5
Atropine	2
Yellow phosphorus	2
Sodium cyanide	2
Arsenic trioxide	2
Strychnine sulfate	1
Nicotine	1
Cobra venom (intravenous)	0.5
Tetrodotoxin (puffer fish toxin)	0.1
Aconite	0.05
Tiger snake venom (intravenous)	0.05
Ricin (intravenous)	0.005
Dioxin	0.001
Botulinus toxin	0.0005
Plutonium-239	0.0001

* LD (lethal dose) 50 is the amount of substance that would need to be ingested, for a given body weight, to prove fatal in 50 percent of cases.

Incidence

Poisoning is seldom the result of a malicious act. Instead, poisoning is usually the result of an accident or of self-administration—either accidental or, in cases of suicide attempts, as a result of intentional self-administration.

The largest number of deaths from poisoning are due to carbon monoxide and barbiturates. Other important pharmaceutical poisons are tricyclic antidepressants, aspirin, and quinine. Almost all cases of pharmaceutical poisoning are self-induced and are called parasuicides, even if the poisoning does not result in death.

Plant and mushroom poisons are far less common, and snake bites, although dramatic, account for few hospital admissions. Marine animal poisons are the smallest group of all.

The prognosis for those suffering from poisoning is generally good. Of those admitted to a hospital, 80 percent need no more treatment than routine nursing. The remaining 20 percent are given various treatments according to the nature of the poison.

Those at risk

Adults suffering from poisoning are usually in their 20s and 30s, and women are most often at risk. Children, especially those under five, are particularly at risk from analgesics, benzodiazepines, and the contraceptive pill. Pharmaceuticals account for 60 percent of child poisoning cases, and the remaining 40 percent are caused by apparently harmless household products—bleach, kerosene, home-grown plants, and seeds.

Symptoms

The symptoms of poisoning are almost as wide-ranging as the causes. Narcotic substances, such as opium and chloroform, lead to dizziness, drowsiness, headaches, and sight disturbance. In extreme cases, narcotics can lead to muscle paralysis.

Corrosive poisons, such as acids and bleaches, can lead to extreme physical discomfort and danger to life. If they are swallowed, the lips may become burned, stained, and blistered. The throat may be affected so much that breathing and swallowing are impaired. As the corrosive passes through the digestive system, intense stomach pain, vomiting, and diarrhea often occur. In the most extreme circumstances, gangrene and perforation of the digestive tract develop.

Irritants such as ammonia, some types of arsenic, and phosphorus have less alarming effects. When taken into the body, they usually result in vomiting and indigestion.

Convulsants can cause distressing symptoms. The most notorious convulsant is strychnine, which can cause spasms in the limbs, trunk, and throat. As poisoning progresses, breathing becomes more and more difficult, and the jaw and fists clench. Death comes when the patient suffocates or becomes totally exhausted. The symptoms are even more horrifying in that consciousness is not affected.

Hypnotics can lead to a characteristic condition often called shock lung. Shock lung happens within 24 hours of a patient taking an overdose of a hypnotic drug. The patient starts hyperventilating but cannot metabolize the oxygen being taken into the lungs. Despite being given oxygen therapy, the patient effectively suffocates.

Treatment

In extreme poisoning, the first priority is often to restore breathing and/or heartbeat. In some cases, such as shock lung, the patient needs a ventilator to survive. If the patient has taken a short-acting barbiturate or is suffering from exposure after collapsing, he or she may suffer hypothermia—body temperature below 95°F (35°C). The usual treatment is to use a foil blanket (a space blanket). Convulsions can often be effectively treated by giving diazepam (Valium).

How the physician deals with the poison depends on both the patient and the substance (or substances) involved. If the poison is noncorrosive, an emetic may be used to make the patient vomit. Although this treatment is usually successful with children, adults usually need gastric lavage—a stomach pump. A large-gauge tube is passed down the throat to the stomach, and warm water is pumped into the stomach and pumped out again. The process is repeated until the stomach fluid runs clear.

In cases of drug overdose, the physician may opt to use activated charcoal instead of gastric lavage. To be effective, the charcoal-to-drug ratio needs to be 10:1. Typical doses are in the range of 1.7 to 3.5 oz. (50–100 g), which may be swallowed or made into a slurry with water and introduced down a nasogastric tube. In cases of barbiturate poisoning, a further 0.7 to 2 oz. (20–60 g) may be used every 4 to 12 hours.

Antidotes

Antidotes are one of the most effective ways of treating poisoning. Broadly, all antidotes counteract the effects of poisons, although there are a number of specific ways in which they act. Many antidotes form an inert complex with the poison.

◀ An Auca Indian using a blowpipe with a dart tipped with the poison curare. Amazonian hunters obtain the poison from the skin of frogs (inset).

Cyanide poisoning, for example, may be treated with dicobalt edetate.

Some poisons interact with specific receptor sites in the body. Oxygen can act as an antidote for carbon monoxide poisoning by competing for those receptor sites. Other antidotes, such as atropine, block the receptor sites for poisons such as cholinesterase inhibitors (a type of insecticide).

Other antidotes bypass the effect of the poison. For example, glucagon bypasses the effect of certain drugs. Finally, a family of antidotes will speed up poison excretion. Chloride may be given as an antidote to bromide and iodide.

Snake venom

Poisoning from snake bite is rare in most of the developed world but is one of the most unpredictable forms. The symptoms can be dramatic. Viper bites can cause rapid swelling. The most common cause of death after viper bites is hemorrhage in a vital organ—usually the brain. Without treatment, between 1 and 15 percent of those bitten would die after about two days.

Elapids—a family of snakes with short, fixed fangs—produce venom that is neurotoxic. The muscles in the eyes, tongue, throat, and chest are often affected by the toxin blocking particular parts of the brain. In extreme cases, the venom can induce respiratory failure. Elapid bites can

◄ The olive sea snake, though highly poisonous, rarely presents any danger to humans.

cause about 10 percent mortality without treatment after about 5 to 20 hours.

The third family of venomous snakes is the sea snakes. For animals, their venom is neurotoxic, but the effect on humans is different. Lesions are often formed in muscles throughout the body. Mortality rates are similar to those from elapid venom, but death normally follows about 15 hours after the bite. All three kinds of venomous snakes affect the kidneys. Acute renal failure, leading to death, may follow any serious snake bite.

Detecting poisons

When someone is suffering from acute poisoning or when poisoning is suspected as a cause of death, the substance involved and the dosage taken or administered must be determined. Often there is little or no evidence to help the experts to make these determinations. Forensic technologists, however, have a battery of techniques available to determine the nature and amount of poison present in body tissues. They include simple chemical tests, liquid-, gas-, and thin-layer chromatographic techniques for separating out complex organic mixtures, mass spectrometry, ultraviolet spectrophotometry, radioimmunoassay, and spectrofluorometry. Only poisons, like ricin, that are lethal in microscopic doses and very quickly broken down are likely to escape detection.

FACT FILE

■ Medieval politicians and courtiers frightened of assassination paid large sums of money for bezoar stones—large gallstones from the stomach of sheep and goats. They were believed to detoxify poisonous substances and change color if held over poisoned food.

■ Japanese chefs expert in preparing fugu fish are awarded a special diploma. Fugu contains puffer fish meat. The puffer's entrails contain deadly tetrodotoxin, which survives cooking, and expert preparation is vital. In one year, there were 259 cases of fugu poisoning in Japan, of which 118 were fatal.

■ Even touching the giant South American toad, Bufo marinus, can result in vomiting and soaring blood pressure. Head glands of the 3 lb. (1.6 kg) reptile exude toxic chemicals that include a nerve poison, a heart stimulant similar to digitalis, and an anesthetic.

 SEE ALSO: CHROMATOGRAPHY • IMMUNOLOGY • MASS SPECTROMETRY • PATHOLOGY

Polarimeter

Many chemical compounds can exist in more than one optically active form. Each optically active form, or isomer, of a compound will be able to rotate the plane of polarized light by an amount characteristic of that isomer (isomers are different arrangements of the same atoms in a molecule). Polarimeters are instruments for measuring this rotation, and they are widely used in research and in the purity control of food, pharmaceutical, and biochemical products.

A polarizing material, for example, a piece of polaroid film, will preferentially transmit light polarized in a particular plane. If a light source is viewed through two polaroid films with planes of polarization at right angles to each other, the field of view will appear dark since the first film will only allow through light that is polarized at right angles to the direction that would pass through the second. If then a glass tube containing a solution of an optically active compound is inserted in the light path between the two films, a certain amount of light will be transmitted by the second film because the optically active compound will rotate the plane of the light emerging from the first film. The angle through which the first film must be rotated to restore the dark field of view will be a measure of the optical activity of the compound in the tube.

Construction

The simplest polarimeters consist of two polarizing elements in series. The first, called the polarizer, is used to produce a polarized beam of light; the second, called the analyzer, is used to observe the polarized light thus produced. The analyzer is mounted at the center of a rotatable metal disk, the perimeter of which is graduated in degrees so that its orientation can be determined. The earliest instruments used a Bunsen burner as the light source, and the flame was made to appear bright yellow by the addition of common salt, since it was important to know the wavelength (color) at which the measurements were made. The light source in a modern visual polarimeter is usually a mercury or sodium discharge tube.

To use a polarimeter, the analyzer is rotated until the zero transmission condition is reached, in which the polarizer and analyzer transmission axes are at right angles to each other and no light passes through the instrument. The reading on the graduated scale is noted. A glass tube containing a solution of the optically active substance is then inserted between the polarizer and the analyzer, and some light will be observed to pass

▲ This polarimeter uses a microprocessor to give instant information on the polarity and therefore the purity of substances being analyzed.

through the analyzer. The analyzer is then rotated until the original dark condition is restored and the new reading on the graduated scale is taken. The difference between the two readings gives the amount in degrees by which the polarized light has been rotated by the optically active solution.

Modern instruments

With modern automatic polarimeters, it is only necessary to place the sample to be measured between the polarizer and the analyzer for the rotation (accurate to about 0.002 degrees) to be determined electronically and presented in digital form in a few seconds.

Sugars are among the compounds that rotate polarized light, and polarimeters are frequently used in the quality-control laboratories of sugar refineries; in this application, they are usually called saccharimeters. Some types of polarimeters automatically record optical rotations in graphical form throughout the visible and ultraviolet spectrum.

Polarimeters have many other applications, for example, in astronomy, where they are attached to telescopes to detect the polarization of different wavelengths of electromagnetic waves emitted by distant bodies. In addition, polarimeters of a somewhat different construction may be used to measure the polarization of beams of subatomic particles such as neutrons and protons.

SEE ALSO: Crystals and crystallography • Electromagnetic radiation • Light and optics • Polarization

Polarization

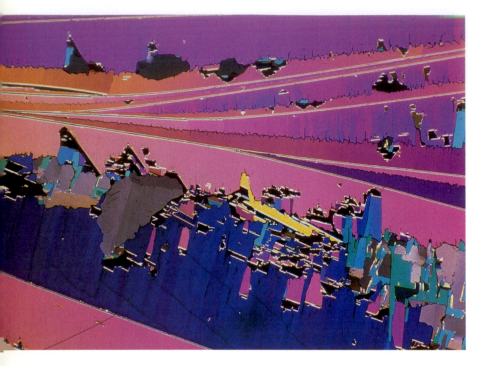

In the 17th century, the Danish physicist Erasmus Bartholinus discovered that crystals of Iceland spar, a form of calcite—natural crystalline calcium carbonate—would split light into two beams. This process was known as double refraction, and differing properties of the two beams led the British physicist Thomas Young, in 1817, to propose that light is a transverse wave, in which the vibrations are perpendicular to the direction of motion of the wave. Birefringent crystals, such as calcite, produce two beams whose directions of vibration are perpendicular to each other (and also perpendicular to the direction of the beam); for example, light traveling horizontally straight ahead might be split into a beam of vertically vibrating waves and one of waves vibrating left to right, known, respectively, as vertically and horizontally polarized beams.

Light is now recognized as being only a small part of the total spectrum of electromagnetic radiation, which consists of transverse electric and magnetic waves, the magnetic field being perpendicular to the electric. It is usual to call the direction of polarization that of the electric field, although it would be just as valid to use the direction of the magnetic field. Electromagnetic radiation is generated by the acceleration of charged particles, usually electrons, and the direction of polarization of the radiation is simply the direction of acceleration of the generating charge.

Ordinary light, from the Sun or a lightbulb, for example, is produced by the random motions of the electrons in a hot body, and because of this

▲ A polarized light micrograph of crystalline sulfur.

▶ Polarized light reveals the high-stress areas in an acrylic injection molding.

random motion, the polarization of the waves is also random. On average, there is as much vertical as horizontal polarization, and the light is usually referred to as unpolarized, even though each individual wave has a definite polarization.

Most methods of producing polarized light involve splitting unpolarized light into two polarized beams and then removing or absorbing one of the beams. Some lasers, however, do produce polarized light directly, because the slanted ends of the laser tube reflect away one of the polarizations and allow the other to dominate.

Dichroic polarizers

The most commonly used polarizers today are made of dichroic materials: substances that transmit only one polarization of light, absorbing the other. Some naturally occurring crystals, such as tourmaline, are dichroic, but plastic dichroic sheets can now be made much larger and more cheaply.

To illustrate the principle of dichroism, consider what happens when an unpolarized beam of radio waves meets a grid of fine vertical wires. The vertical component of the electric field causes eddy currents in the wires, and these are damped by the resistance of the wire until their energy is dissipated as heat. All the energy of the vertical component is therefore absorbed. The horizontal component of the field, on the other hand, can induce currents only across the wires,

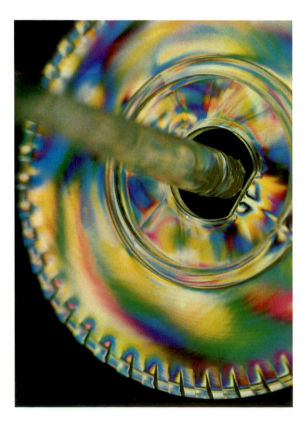

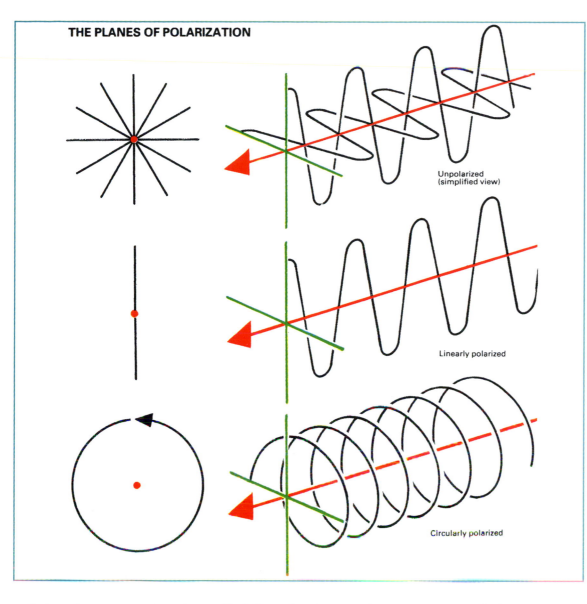

THE PLANES OF POLARIZATION

Unpolarized
(simplified view)

Linearly polarized

Circularly polarized

◀ Unpolarized light vibrates in an infinite number of planes in three-dimensional space. Polarizers restrict the vibration to one plane only.

and since the wires are thin, there is little loss of energy. The emerging radiation is thus completely horizontally polarized, providing the wires are thin and the spacing between them is less than about a wavelength.

It is very difficult to make metal grids that polarize radiation of wavelengths as short as those of light (less than 0.00004 in., or 0.001 mm), and in practice, the very long, thin molecules in plastics are used. A sheet of polyvinyl alcohol, for example, is softened by heating and then rapidly stretched to several times its original length to pull the long molecules into line with each other. It is then fixed to a rigid backing, such as cellulose acetate, and dipped into a solution containing iodine, which reacts with the plastic molecules. The long parallel strings of iodine atoms so formed act as the fine conducting grid needed to polarize the light. Various grades of polarizers are made that leak different amounts of the unwanted polarization, although cutting down the leakage also reduces the amount of wanted polarization. The wanted polarization is reduced from the

theoretical 50 percent to typically 40 percent, while the unwanted polarization amounts to around 0.05 percent.

Other polarizers

Dichroic sheet polarizer, such as Polaroid, which can be produced up to 19 in. (48 cm) in width and in any length, is by far the most commonly used polarizer today. Until its invention in 1928, the most popular polarizer was the Nicol prism, a calcite crystal that had been cut in half and cemented together again with Canada balsam, a type of resin. The crystal is shaped so that one of the doubly refracted beams is totally internally reflected at the balsam, while the other passes straight through to be used in the polarization experiment. Another type of polarizer depends on the fact that light reflected obliquely from a surface, though not from a metal, is always polarized to some extent. (Metals, having good electric conduction, will not work. For this reason, a reflection from a normal silvered mirror will not be polarized.) The beam is completely polarized if

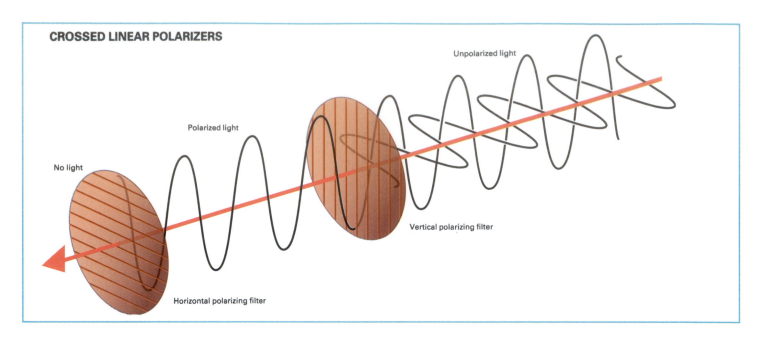

CROSSED LINEAR POLARIZERS

Unpolarized light

Polarized light

No light

Vertical polarizing filter

Horizontal polarizing filter

the reflected light is at right angles to the beam refracted through the surface. The angle between the incident beam and the normal to the surface when this occurs is called the Brewster angle and is about 57 degrees for glass. A pile-of-plates polarizer is simply a number of glass plates set at this angle in a tube: as light passes through it, some of the polarization is reflected off each plate and absorbed in the blackened sides of the tube.

Uses of polarized light

Polaroid sunglasses are dichroic sheets that transmit only vertically polarized light. They cut down the general illumination because only 40 percent of the light falling on them is transmitted, but, more important, they reduce glare to an even greater extent.

There are many industrial applications of polarized light, two of the most important being polarimetry and photoelastic stress analysis. The former is used to measure the concentration of solutions of certain compounds, such as sugar, that consist of asymmetric molecules. These optically active substances rotate the direction of polarization of light, and the amount of rotation depends on the concentration of the solution.

Photoelastic analysis is used to investigate the positions of maximum stress in mechanical components. A model of the component is made in a plastic such as transparent Bakelite, which is birefringent when stressed, and placed between crossed polarizers in a polariscope. Appropriate forces are applied to the specimen, and the regions under stress show up as light areas, because they rotate the polarization of the light from the first polarizer so that it is no longer perpendicular to the transmission direction of the second polarizer. The amount of rotation

depends on the wavelength of light used, and therefore, by illuminating the specimen with white light, regions of differing stress will be brightest at different wavelengths.

Circular and elliptical polarization

As well as the linear polarization discussed so far, light can also be circularly or elliptically polarized. In this case, the electric field of a light wave is not oscillating in a fixed direction in space but moves around the direction of propagation. A circularly polarized wave has an electric field that is constant as it rotates, whereas the electric field of an elliptically polarized wave is stronger in one particular direction than in the perpendicular direction. A linearly polarized wave can in fact be regarded as an extreme example of elliptical polarization, where its strength in the perpendicular direction is zero. Circular and elliptical polarized waves are also either left or right polarized. If the electric-field vector of the electromagnetic wave is rotating clockwise as the wave approaches an observer, the wave is said to be right-circularly polarized or right-elliptically polarized; if it is is moving counterclockwise, the wave is left-circularly polarized or left-elliptically polarized.

One form of polarization can be converted to another by an appropriately cut thin piece of birefringent crystal. For example, circularly polarized light may be obtained by directing a beam of linearly polarized light through such a crystal.

Circular polarized electromagnetic waves have a variety of uses, for example, as in high-powered FM radio transmissions and in light spectroscopy.

▲ Crossed linear polarizers. White light, represented as vertical and horizontal vibrations, approaches a vertical polarizing filter, which allows only vertical light to pass through. When the vertically polarized light reaches the horizontal polarizing filter, the remaining vibrations are blocked, so no light is able to pass through.

SEE ALSO: ELECTROMAGNETIC RADIATION • LIGHT AND OPTICS • POLARIMETER • SPECTROSCOPY

Pollution Monitoring and Control

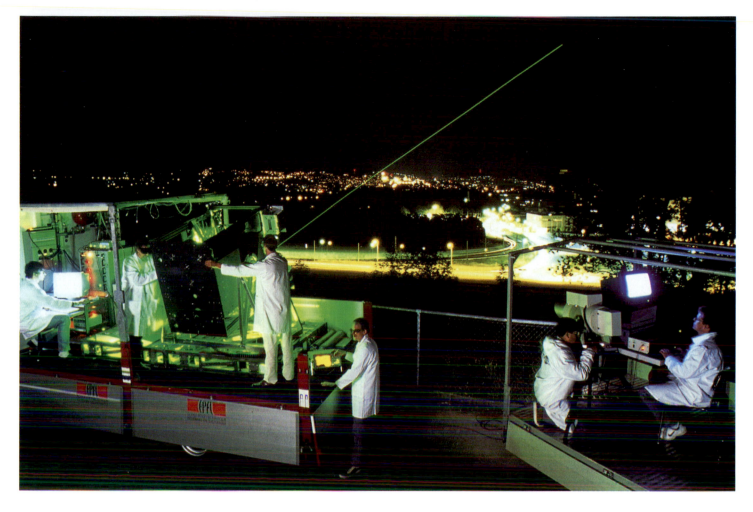

Pollution control describes a system of procedures and techniques aimed at limiting chemical and physical contamination of the environment by industrial, domestic, commercial, and agricultural activities. It is a wide and developing field in which science and technology have an important but not dominant part to play. Other advances must take place in the legal, economic, social, and political spheres if progress is to be made.

In our haste to exploit the benefits of particular processes, humans have for many centuries used the environment—the air, water, and land that surround us—as a convenient depository for unwanted by-products of reactions. Originally, for example, the smoke from burning wood or coal was acceptable as long as the processes remained limited in scale and sparsely distributed. The last hundred years have seen an unprecedented use of Earth's resources of fuel and materials in meeting the expectations of hundreds of millions of people for convenience and comfort. Taken together with an increasing awareness of our relationship to and dependence on our environment, however, such a solution is no longer always satisfactory.

Even though the 1990s witnessed a considerable change in emphasis, the application of scientific and technical knowledge in making possible new products and services still far outstrips its application in dealing with potentially harmful side effects. The minimization of such effects is the aim of environmental protection, which seeks to protect people from damage or irritation by pollution and, on a broader scale, to protect the natural balance of Earth's ecosystem, including all living organisms, as well as humans. Most countries have some form of legislation to try and restrict pollution, and in the United States its enforcement is the responsibility of the Environmental Protection Agency.

Local and global pollution

Locally, pollution effects are most serious in and near large centers of population or industry. Smoke, grit, fumes, and noxious gases in the discharges of domestic, industrial, and power plant chimneys and of traffic exhausts make the air often unpleasant and sometimes hazardous to breathe. In periods of still and stable air, pollution has built up to levels sufficient to cause many

▲ Concentrations of atmospheric pollutants can be measured using LIDAR (*light detection and ranging*), a form of radar that uses a green laser. The type of lidar used to measure pollution uses two different wavelengths of light, selected so that one of the wavelengths is absorbed by the molecule being measured. The difference in the intensity between the two returned signals indicates how much pollutant is present in the atmosphere.

◀ Discharges of smoke and steam are subject to legal restrictions on the amount and type of emissions that can be released to the atmosphere. Refineries are also subject to regulations on storage of oil so that the soil and groundwater are not contaminated, and wastewaters have to be treated to high standards before they can be discharged back into the environment.

deaths—especially among those with respiratory ailments, the very young and the aged. Inadequately treated domestic or industrial sewage, runoff from contaminated land, and the careless disposal of poisonous wastes can render rivers and streams unfit for higher forms of aquatic life and make them unsuitable for recreation or water supply. Often the pollution is caused by small firms or individuals who may not realize the damage they are doing. However, the costs of disposing of some hazardous materials legally are often an economic burden that a small company may not be able to afford. There is also the problem of subcontractors not complying fully with disposal regulations. Cyanide and asbestos are typical of illegally dumped substances that have caused concern among environmentalists.

There have been cases where rivers have become so polluted by organic waste that they have been declared fire hazards: the fermentation of organic wastes may produce methane gas, for example. Fertilizers used on the land may get into rivers, causing the accelerated growth of weeds that then choke the river flow, causing further difficulties downstream. Local dangers from land pollution by mine spoilings or home and industrial dumping are that water supplies can become contaminated and that harmful substances make the plants grown in the ground potentially poisonous, if they grow at all.

To date, most effort in pollution control has concentrated on reducing local problems, but there are causes for concern on the international

and even global scales. This is especially the case for air and water pollution because of their easy movement across political boundaries. Some of the sulfurous discharges from the chimneys of Britain and Europe are believed to fall as acid rain in Scandinavia, complicating crop cultivation because of the nature of the soil. Similarly, acid rain in New York and New England is believed to originate in the industrialized regions of the Ohio River basin. The waters of the Rhine River are used and polluted by four nations before they reach the North Sea.

More widely, it has been calculated that the chlorofluorocarbon compounds widely used as aerosol propellants (such as in hair sprays) could weaken the stratospheric ozone layer by the catalytic action of chlorine atoms. (The ozone layer protects life from heavy doses of ultraviolet radiation from the Sun, and a decrease in its strength might lead to increased incidence of skin cancers.) Methane produced by the digestive processes of domestic animals is also believed to affect the ozone concentration. There is lively debate on the safety of widespread use of biodegradable plastics, which eventually rot away like paper, to aid litter control.

Techniques

Scientific and technical knowledge is essential for providing methods and instrumentation in certain areas of pollution control. They include measurement and monitoring of pollutant concentrations in the environment; deriving reference concentrations (related, for example, to public health) against which potential hazards can be assessed; reducing emissions at their source, either by making possible the construction of purifying units for the effluent or by invention of inherently cleaner new processes; and background knowledge and equipment for use in dealing with specific problems, such as oil spills at sea.

In spite of considerable activity in all of these areas, much remains to be done. There is such a wide range of agencies creating pollution, of types of pollutants and their concentrations, and of practical limitations, such as cost and reliability of equipment, that almost every discipline known to modern science has been involved in finding answers. For example, nuclear physics techniques such as neutron activation and biological studies of the rate of growth of lichens have been used to monitor atmospheric pollution; electrostatics and bacteriological growth have been used to control effluents; and electronics, statistics, and medicine have been involved in the derivation of reference levels for use by monitoring bodies.

◄ Examining fish caught in the once heavily polluted Thames River in London. A concerted effort to prevent industrial wastewaters and agricultural runoff from entering the river has restored it to health. Salmon, an indicator of clean water, are now commonplace, and even dolphins have been seen swimming under Tower Bridge in recent years.

Some monitoring devices

Environmental monitoring is an important factor in pollution control for a number of reasons. First, in conjunction with reference levels, it enables potential hazards to be confirmed or dismissed; second, if continued for sufficient lengths of time, it demonstrates how effectively new remedies for control are reflected in environmental improvement; and third, it provides the data on pollutant concentrations that, together with observed effects (for example, the occurrence of a particular disease), is needed for the setting of reference concentrations.

Perhaps the most easily accessible monitoring devices, and in some cases the most relevant, are the human senses. They are extremely responsive to some pollutants (odors) but, unfortunately, completely insensitive to others (heavy metal contamination or carbon monoxide). In addition, their responses are relative rather than absolute and therefore suffer difficulties of interpretation and reliability. Careful individual observation is, however, still one of the best ways of detecting likely pollution hazards. Wildlife forms are often related to pollution levels. It is standard practice on many rivers to note the population of flatworms, caddis flies and mayflies, and even trout and salmon that they support. Thus, the environment can act as its own monitor.

A widely employed monitoring method applicable to air, water, and land is to take samples at various points of interest and carry them to the laboratory for detailed analysis. There, a wide range of chemical and physical techniques, such as microscopy, chromatography, atomic and gamma-ray spectroscopy, X-ray fluoroscopy, and neutron activation, is available to identify pollutants and measure their concentrations.

Often it is found that the concentration of a pollutant varies markedly during the day or from one day to another. In such instances, spot samples are of limited value, and average concentrations must be measured over a period of time. For example, in the measurement of daily average concentrations of atmospheric sulfur dioxide, the air sample is filtered first to remove small particles, and then bubbled for a day at a fixed rate through a solution of hydrogen peroxide. Sulfur dioxide is converted to sulfurous acid, whose amount is determined by titration against an accurately standardized sodium carbonate solution. The average sulfur dioxide concentration then can be calculated knowing the volume of air passed and the quantity of sulfurous acid it created.

There is frequently a need to establish how the pollution changes from minute to minute, especially in air pollution work where wind speed and direction can vary rapidly. An instrument for determining dust and smoke concentrations makes use of a vibrating crystal like those employed in some modern watches. The air sample is drawn through a high-voltage discharge that electrically charges the dust particles and deposits them on one surface of the crystal. This action causes the vibrations of the crystal to slow down in proportion to the mass of dust deposited, a change that can be accurately metered and recorded electronically.

The development of equipment giving continuous, on-the-spot recordings of pollutant concentrations makes possible the assembly of advanced monitoring systems that can be used not only for collecting data for subsequent interpretation but

► The peppered moth has adapted its coloration so that it blends in with an environment first blackened by pollution and then lightened by measures to prevent soot and other atmospheric contaminants from being emitted by industrial chimney stacks.

also as the basis for immediate decisions on how to control polluting emissions. A system for water pollution is made up of a number of monitoring stations located at carefully chosen points along a river or network of rivers. At each station, acidity, electric conductivity, dissolved oxygen content, chloride concentration, turbidity (transparency), and temperature are measured and the data transmitted, usually through telephone lines, to a central control room. There the results can be fed to computers for immediate analysis and display. Remote sensing systems like these are particularly useful for spotting water pollution incidents upstream of a drinking water intake, allowing operatives to shut off the intake valves until the pollutant has passed.

Emission control

Certain remedies can be used to alleviate local pollution problems without cutting down on overall polluting emissions. For example, tall chimneys permit the dilution of effluents to tolerable concentrations before they reach the ground, local traffic fume problems may be reduced by road design and traffic control, and industrial waste can be discharged through a pipeline out to sea. This type of solution is inherently unsatisfactory on the global scale, however. We are unlikely ever to be capable of purifying the atmosphere, oceans, and land once they become dangerously polluted. The environmentally safer method of control is thus to reduce emissions at the source whenever it is possible.

As with monitoring, numerous ways have been developed to cope with the widely different characteristics of polluting sources. Sources are usually classified as point sources when there is a single, clearly defined outlet, such as a factory

▲ The pristine Arctic and Antarctic environments are subject to monitoring for pollutants even though activities are severely restricted in these areas. They provide valuable information on changes over time and the global movement of atmospheric and waterborne contaminants.

▶ Measurement of ice-core samples can reveal present and past levels of carbon dioxide in the atmosphere, useful information for predicting the effects of global warming.

wastepipe; pollution occurring over a wide area or from more than one outlet is described as diffuse, or nonpoint. The major approaches used for controlling the pollution of land and waterways involve the use of appropriate waste disposal methods and wastewater treatment.

Some liquid effluents from industry are not, however, amenable to purification by the bacteriological processes of wastewater treatment. For them, chemical or physical methods have to be used, such as electrolysis, acid or alkali neutralization, evaporation, and incineration. In many cases, it is possible to recover the costs of operating a pollution abatement plant by reclaiming or recycling material from the effluent for reuse or sale. For example, substantially pure copper can be recovered by electrolytic treatment of acid pickling baths in the metal-processing industry.

The most common type of contaminant in the atmosphere is probably particles with diameters in the range 0.01 to 100 microns. This range includes easily visible smokes as well as grits and dusts and barely visible aerosols (in this case, particles or droplets suspended in the air). Particles may be removed in many ways, most obviously by filter bags that are periodically changed or replaced. Another method is to use electrostatic precipitators, in which the particles are forced by electric fields onto collecting plates that are cleaned mechanically as the deposit grows. Water sprays are sometimes a reliable way to remove small particles and any soluble gaseous pollutants, and chemical scrubbers, using various compounds in aqueous solution, are used for some gases, such as sulfur dioxide. Alternatively, if the effluent gases are made to swirl sufficiently, the centrifu-

AS MAD AS A HATTER

The cats, whose diet was almost exclusively fish scraps, were the first to react. In the fishing towns and villages up and down the west coast of the island of Kyushu in Japan, the cats began to stagger and lurch around, their eyes glazed. They had fits and seemed to go mad. Eventually, they fell into coma and died. Before the year was out, the first human was stricken.

The mercury that poisoned fish, birds, animals, and humans throughout the Minamata region of Kyushu originated in a vinyl chloride factory. Mercury is one of the many toxic metals known as heavy metals, and it is poisonous in all forms. The three main forms encountered are the mined metal (quicksilver), inorganic compounds, such as mercuric chloride and mercuric sulfate, and organic forms, such as phenyl and dimethyl mercury. The organic forms are far more lethal than the others. At Minamata the factory effluent started out as an inorganic compound, but it changed to an organic form on its way through the settling ponds and ditches.

The epidemic that became known as Minamata disease was the first big pollution scandal in the postwar years, and it brought home to a shocked world the fact that there could be a high price to pay for unregulated industrial expansion. In an eight-year period, starting in 1953, 43 Japanese people were to die as a result of the mercury poisoning, and 68, including many children, were crippled and left horribly handicapped. The adults died in a matter of months, but the agony of the children was drawn out in many cases for years. All were the victims of chronic mercury poisoning caused by eating contaminated fish or, as with some of the children, as a result of their mothers doing so before they were born. Like the cats, the victims lost muscular coordination and then experienced a numbness in hands and feet, loss of hearing, impaired speech, and clumsy gait. This stage was followed by violent laughing and crying without apparent reason and a high fever and seizures, culminating in death.

In *Alice in Wonderland* the Mad Hatter at Alice's tea party was so called for the same reason that the phrase "as mad as a

▲ The Mad Hatter in *Alice in Wonderland* was so called because of a real phenomenon observed in hat industry workers who used mercury. Heavy metals have caused a number of poisoning incidents with devastating effects on organisms in the environment.

hatter" became common usage in the English language. Nineteenth-century hatmakers sometimes used a compound containing mercury when preparing beaver fur for hats. They were poisoned by the mercury fumes and experienced symptoms such as lack of concentration, hallucinations, irritability, excitability, and even complete personality change. Humans can absorb mercury through any mucous membrane, and it can also enter the body through the skin. Hatters no longer go mad for their trade, but modern industries use mercury in a number of ways. The paper industry uses it, and it is used for the electrodes necessary for the manufacture of caustic soda. It is also used as a fungus and mold deterrent in several industries, including laundries, home decorating, building, and agriculture. One of the more recent uses is as a catalyst in polyvinyl chloride (PVC) manufacturing processes. Heavy metals, such as mercury, have a long survival time. They become increasingly concentrated in their progress through food chains and are particularly dangerous to those feeding at the top end of the chain, such as cats and humans.

In addition to mercury, heavy metals include lead, iron, cadmium, zinc, copper, nickel, and arsenic. Our body needs small quantities of some metals—iron in the blood's hemoglobin is an example—and copper, nickel, and zinc all have a function

as tiny trace elements in the body's metabolism. The amounts encountered as a result of industrial pollution are far in excess of anything usable by the body. Some heavy metals—notably mercury and lead—have no natural function in the human body.

Most Americans accumulate up to 0.0004 oz. (10 milligrams) of cadmium, mainly in their kidneys, by the time they are 20. It can be passed along the food chain from the ground up from phosphate fertilizers with a high cadmium content. Mine workings and field drainage flush it into water supply sources. We eat it, drink it, and inhale it. Probably the main industrial source is the flue dust from the chimneys of zinc, lead, and copper smelters. Zinc and cadmium together seem to have an intensifying effect, and the cadmium that gathers in the kidneys combines with zinc in a special protein. Cadmium poisoning attacks the kidneys and central nervous system, causes anemia, and in heavy doses, can cause loss of sexual potency and fertility. It lingers in the body, sometimes not taking effect for years. It speeds up tooth decay and deadens the senses of smell and taste. It has been linked strongly with the incidence of high blood pressure. As with mercury and lead, one of cadmium's most disconcerting effects is the damage it can inflict on unborn children.

turbine principle. One of the most worrying pollutants in car emissions—tetraethyl lead—is now being phased out as an additive in fuel as a result of improvements in octane ratings and cleaner-burning engines.

Other forms

Noise and light are also now regarded as environmental pollution. Noise abatement is as important near major roads and airports as control of emissions, at least as far as the local inhabitants are concerned. Adequate shielding of housing areas, in terms of muffling walls along roads and storm windows near airports, solves part of the problem, but the real answer is to develop forms of transport that make less noise.

Light pollution from street lights and signs is of concern to astronomers and naturalists. Many young people in city areas have never seen the Milky Way properly; in some areas, there is so much light during the night that biological processes are upset, and some plants remain in their daytime cycles of operation. It is possible to design street lights so that they throw all their light downward, rather than allowing some of it to shine upward. With the growing tendency to illuminate all roads for safety reasons, controls may eventually become desirable. Noise and light pollution are not as serious as other forms, because they do not have a foreseeable lasting effect on the environment.

Natural remedies

Not all pollutants require sophisticated chemical and technological methods of removal. Bioremediation uses naturally occurring microbes and bacteria to treat organic pollutants in situ, particularly in areas where the soil or groundwater has been contaminated. The microorganisms use the organic substance as food, releasing harmless

gal forces can be large enough to throw particles to the walls of a container, where they can be collected. Grit and dust blown off industrial stockpiles can be controlled to a certain extent by periodically hosing the material with water or, if necessary, by using sealed containers for storage and transportation.

An important way to reduce air pollution from combustion sources is for authorities to place restrictions on fuel composition. A very successful example of this is the implementation of smoke-less zones, in which only approved fuels and appliances may be employed for all heating needs. Some cities have taken action to limit the sulfur content of oil and coal burned within their boundaries, and many countries specify upper limits for the lead content of motor fuels.

Undesirable trace gases can also be removed in a variety of ways, depending on several factors, such as the nature of the gas and its concentration, flow rate, and so on. Catalytic combustion, in which the pollutant is oxidized to a safer substance, is widely used. The importance of the catalyst in the industrial context is that it permits the oxidation to take place at a low temperature so that large quantities of heat are not wasted in dealing with the pollution.

Catalytic units have also been developed to remove carbon monoxide and hydrocarbons from the exhausts of gasoline-engined vehicles. Catalysts speed up the oxidation sufficiently so that it is completed by the time the exhaust has passed through the system. Other methods of cleaning vehicular emissions include the use of electric drives and attachments to limit crankcase and fuel tank evaporation, and basic redesign of the engine, even to the extent of using the gas-

▲ The dark coloration on the shore of eastern Trinidad, West Indies, is caused by iron ore waste. The pollutant lies thickly on the shore and is toxic, harming wildlife and vegetation. It was brought ashore by currents from a dumping ground at sea.

▶ An aerial shot of Auckland, New Zealand, shows tons of potentially dangerous effluent pouring into the city's harbor (bottom left).

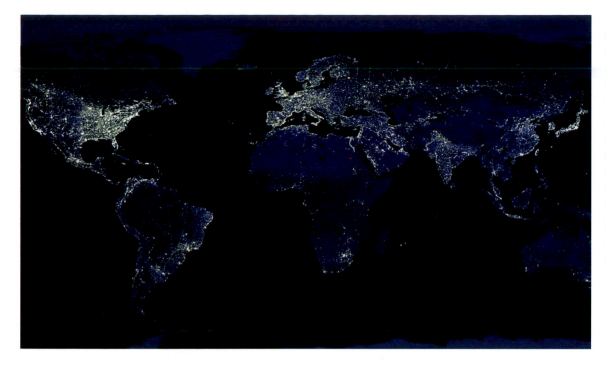

◀ This picture taken at night by satellite shows the extent of light pollution from cities all around the world. The outline of many countries can be seen clearly, though the least developed and those with small populations are much darker than the wealthy and highly populated countries such as those in Europe and North America.

waste products such as carbon dioxide and water. When the food source is exhausted, the microorganisms begin to die off, leaving no threat to the environment. Often, the indigenous microorganisms can be used, but most forms of bioremedia-

tion assist the natural process by adding extra nutrients or injecting oxygen to ensure that the maximum amount of contaminants is removed. If the microbe needed to remove the pollutant is not present naturally, it can be brought in from elsewhere and the conditions adjusted to favor its growth. In situ techniques are cost effective as they do not require expensive removal of the soil for treatment, thus avoiding the spread of dust and contamination over a wide area, and a larger volume of soil can be treated at any one time.

Economic and moral factors

Mankind now has the ability to monitor and measure the impact it makes on the environment. Great strides have been taken toward building cleaner engines, limiting the use of toxic chemicals, and recycling materials to conserve resources. What is lacking, however, is a universal will to put all these measures into practice. Economic factors are frequently cited as a reason for not installing pollutant controls or shifting polluting industries to countries with lax regulation. As a result, some developing countries are prepared to suffer environmental degradation for the money industry brings into their economy. Changes will happen only when the prevailing attitudes and values focus on long-term conservation of resources rather than immediate survival, and when individual countries are willing to cooperate on setting international standards.

FACT FILE

- A pollution-control system devised at Woods Hole Oceanographic Institute, Massachusetts, involved growing marine algae in a mixture of sewage and seawater and then feeding the algae to shellfish. Other fish were fed on the shellfish wastes, and the final effluent was polished (the last stage of cleaning) by commercially grown seaweed.

- At NASA's Bay St. Louis laboratory, water hyacinths are used to clean domestic and chemical wastewaters. About 15 acres (6 ha) of water hyacinth ponds can efficiently clean up to 141,000 cu. ft. (3,950 m³) of water in 24 hours.

- Columbia University, New York, has developed the Toxiplex system for heavy metal waste disposal. Coal and municipal wastes are made into briquettes and burned to form a fuel gas. Metals, such as chromium and lead, are added during gasification and become trapped in the slag, which in turn can be made into a construction material.

SEE ALSO: CHEMISTRY, ANALYTICAL • ENVIRONMENTAL SCIENCE • NOISE MEASUREMENT • NUCLEAR WASTE DISPOSAL • RECYCLING • WASTE DISPOSAL • WASTEWATER TREATMENT

Polyamide

◀ Kevlar—an aromatic polyamide, or aramid—is used as the skin for the foam hulls of racing sailboats and yachts such as this. The material is chosen for its low density, high tensile strength, and abrasion resistance.

Polyamides form a class of polymers whose macromolecules consist of small hydrocarbon blocks linked together by amide (–CO–NH–) groups. The class includes the nylon polymers that can be spun as fibers for weaving as textiles as well as engineering nylons, which are strong enough to replace alloys for making components such as pulley wheels and zippers.

Aromatic polyamides, or aramids, form a sub-class that includes Kevlar, a tough polymer used to make body armor. Polyimides are polymers in which the two carbonyl (–CO–) groups of a diacid both form amide linkages with the nitrogen of a single amine (–NH$_2$) group.

Provided the monomers are simple diacids and diamines, polyamides are strictly linear polymers (unlike polyethene, for example). Furthermore, the carbonyl oxygen and the hydrogen of amide groups in adjacent chains can form hydrogen bonds together. The combination of linearity and hydrogen bonding promotes the formation of crystalline regions, in which polyamide chains lie neatly alongside one another. A proportion of triacid or triamine in the monomer blend causes branching, which reduces crystallinity.

Water molecules can also form hydrogen bonds with amide groups, so some polyamides can absorb water on soaking. The tendency to absorb water reduces as the number of carbon atoms in the monomers increases, increasing the hydrophobic hydrocarbon content of the chain.

Types of nylons

The original Nylon was synthesized in 1935 by Wallace Carothers of the U.S. chemical company Du Pont. He heated hexane-1,6-dioic acid with 1,6-diaminohexane, causing water to boil off as the polymer formed:

$$n\text{HOOCC}_4\text{H}_8\text{COOH} + n\text{H}_2\text{NC}_6\text{H}_{12}\text{NH}_2 \rightarrow$$
$$\text{HO–(OCC}_4\text{H}_8\text{CO–NHC}_6\text{H}_{12}\text{NH)}_n\text{H} + (n{-}1)\text{H}_2\text{O}$$

This polyamide is nylon-6,6—the first six refers to the number of carbon atoms in the diamine, the second to the number of carbons in the diacid.

The next nylon to be developed was nylon-6. This polymer was made by polymerizing caprolactam (C$_5$H$_{10}$CONH), a cyclic amide in which the amide group forms part of a seven-membered ring. As the rings open, the carbonyl group of one molecule forms an amide linkage with the amine group of the next:

$$n\text{C}_5\text{H}_{10}\text{CONH} \rightarrow$$
$$\text{HO–(OCC}_5\text{H}_{10}\text{NH)}_n\text{H} + (n{-}1)\text{H}_2\text{O}$$

Nylon-6 is similar to nylon-6,6 in that both have groups of six carbon atoms in their monomer blocks; the difference is that the amide groups of nylon-6 all lie in the same direction along the chain, whereas those of nylon-6,6 alternate.

Nylon-6,10 is another important polyamide. It is made by reacting the C-10 diacid chloride with 1,6-diaminohexane. The reaction is rapid, but the monomers do not mix, so the polymer forms only at the interface between the two layers. Left alone, a film of nylon-6,10 would form at the boundary, and the two layers would remain intact. In industry, the film is picked out from the center of the interfacial layer and drawn out of the vessel. More nylon forms as soon as the two monomer layers are exposed to one another, and the nylon can be drawn out of the vessel as a continuous filament as long as the monomers are replenished. This process forms the basis of the "nylon rope trick"—a popular laboratory demonstration.

Any amino acid or combination of diamine and diacid can form a polyamide. Proteins are polyamides, and important nylons include 4,6; 6,6; 6,10; 6,12; 12,12; and 6; 11; and 12. As a general rule, flexibility increases with the number of carbon atoms in the monomer blocks, since chains of $-CH_2-$ groups are highly flexible, whereas amide groups are less so.

Raw nylons are processed into fibers by melt spinning: the polymer is melted and extruded through fine holes into a stream of cooling air, where it solidifies as fibers. They may also be chopped and melted for injection molding.

Aramids

The term *aramid* is a contracted and modified form of "aromatic polyamide," and it refers to polyamides in which at least 85 percent of amide linkages are attached directly to two aromatic rings—hexagonal rings of six carbon atoms; polyamides in which fewer amide linkages join two aromatic rings are classed as nylons.

The presence of aromatic rings in aramids has a profound influence on their properties when compared with other polyamides. The bonding in aromatic rings makes them rigid and also interacts with the bonding in the amide groups, locking them into position. As a consequence, aramid chains are much more rigid than those of other polyamides. The rigidity of aramid chains helps them pack closely together in the solid state, resulting in extreme physical strength and chemical resistance when compared with other polymers. Nevertheless, aramids still have lower densities than metals and alloys, for which they are useful replacements in many applications.

The most widely known aramid is Kevlar, formed by the reaction between 1,4-diaminobenzene (p-phenylenediamine, $H_2N–C_6H_4–NH_2$) and benzene-1,4-dioyl chloride (terephthalyl chloride, $ClCO–C_6H_4–COCl$). Molecules of

▲ Space shuttle rocket-booster casings are made with a high proportion of Kevlar. It is also now used to line the wing fuel tanks of Concorde following a disastrous crash outside Paris, France, in 2000.

Kevlar consist of benzene rings linked together by amide groups at diametrically opposed carbon atoms. For this reason, Kevlar is classified as a *para* aramid, *"para"* being the term used to identify the relative positions of chemical groups on opposite sides of the same benzene ring.

Aramids are much more difficult to synthesize than are other polyamides, since the aromatic rings sap reactivity from both carboxylic acid and amine groups. However, highly reactive diacid chlorides are capable of reacting with diamines, the by-product being hydrogen chloride (HCl).

The great tendency of *para* aramids to form crystals also makes them difficult to spin as fibers, so Kevlar is spun from liquid mixtures with concentrated sulfuric acid. The acid protonates some of the amide groups, thereby reducing the opportunity for hydrogen bonding between like-charged polymer chains. Nevertheless, the rod-shaped molecules become aligned with the flow through the spinneret (the perforated cap used for spinning), and the polymer crystallizes in alignment with the fiber when the sulfuric acid is removed. Kevlar is supplied in pulp, fabric, and fiber forms, depending on the intended use.

The alignment and crystallinity of Kevlar gives its fibers excellent tensile strength, breaking only at a tensile stress of 400,000 psi (2,800 MPa)—a value comparable with some steels—and an elongation at fracture as low as 1.9 percent, depending on the grade of Kevlar. The relative density is only 1.44, however, so Kevlar has a weight-to-strength ratio five times that of steel.

Kevlar is resistant to abrasion, mildew, most solvents, and many common chemicals, such as fuels and lubricants. It retains most of these properties at temperatures as high as 350°F (180°C) and is difficult to ignite. Kevlar decomposes at around 7200°F (4000°C) without melting.

While the strength of Kevlar makes it an extremely useful material, it also makes it a difficult substance to cut and machine. Conventional cutting tools—serrated scissors, shears, and saws, for example—can be used provided due attention is paid to sharpness and the conditions of use. Advanced cutting tools, such as lasers and high-energy water jets, are better suited to the job.

A weak point of Kevlar, its low compressive strength, which makes it prone to crumble under large compressive forces, can be overcome by using Kevlar in composites with materials of high compressive strength, such as glass fiber.

Applications of Kevlar

One of the first uses of Kevlar was as the belting material for high-performance radial tires. In addition to improving ride characteristics when compared with steel, there is typically a weight saving of up to 80 percent. The fuel economy achieved with Kevlar belts offsets its high cost relative to steel. Kevlar fibers are also used to reinforce many other rubber products, such as pressure hoses, drive belts, and conveyor belts.

The high strength-to-weight ratio of Kevlar and its composites makes it attractive for use in aviation and sports equipment. The Rolls Royce RB 211/535 C turbofan engine uses Kevlar fibers for the containment ring that catches engine fragments in the case of a turbine or compressor breakup. The Kevlar component weighs 200 lbs. (90 kg) less than an equivalent titanium-steel unit.

The hulls of racing sailboats often have Kevlar-reinforced skins over foam cores, while racing and rally car bodies made from Kevlar composites achieve high stiffness, impact resistance, vibration damping, and weight reduction. Other sporting applications include downhill skis and tennis rackets, where the damping characteristics of Kevlar reduce vibration effects.

Textiles woven from Kevlar fibers are used to make gloves that protect against cuts, abrasion, and sparks and have working lives five times greater than traditional leather gloves. The low thermal conductivity of Kevlar makes such gloves useful for handling hot objects. The thermal insulating property of Kevlar combined with its reluctance to catch fire make Kevlar a useful fabric for firefighters' uniforms.

Woven Kevlar is used to make bullet-proof garments, sometimes with resin-impregnated Kevlar panels. When hit by a projectile, the Kevlar fibers stretch and eventually break, absorbing some of the energy of the projectile. The remaining energy is spread over time and area to minimize the shock of impact while stopping the projectile in its path. Kevlar with ceramic inserts can even stop armor-piercing projectiles: the ceramic shatters as it breaks up the projectile and absorbs some of its energy while the Kevlar catches the resulting fragments.

Kevlar fibers are also used to make mooring ropes and towing cables that are stronger and lighter than fiber ropes and steel cables. Parafil rope, which consists of parallel Kevlar fibers encased in a tough protective sheath, is used to moor deep-sea oil-production platforms. In tests, a 5.5 in. (14 cm) diameter Parafil rope had a breaking load of almost 1,500 tons (1,360 tonnes) with an extension at failure of 2.5 percent.

Other aramids

Increased flexibility can be achieved by including a proportion of aliphatic monomer, such as 1,6-diaminohexane, in the monomer blend. There is some loss of strength in this case.

Nomex is an aramid formed from benzene-1,3-dioyl chloride and 1,3-diaminobenzene. The resulting polymer has zigzag chains that are more flexible than Kevlar, but also less strong.

Polyimides

Polyimides are made by reacting dianhydrides with diamines. The initial product is a polyamide in which each amide group is next to an acid (–COOH) group. In this form, the polymer is easy to mold or apply in a spray coating. Once in place, heating to 390°F (200°C) makes the acid and amide groups condense to form imide groups, resulting in an extremely tough polymer that resists chemical attack. Polyamide-imides have greater flexibility than polyimides, making them useful as internal coatings for aerosol cans.

FACT FILE

■ The annual production of Kevlar soared from 50 tons (45 tonnes) in 1972—the year of its introduction—to 22,000 tons (20,000 tonnes) in 1982. The increase in demand was spurred on by a widening range of applications for the material.

■ Kevlar, impregnated with epoxy resin, is used as a reinforcing cover for aluminum pressure vessels used to hold air for inflating the life rafts and emergency escape chutes of Boeing 747 airliners. The bottles have diameters of 7.9 in. (20 cm) and lengths of 33 in. (83 cm). They work at 3,000 psi (21 MPa) and burst only at more than three times that pressure. Such a bottle weighs around 20 lbs. (9 kg) less than its steel equivalent.

■ Kevlar fuel-tank linings were one of the improvements made to return Concorde aircraft to airworthiness after a fatal crash in 2000 near Paris, France. On takeoff, debris punctured a fuel tank and released a stream of fuel, which caught fire as the doomed aircraft started its climb.

 SEE ALSO: Amino acid • Fiber, synthetic • Protective clothing

Polygraph

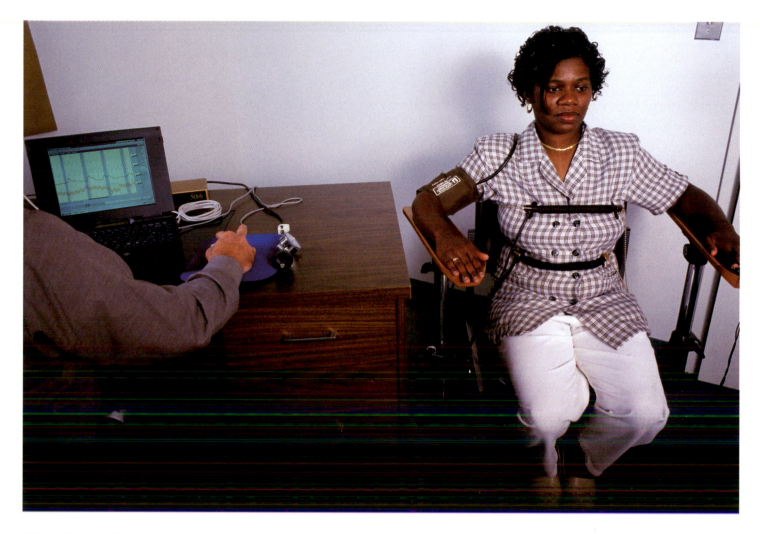

The polygraph is one of the mainstays of experimental psychology and of lie detection. Polygraphs produce graphical representations of physiological changes such as electric activity in the skin or the brain, breathing, pulse rate, and blood pressure. The graphs are recorded on moving graph paper from a roll by three or more pens driven by amplification circuitry. The resulting graphs are a permanent record of the reactions of the subject.

Polygraph applications

Polygraphs used for measuring different kinds of changes are often given specific names. A galvanograph records variations in the resistance of the skin to the passage of electric current. Skin has a certain capacity for conducting electricity, called galvanic skin response (GSR), which varies with the amount of surface fluid on the skin. Changes in the pattern recorded by the polygraph therefore reflect changes in the amount of perspiration on the skin.

A pneumograph is used for measuring breathing patterns in conjunction with a rubber tube placed around the subject's chest. Movements of the chest stretch and relax the rubber tube, causing variations in the pressure of the air in the tube. These changes are plotted on the polygraph.

A cardiosphygmograph is a polygraph used to record relative pulse rate and blood pressure. A bladder and cuff are placed over the brachial artery, which is the one running between the armpit and the elbow. A bellows and lever system transmits changes to the polygraph.

Lie detection

The origins of lie detection came from the ancient Greeks. In the fourth century B.C.E., a physician reasoned that a quickening pulse was a sign of emotional stress caused by lying. More work was done by the Italian scientist Lambroso in the 19th century; he tried to correlate changes in blood pressure with stress. By the 1920s, two Americans, Larson and Keeler, had developed new techniques to enable the measurement of blood pressure and the patterns of respiration, which are two of the main cornerstones of lie detection as it is used today.

▲ All new recruits to the FBI and CIA undergo lie detection tests using instruments that measure the subject's pulse rate, blood pressure, breathing, and skin resistivity.

Lie detection is sometimes used when interviewing suspects in criminal cases, particularly where there is little supporting witness evidence. However, in 1998 the Supreme Court ruled that polygraph evidence was inadmissible in court, citing evidence from recent studies by a U.S. psychologist, David Lykken. However, polygraphs remain popular in preliminary investigation work and in other fields. Other uses found for lie detectors include employment screening and security screening—it has been estimated that over one million polygraph tests are carried out annually in these two areas. The FBI and CIA both use polygraphs when interviewing potential employees.

A number of different lie detection techniques have been developed, but they all follow the same basic format. The subject is connected to the polygraph, and a series of questions is asked of him or her by the polygraph operator. The operator interprets the readings plotted by the polygraph.

Polygraph operators receive training in interpreting the printouts from the polygraph, and commercial lie detecting concerns claim up to 95 percent accuracy when detecting lies. A technique called control question test (CQT) is most often used in criminal investigation. The polygraph operator asks three different sorts of questions—neutral or irrelevant questions, key questions, and control questions—each to elicit a different response.

The neutral questions—such as, "Are you wearing a green sweater?"—should not be emotionally arousing and should not in theory cause abnormal plots on the polygraph. Key and control questions, though, are designed to be emotionally arousing, causing movement in the polygraph pens. Control questions are of the type, "Before the age of 25, did you ever think of hurting someone for revenge?"

The key questions relate to the crime that is being investigated. An innocent person is expected to react at least as much to the control questions as to the key questions, while a guilty person will react more strongly to the key questions than to the control questions.

Voice-stress analysis

Another method for determining whether someone is telling the truth is the computer voice-stress analyzer (CVSA), which was first used during the Vietnam War. In relaxed conditions, the human voice produces both AM and FM sounds, though only the AM component is audible. A truthful response to a question results in diagonal pattern of peaks on the CVSA. However, the onset of stress sends the voice response into an abnormal range, and the FM component starts to

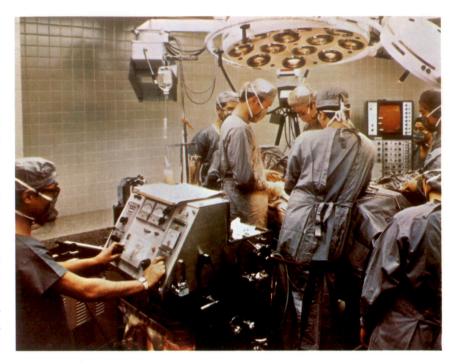

diminish, changing the display on the CVSA to squared-off blocks. The patterns can then be interpreted on the basis of the levels of peaks and blocking shown on the chart.

Problems with lie detection

The wide adoption of lie detection techniques and the accuracy claims made by the practitioners have not deterred their critics. Many psychologists now question the effectiveness of lie detection and the theories behind the technique.

For example, some question whether anything measured by the polygraph actually constitutes a unique measure of lying; in other words, are there other factors at work that are contributing to the polygraph's readings? The detractors argue that the polygraph detects the quantity of arousal, not the nature of the arousal. The polygraph cannot tell the difference between guilt and fear, for example. While some studies have shown accuracy to be in the region of 87 percent, others suggest it is little better than can be obtained by the toss of a coin—that is, 50 percent.

Probably the most worrying case against lie detection comes from a body of laboratory research that has found that lie detection tends to throw up many false positives, that is, when the innocent are detected as being guilty. Lie detection normally detects almost all those who are guilty but also a large number of others who are innocent. Until such effects are solved, polygraphs are likely to remain inadmissible in court.

▲ A polygraph is not only used for lie detection—here it is being used in an operating room to monitor the patient's condition. Polygraphs can also be used in psychiatry to pinpoint anxieties of which the patient may be unaware. A great deal of research still needs to be done into the nature of the autonomous nervous system, the behavior of which is triggered by fear or stress.

 SEE ALSO: BRAIN • ELECTRONICS IN MEDICINE • OPERATING ROOM • PEN RECORDER • PSYCHIATRY

Polymer and Polymerization

The word *polymeric* is derived from the Greek word *polymeres* (of many parts). Polymers are materials that consist of molecular chains or networks of simple units that repeat hundreds, thousands, or even millions of times in each molecule.

Polymers may be natural or synthetic and are either organic (based on carbon and hydrogen) or inorganic (based on salts and minerals). Natural organic polymers include rubber, cellulose, and proteins. Natural inorganic polymers include silicates, such as asbestos, and polyphosphates.

Some important inorganic polymers are synthetic—silicone oils and rubbers, for example—but the polymer-manufacturing industry is predominantly concerned with the manufacture of synthetic organic polymers, such as polyacrylates, polyamides, polyethene, polypropene, polystyrene, polyvinyl chloride (PVC), and polyesters. These polymers are the principal materials in plastics, coatings, and synthetic rubbers.

Polymerization reactions

Synthetic organic polymers are made by reacting together a multitude of simple molecules, such as ethene (ethylene, $C_2=H_4$) and phenylethene (styrene, $C_6H_5CH=H_2$), to form long, chainlike molecules. The reactions that form polymers include esterification, amide formation, and additions at double bonds:

$$-COOH + HO- \rightarrow -COO- + H_2O$$
$$-COOH + H_2N- \rightarrow -CONH- + H_2O$$
$$-C=C- + -C=C- \rightarrow -C-C-C-C-$$

These reactions are also used in simple organic chemistry, but their product mixtures in polymerization are much more complex. For example, whereas a simple chemical reaction forms a target compound at a greater or lesser degree of purity, polymerization reactions form blends of molecules that are similar in structure but with molecular weights spread across a wide range.

Polymers are therefore characterized by their mean molecular weights and by the standard deviation of molecular weights from that mean. Other defining features include the viscosities of liquid and solution polymers, the percentage by weight of polymer in solutions, and their functional values—indicators of the numbers of hydroxy (–OH), carboxylic acid (–COOH), and other functional groups—per unit mass of polymer. Another important value is the glass transition temperature (T_g), the temperature at which a polymer changes from its brittle, glassy state to a flexible, elastic state as it is heated.

▲ Crystals of polypropene magnified 120 times. Highly regular polymers tend to form regions of crystallinity. These regions increase the hardness of a polymer but can also detract from its flexibility.

Polymerization processes

There are four broad classes of industrial and laboratory-scale polymerization techniques: bulk, solution, suspension, and emulsion. The choice of method for an individual polymerization reaction is influenced by the characteristics of the reaction and the properties required of the final product.

Bulk polymerization. In a bulk polymerization, the reactor is fed with monomers and catalysts, or initiators, and nothing else. Heat initiates the reaction, which proceeds until the monomers or initiators are used up or until the heating ceases.

For exothermic (heat-releasing) reactions, the excess heat of reaction must be removed through water-cooled coils immersed in the reactor or through a cooling jacket in the reactor walls. Nevertheless, there is a risk of potentially explosive runaway reactions caused by hot spots developing in poorly cooled parts of the reactor.

Bulk polymerization is best suited to the manufacture of condensation polymers, since the evaporating condensate helps carry away any heat developed by the reaction. Where the technique is used for addition polymerizations, which can be strongly exothermic, there is a greater risk of runaway reactions. Such reactions tend to be stopped at less than 10 percent conversion so that the mixture remains easy to stir as a means of avoiding

ADDITION POLYMERIZATION

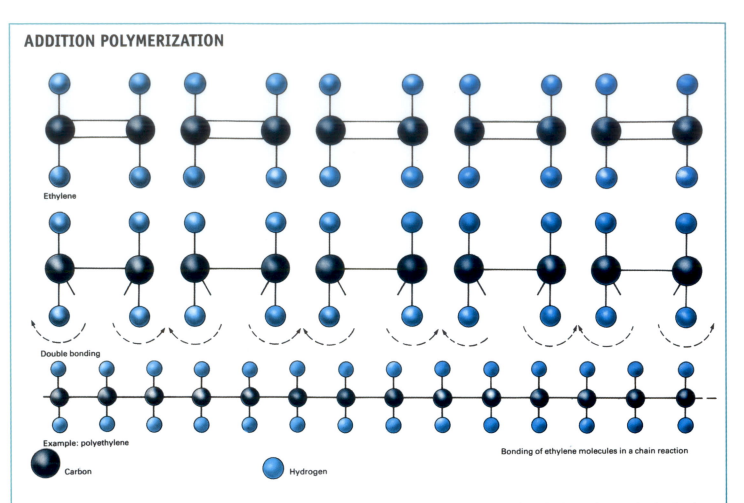

Ethylene

Double bonding

Example: polyethylene

● Carbon

● Hydrogen

Bonding of ethylene molecules in a chain reaction

Addition polymerization is one of the principal mechanisms by which monomers join together to form polymers. The reaction is characteristic of compounds that contain the ethenyl ($CH_2=CH-$) group, formerly called the vinyl group—thus explaining why this type of reaction is often called vinyl polymerization.

The simplest molecule to undergo vinyl polymerization is ethene (ethylene, C_2H_4), which forms polyethene (polyethylene) as illustrated in the above diagram. Other substances that polymerize in this manner include propene (propylene, $CH_3CH=CH_2$), chloroethene (vinyl chloride, $CH_2=CHCl$), phenylethene (styrene, $C_6H_5CH=CH_2$), propenonitrile (acrylonitrile, $C_2H=CHCN$), and esters of ethenoic acid (acrylate esters, general formula $C_2H=CHCOOR$). Polymers built from a single type of monomer are called homopolymers, whereas polymers made from blends of monomers are called copolymers. Copolymers often have better properties than equivalent blends of homopolymers.

Polymer-chain formation by addition polymerization consists of three stages: initiation (also called activation), chain growth, and termination. They can be represented as follows:

$M + A^* \to M^*$	(activation/initiation)
$M^* + M \to M-M^*$	(chain growth)
$M-M^* + M \to M-M-M^*$	(chain growth)
$M-M-M^* + M^* \to M-M-M-M$	(termination)

A* is the active form of an initiator, M is an unactivated monomer molecule, and M* is activated monomer. The average length of the chains that form depends on the rate of chain-growth reactions relative to termination reactions.

▲ In the simplest addition polymerization, ethene molecules (top) rupture one bond of their double bonds (center) and form long chains of polyethene (bottom) that have extremely high molecular weights.

One type of addition polymerization is triggered by initiators, such as benzoyl peroxide ($C_6H_5CO-OO-COC_6H_5$). This substance produces its active form, the phenyl radical ($C_6H_5^\bullet$), on heating. When the phenyl radical reacts with the double bond of a monomer, it forms a single bond and creates a new radical:

$$C_6H_5^\bullet + C=C \to C_6H_5-C-C^\bullet$$

Chain growth then proceeds rapidly until halted by two growing chains meeting. Alternatively, chain growth can be terminated by a chain-transfer agent, which terminates one chain and in doing so becomes able to start another chain growing.

Ionic polymerizations are initiated by powerful acids and bases, such as the acid HBF_3OH, formed by boron trifluoride (BF_3) and water, and potassium amide (KNH_2). The respective ions from which chains grow are formed as follows:

$$HBF_3OH + C=C \to HC-C^+ + BF_3OH^-$$
$$KNH_2 + C=C \to NH_2C-C^- + K^+$$

Ziegler–Natta catalysts for alkene polymerization have their own mode of action. Such a catalyst is formed by triethyl-aluminum ($Al(C_2H_5)_3$) and crystalline titanium trichloride ($TiCl_3$). Ethyl groups from the aluminum compound attach to the surface of $TiCl_3$ crystals. The chain grows as successive ethene molecules insert between the titanium and the ethyl group.

STEP-GROWTH POLYMERIZATION

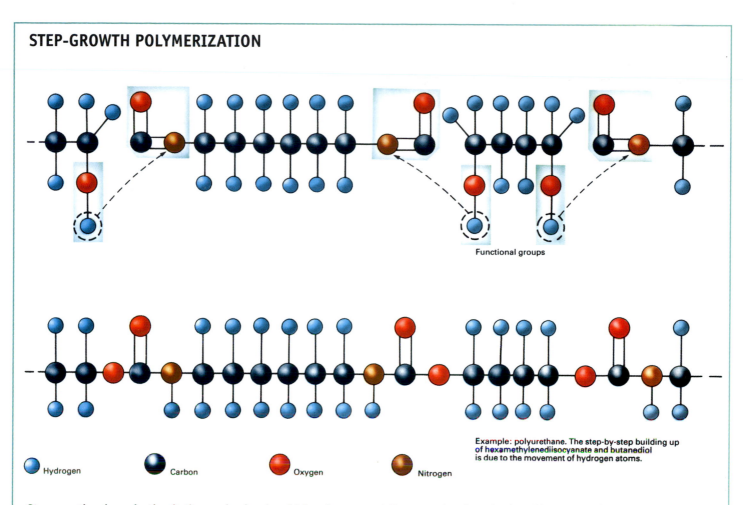

Functional groups

Example: polyurethane. The step-by-step building up of hexamethylenediisocyanate and butanediol is due to the movement of hydrogen atoms.

● Hydrogen   ● Carbon   ● Oxygen   ● Nitrogen

Step-growth polymerization is the mechanism by which polymers such as polyesters and polyamides, including nylons, are formed. It is characterized by monomers that each have two functional groups that take part in the polymerization reaction.

In many cases, the reaction that forms the polymerization linkage also yields a low-molecular-weight species, such as water (H_2O). Such reactions can be driven toward completion by boiling the low-molecular-weight species out of the reaction mixture and making it condense elsewhere, so step-growth polymerizations are also called condensation polymerizations.

One subclass of step-growth polymerizations occurs between two different monomers: each has a pair of similar functional groups, but the functional groups of the two monomers differ. This type of reaction is represented as follows:

$$x(A\!-\!A) + x(B\!-\!B) \rightarrow \left(\!A\!-\!B\!-\!B\!-\!A\!\right)_x$$

A and B are functional groups that react together to form the A–B linkage, the longer lines stand for the "backbones" of the monomers, and x is the number of repeated units. In theory, an exact one-to-one blend of the two monomers could eventually form a single huge molecule. In practice, such an exact blend is hard to achieve, so several smaller chains form and then stop joining together when one or other monomer is used up.

Pairs of monomers that undergo this type of reaction include dimethyl benzene-1,4-dioate acid (dimethyl terephthalate, $CH_3OOC\!-\!C_6H_4\!-\!COOCH_3$) and ethane-1,2-diol (ethylene glycol, $HO\!-\!C_2H_4\!-\!OH$), which form polyethylene terephthalate (PET) and methanol, the condensate. The linkages that join the monomers

▲ Step-growth polymerization of hexane-1,6-diisocyanate (top center left, $OCN\!-\!C_6H_{12}\!-\!NCO$) with butane-1,4-diol (top center right, $HO\!-\!C_4H_8\!-\!OH$). The product is a polyurethane.

together are ester groups, $-CO\!-\!O-$, so PET is an example of a polyester. Another type of polymer is formed by the reaction of 1,6-diaminohexane (hexamethylene diamine, $H_2N\!-\!C_6H_{12}\!-\!NH_2$) with hexane-1,6-dioic acid (adipic acid, $HOOC\!-\!C_4H_8\!-\!COOH$). The product of this reaction is nylon-6,6, so called because each of its monomers has six carbon atoms; the monomers are linked together by amide groups, $-CO\!-\!NH-$, so nylons are polyamides.

In the case of nylon-6,6, the two monomers form a salt by the acid groups donating protons to the amide groups. This salt, whose formula is $(^+H_3N\!-\!C_6H_{12}\!-\!NH_3{}^+)(^-OOC\!-\!C_4H_8\!-\!COO^-)$, can be purified to form an exact one-to-one monomer blend. Thus, it can be heated to form polymers of extremely high molecular weight, the progress of reaction being monitored by the yield of water. If required, a small excess of diacid or diamine can be added to prevent the molecular weight from becoming too great.

The same one-to-one blend of reactive groups is achieved in another type of reaction, where a single monomer has one each of two types of reactive group that link the polymer together. Such a monomer has general formula A—B in terms of the earlier equation, and the polymer is —A—B—A—B—, and so on. An example is caprolactam, a cyclic amide $C_5H_{10}CONH$. A trace of water breaks open caprolactam to make an amino acid, 6-aminohexanoic acid ($H_2N\!-\!C_5H_{10}\!-\!COOH$), which breaks open other caprolactam molecules to form nylon-6 on polymerization.

hot spots. The polymer is then isolated by adding a liquid that dissolves excess monomers but makes the polymer precipitate as a solid.

Where bulk polymerization is taken to completion, polymer runs out of the reactor and is barreled after cooling if still liquid. Polymers that are solid at room temperature run onto a cooling belt where they solidify before being broken into chips, or they are sprayed into a cold fluid, where they form solid prills (roughly spherical pellets).

Solution polymerization. Solution polymerization is similar to the bulk method, but a solvent is also present in the mixture. It does not become part of the polymer but can influence the progress of the reaction and the shapes of the polymer chains that form. Often the reaction occurs at the boiling point of the solvent mixture. A condenser above the reactor returns the liquid solvent to the reactor after removing its heat of evaporation. This process, called reflux, acts as an automatic safety device, removing excess heat and helping prevent runaway reactions.

Emulsion polymerization. In the emulsion polymerization method, water-insoluble addition monomers are added to vigorously stirred water at around 158 to 212°F (70–100°C). The water contains an emulsifier and a water-soluble initiator. The function of the emulsifier is to stabilize most of the monomer as droplets dispersed in water.

The initiator decomposes at the reaction temperature to form an active ionic species, such as the sulfate radical ion ($SO_4^{\bullet-}$). The radical ion, which is insoluble in monomer, initiates polymerization when it comes into contact with a monomer in the water phase. As the chain grows, fed by monomer diffusing from the monomer droplets, the ionic tip from the initiator helps keep the polymer dispersed in water.

The product is a polymer emulsion that consists of droplets of addition polymer, around 0.00004 in. (1 μm) in diameter, distributed in water. The polymer can be used in this form—in emulsion paint, for example—or it can be coagulated and recovered from the emulsion.

Suspension polymerization. Suspension polymerization resembles emulsion polymerization in that it is an addition polymerization performed in water; it differs in that the droplets in suspension polymerization are much larger than in the emulsion method—typically 0.008 to 0.059 in. (0.2–1.5 mm) in diameter. The other difference is that the initiator for suspension polymerization is soluble in monomer, so it enters the monomer droplets and converts them into beads of pure polymer. The water absorbs the heat of the addition reaction, and the polymer product is then separated from the water, dried, and packaged for sale.

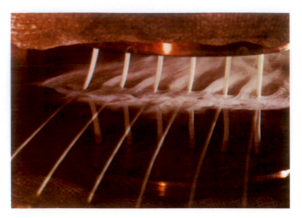

◀ Liquid nylon emerges from a polymerization reactor. The strands solidify rapidly in the cooling water below.

Copolymers

When two or more similar monomers are polymerized together, such as when a mixture of acrylate esters is polymerized, the distribution of the different monomers along the polymer chains affects the properties of the product. In random copolymers, the different monomers are scattered more or less randomly through the chains. In alternating copolymers, there is an almost perfect alternation between two types of monomers; this phenomenon is often a consequence of a favorable interaction between the different monomers.

Block copolymers contain long stretches of single monomers. They can be made by anionic polymerization initiated by a metal alkyl, such as butyl lithium (C_4H_9Li): when the first monomer is added, it repeatedly inserts itself between the carbon and lithium atoms to form the first stretch of homopolymer. When the first monomer is depleted, the second monomer is added to make the second stretch of homopolymer, and so on.

Polymer architecture

The simplest polymer architecture is the straight chain: monomers joined together in a linear molecule. Branched copolymers have side chains that are created by the initiator forming a radical along the chain of a straight-chain polymer and a branch growing from that point or by including a proportion of trifunctional monomer in the starting materials for a step-growth polymerization. Dendrimers are treelike polymers made from trifunctional monomers: the chain branches at each layer out from a central core.

In the case of an asymmetrical monomer, such as propene, the properties of the polymer are influenced by whether the monomers join head to head or head to tail. The tendency for the side groups to join on the same or alternating sides of the chain is also an influence on properties.

 SEE ALSO: Chemistry, organic • Chemistry, organometallic • Fiber, synthetic • Plastics • Plastics processing

Polytetrafluoroethylene (Teflon)

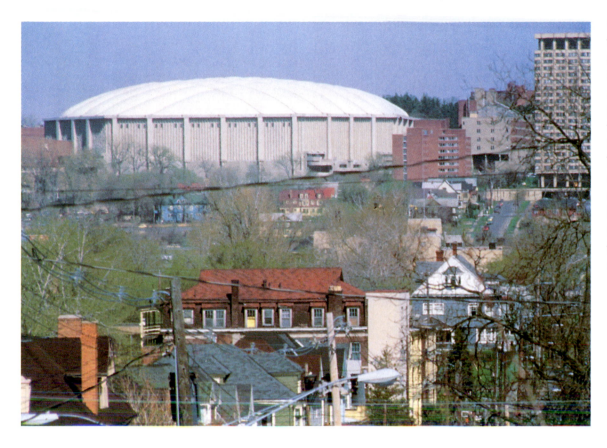

◀ The domed roof of this university building at Syracuse, New York, benefits from two of the notable properties of polytetrafluoroethylene: its nonstick property and low thermal conductivity. The nonstick property deters the accumulation of dirt on the roof, while the low thermal conductivity makes it as good a thermal insulator as much denser conventional materials.

Polytetrafluoroethylene is a polymer of carbon and fluorine that is also known by the systematic chemical name polytetrafluoroethene, by the abbreviation PTFE, and by the Du Pont trade name Teflon. Its chemical composition and structure lend it remarkable properties, including an extremely low coefficient of friction, thermal and electrical insulating properties, and resistance to attack by corrosive chemical compounds.

PTFE was discovered by chance in 1938 by a chemist at the Du Pont chemical company. It was used as a corrosion-resistant coating during World War II and launched as a coating for nonstick cookware in the 1960s. It has since found numerous applications, ranging from a physiologically inert material for surgical implants to a material for lubricant-free bearings.

Structure

Polytetrafluoroethene is essentially polyethene in which fluorine atoms take the places of hydrogen atoms, so it is a chain of repeating $-CF_2-$ units:

$$-CF_2-CF_2-CF_2-CF_2-CF_2-CF_2-CF_2-$$

The chemical stability of PTFE stems in part from the great strength of the C–F bond: any chemical reaction would require this bond to break, so its strength deters reactions. The other factor is the size of the fluorine atom: whereas the hydrogen atoms are small relative to carbon atoms so that chains of polyethene are highly flexible, the much greater radius of the fluorine atom forces PTFE into a twisted form with fluorine atoms arranged in a double helix around the core formed by the carbon atoms. In effect, the fluorine atoms form a protective sheath around the carbon core, preventing potentially aggressive chemical species from reaching the carbon backbone.

The structure of PTFE is also responsible for its physical properties. The tight packing of the fluorine atoms gives a stiff molecular structure, which encourages crystallinity and leads to a high melting point and good thermal stability. The sheath of fluorine atoms provides little opportunity for the physical attractions that underlie ease of wetting and friction, thus accounting for the low surface energy and coefficient of friction.

Manufacture

Early laboratory techniques for the production of fluorocarbon compounds reacted carbon with fluorine in the presence of a catalyst such as mercury. Such processes are unsuitable for large-scale production of single compounds such as PTFE, however, and commercial production is based on the formation and polymerization of tetrafluoroethene (tetrafluoroethylene, $CF_2=CF_2$).

▶ The good chemical resistance of PTFE makes it the ideal material for these trays, which are used to support silicon wafers in etching baths. The low surface energy of the material makes it difficult to wet, so etching solution drains away with ease when the tray is removed from the bath.

The manufacturing sequence starts with the production of hydrogen fluoride (HF) gas by reacting fluorspar (calcium fluoride, CaF_2) with sulfuric acid (H_2SO_4):

$$CaF_2 + H_2SO_4 \rightarrow CaSO_4 + 2HF$$

The hydrogen fluoride so obtained then reacts with trichloromethane (chloroform, $CHCl_3$) to form chlorodifluoromethane ($CHClF_2$):

$$CHCl_3 + 2HF \rightarrow CHClF_2 + 2HCl$$

When heated to around 1290°F (700°C), chlorodifluoromethane loses hydrogen chloride as it forms tetrafluoroethene:

$$2CHClF_2 \rightarrow CF_2=CF_2 + 2HCl$$

The product mixture is then scrubbed to remove hydrogen chloride and distilled to separate pure tetrafluoroethene from other compounds.

The final stage in the production of PTFE is polymerization, which is done in solution or by dispersing a suspension of monomer in water. Oxygen or a free radical initiator triggers the reaction, but the exact details of the process are commercial secrets, since they determine the precise characteristics of the end product and hence its properties. However, there are at least two main approaches, one of which gives a finely dispersed polymer of comparatively low molecular weight, while the other gives a more granular polymer with a higher molecular weight. Typical values for the molecular weight fall in the range 400,000 to 9,000,000, corresponding to 4,000 to 90,000 molecules of monomer joining together.

Properties

Although the detailed properties vary with the method used to produce the PTFE and the way the material is used, the general characteristics remain the same. As noted above, the helical covering of fluorine atoms confers good chemical stability. At working temperatures of up to 500°F (260°C), PTFE resists attack by virtually all solvents and other chemicals, including boiling acids and alkalis. PTFE is vulnerable to chemical attack by molten alkali metals, such as sodium and potassium, and by fluorine at high temperatures.

Long-term weathering tests, lasting for up to 15 years, show that PTFE is resistant to ultraviolet light as well as to extremes of heat and cold. The thermal stability of PTFE is high, with some types being apt for use at temperatures up to 500°F (260°C), while good mechanical properties persist at temperatures down to –450°F (–268°C).

The nonstick properties of PTFE, exploited in applications such as coatings for cookware, stem from its low coefficient of friction, which is typically in the range 0.02 to 0.1. These values apply to both static and dynamic friction, so there is no slip/stick effect. In most cases, the abrasion resistance of PTFE is high, and it has moderately good mechanical and impact strengths. One limitation is that PTFE tends to show significant creep under the initial application of a load. Creep resistance can be improved by the use of fillers, such as glass fiber and graphite.

The electrical insulating properties of PTFE are excellent: the volume resistivity is greater than 10^{18} ohm cm, and the surface resistivity is greater than 10^{16} ohms. The dielectric constant is low—approximately 2 over a wide frequency range—while the dielectric strength is high.

Applications

The combination of properties described above is exceptional and means that there is a wide range of applications for PTFE products. However, these materials are expensive, and the solid form—rather than thin films—is generally only used for relatively small components. Fortunately most of the advantages of the material can be obtained by applying a coating of PTFE to items made of some other material.

When compared with other polymers, PTFE is unusually difficult to mold and apply to surfaces. Although PTFE is a thermoplastic—a material that softens at high temperature—at around 620°F (320°C), it turns into a viscous gel that cannot be formed by conventional molding techniques. Instead, PTFE is worked using techniques similar to those of powder metallurgy. To make solid objects, powdered or granular PTFE is evenly loaded into a mold and subjected to a pressure of around 1 ton per sq. in. (around 14 MPa). The result is a preform: a mass of polymer particles held together by physical forces. The preform is then sintered at around 700°F (371°C), causing the particles to fuse together and turn into an integral solid when the product cools.

Solid items made in this way can be machined using conventional metalworking techniques, provided allowance is made for the fact that the PTFE is soft but springy. The low thermal conductivity means that heat can build up at the cutting edge and lead to overheating, so efficient cooling is needed. For most applications, a machining tolerance of ± 0.005 in. (± 0.13 mm) is satisfactory, since the natural resilience of the material allows it to take up minor discrepancies. Where the application demands, tolerances as fine as ± 0.0001 in. (± 2.5 μm) can be achieved.

Linear forms, such as rods and tubes, can be produced by extrusion. The powdered polymer is forced into a long, heated die whose cross section is that of the finished object. Compaction, sintering, and initial cooling occur in sequence.

Surface coating

PTFE is applied to a variety of substrate materials, including metals, such as steel and aluminum, glass, rubber, and some plastics. A wide range of coating systems is available to suit specific applications; some are single-coat systems, while others consist of a primer and a topcoat.

The polymer may be suspended in an aqueous or solvent-based medium, and application is generally by spraying. Good surface preparation is essential to ensure a satisfactory bond between the coating and the substrate. Typically, this consists of roughening by shot or grit blasting and washing to remove oil and grease. After application, the coating is cured by baking so that the polymer particles fuse together. Care is needed during application to ensure that all parts of the surface are covered and that the coating fuses without leaving pores through to the substrate.

Uses

PTFE coatings are used both for home cookware and for industrial food-processing equipment: the nonstick properties of PTFE make it easy to clean, thereby assisting hygiene, and help prevent food from sticking and burning while cooking.

PTFE coating is also useful for some tools: a coated handsaw does not stick in timber as it cuts, and the coating helps prevent corrosion of the blade. Similarly, handling equipment, such as chutes and conveyors, runs more smoothly if coated with or made from PTFE. Another major

application is for bearings, which can be made from solid PTFE or simply lined with a coating. The combination of low friction and creep under stress is used in sealing tapes for threaded joints in gas and water pipes, for example. Such tapes stretch over the thread, acting as a lubricant and sealing any gaps in the joint. The chemical resistance of PTFE makes it a lightweight and flexible alternative to glass for lining tanks and pipes that are intended to hold corrosive chemicals.

Other fluorocarbon polymers

While the hardness of PTFE is an asset in many applications, it is sometimes desirable to use a softer material that has corrosion resistance and nonstick properties comparable to PTFE. In such cases, copolymers of tetrafluoroethene with other perfluoroalkenes are used. One such polymer, called FEP (fluorinated ethylene–propylene), uses blends of tetrafluoroethene and hexafluoropropene (hexafluoropropylene, $CF_3CF=CF_2$). The $-CF_3$ groups disrupt crystallization, making the copolymer more elastic than PTFE and reducing its softening point to around 400°F (204°C). FEP can be processed by conventional plastics molding and extrusion techniques and is also available as a coating dispersion. It is widely used for seals and gaskets, where its increased elasticity relative to PTFE is of benefit.

▼ PTFE coatings provide the easy-cleaning properties of nonstick cookware and help this iron glide over clothing. Items coated in this way cannot be scoured and must be protected from metal tools that could scrape the coating away.

SEE ALSO: CHEMISTRY, ORGANIC • FRICTION • HALOGEN • LUBRICATION • MATERIALS SCIENCE • POLYMER AND POLYMERIZATION

Population

World population in mid-2000 was estimated to be over 6.1 billion. Fifty years before, in 1950, the population was 2.5 billion, while in 1900 the figure was less than 1.7 billion. Earlier figures are less certain, and reliable records exist only in a limited number of countries, but the figure for 1800 was around 900 million. Even further back in time, the estimate for the year 1000 is 250 to 300 million, a figure that is about 50 million more than a thousand years earlier. Although by no means exhaustive, these figures give a general picture of the growth in population: slow at first but accelerating from the beginning of the 20th century.

More important than past figures, however, is the present growth rate, which is put at around 1.3 percent. This value may not appear excessive, but at this steady rate, the world's population could reach 9.3 billion by the year 2050. However, this growth rate is not even between developed and developing countries and is projected to slow down in both.

Opinions vary on what is an acceptable level of world population, but it is clear that present expansion rates cannot be sustained indefinitely. Resources are limited and, if devoted to sustaining additional population, will not be available to improve the quality of life for the large numbers already at subsistence level. It is estimated that if the world's food supply were to be distributed at

▲ China has the biggest population in the world. To reduce and control the increase in numbers, Chinese families are encouraged by the state to have only one child. As a deterrent, benefits are not increased if a second child is born.

the sort of level currently enjoyed in the United States and Europe, there would be enough to feed only about one-third of the world's population.

Problems are also likely to occur in individual countries; they will be more immediately obvious. Some form of population control—on both global and local levels—seems to be one way of solving the problems.

Death rates

The main reason for the rapid increase in population is the success enjoyed by modern medicine in overcoming the major killing diseases that used to provide a natural check on populations. The death rates from some of these diseases are potentially very high; for example it is estimated that the Black Death killed some 40 percent of the population of England in the middle of the 14th century. Not all epidemics were so severe, but other diseases, such as cholera, smallpox, and tuberculosis, caused a steady flow of premature deaths. Similarly, crop failures and outbreaks of animal diseases often lead to widespread starvation.

Improved living conditions with better sanitation and standards of hygiene, together with the better diet of the late 19th and early 20th centuries, played a large part in reducing the worst effects of such diseases in the developed, industrial countries. Elsewhere, little change was apparent. Then a series of medical discoveries, including vaccines, the use of antiseptics, and drugs such as the sulfonamides and antibiotics, allowed control of many of the major killing diseases. The result was a rapid fall in the death rate, while the birth rate remained at around previous levels, leading to a significant growth in population. Particularly notable were the reductions in deaths of mothers during childbirth and in infant mortality, both of which tended to increase the effective breeding population.

In the developed countries, the initial surge of population was restricted to some extent by the fact that birth rates had also been falling. The exact reasons for this trend are not altogether clear but seem related to increasing prosperity, a reduced probability of child deaths, and the availability of effective contraceptive methods.

In the less developed countries, the application of modern medicine was equally effective in reducing death rates, but since the social conditions were otherwise unchanged, there was no corresponding decline in the birth rate, and thus, high rates of population growth have continued.

The age structure of the population is also significant. In the countries experiencing the highest rates of growth, a very high proportion of the population (40 percent or more) is under the age of 15 and not yet in the reproductive phase. As this section of the population starts to raise children, a further significant growth in population will occur, even if family sizes are then limited. In contrast, in areas such as Europe and the United States, the population age profile is more balanced, and limitation of family size offers the likelihood of achieving a negative population growth after the year 2025.

Growth limits

In addition to the natural checks imposed by disease and lack of food, many societies developed customs that tended to limit their population growth. In some countries, unwanted (often female) or sickly children were killed at birth. In others, the practice of prolonged breast feeding acted to reduce fertility (owing to hormonal effects) while in some societies, lengthy segregation of women occurred following childbirth. Another approach relied on the combined effects of late marriage and celibacy for a significant proportion of the population.

Wars were another aspect of human behavior that had a limiting effect on population growth. Here the reduction was not particularly due to direct effects of military action—in both world wars the total civilian and military deaths were not much more than one year's normal population growth. However, wars created conditions for the rapid spread of killing diseases and also limited food production and caused starvation.

For individual countries, another major controlling factor on population is emigration. For example, during the last decade of the 20th century the net emigration from other countries to the United States was running at a rate of nearly one million per year. Emigration may be forced, as in the displacement of refugees from war, or may be economic, as where people from poorer

◄ As developing countries industrialize, people tend to migrate from rural areas to the big cities in search of work. This influx produces pressures on the local environment to build more houses and in turn to provide more services to support the new population. As wealth increases, poorer people are often left behind in areas that become ghettoes. While poorer families often have more children, poverty, overcrowding, and disease can lead to high levels of infant mortality.

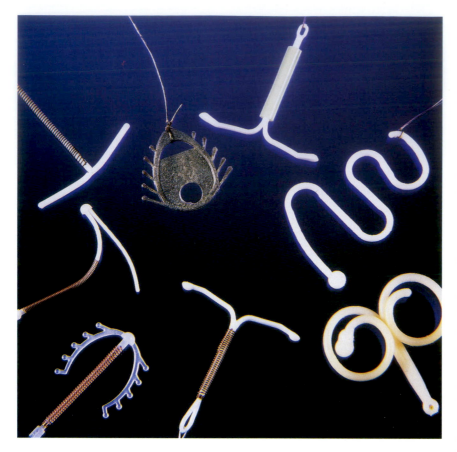

▲ The intrauterine device, or IUD, is a cheap and effective method of contraception. It works by preventing the implantation of a fertilized egg in the uterus. Providing women with the means to control their own fertility is seen as an essential part of meeting United Nations agreements on population control.

countries seek to improve their standard of living or have labor skills that are in short supply in more developed countries.

Controlling fertility

Without large-scale health epidemics or wars to reduce numbers, other means are necessary to contain the population at levels that can be supported. Modern methods of population control rely on the use of various forms of contraception. Some of these methods have a long history; for example Egyptian records exist of contraceptive pessaries made from dried crocodile dung and honey (modern analysis indicates that it was probably fairly effective).

Barrier methods rely on the use of a solid barrier—the condom for males and the diaphragm or cap for females—to prevent sperm from reaching the fertile ovum. The condom is a simple and inexpensive technique with high efficiency when properly used and for many years was the major method. It is still widespread and often strongly promoted by family planning organizations in developing countries, particularly because it can prevent the transmission of HIV and other diseases. The diaphragm has not achieved the same popularity, even though it too is a very effective technique. Barrier methods are often reinforced by the use of spermicidal (sperm killing) creams, foams, or jellies; these substances may also be used on their own, although with a lower efficiency.

Another mechanical means is the IUD (intrauterine device), which is inserted into the uterus and acts to prevent implantation of any fertilized ova. This is a low-cost method that requires only periodic checks once fitted and has been widely used in government family planning programs. However, pregnancy can still occur, and some adverse side effects have been reported.

Surgical sterilization—vasectomy for the male and tubal ligation (cutting the Fallopian tubes) for the female—is the most effective technique and widely practiced in some countries, such as India. It has the disadvantage of sometimes being nonreversible and so is often restricted to people who are confident they have completed their family.

In the developed nations, the most popular form of contraception is the pill, a hormone treatment that suppresses ovulation and thus makes conception impossible. It is a very efficient method but relies on the woman taking a regular course of pills. Some side effects have been reported, but the method is generally considered to be safe. A development of the technique uses an injection or implant of hormones, which are gradually released into the body, giving protection over a period of up to a year. This approach is finding increasing use in underdeveloped countries, since it needs a minimum of medical expertise and is very effective. However, it is thought to have dangerous side effects and is unpopular and rarely used in developed countries.

The aging society

Although the world population continues to rise, declining fertility rates and an increase in life expectancy are creating a new problem in developed countries—an aging of the population. In most of Europe, North America, and Japan, fertility levels have been declining since the post–World War II baby boom and are now below the replacement level of 2.1 children per woman.

Overall, the proportion of children in the global population dropped from 34 percent in 1950 to 30 percent in 2000 and is expected to be only 21 percent by 2050. In contrast, the number of older persons (60+ years) grew from 8 to 10 percent in the same time but is predicted to rise to 21 percent by 2050.

In the more developed countries, the ratio of children to the elderly was already 27 to 12 percent, respectively, in 1950 and was almost equal at 19 to 18 percent in 2000. However, by 2050 older people are expected to outnumber children at 33 percent to 16 percent.

On a global scale the effect of population aging will cause a rapid increase in the number of older people, from 606 million in 2000 to nearly 2 billion in 2050. Although the more developed countries already have a higher proportion of old people, this effect will be even more marked in less developed regions, where numbers will quadruple from 374 million to 1.6 billion.

Consider just a few implications of this population change. Already, in some Western countries, the health services are overburdened with the demands of the elderly—a situation that is likely to escalate dramatically as we move toward the next century. The ratio of dependents to producers in society will increase if the population declines—there will be fewer producers and fewer consumers, a recipe for economic stagnation. Increases in taxation may be needed to meet the extra burden of medical care and pensions, increases that will have to be met by the young producers, creating possible social tensions between the young and the old.

On the other hand, increasing life expectancy has been the result of improved health care and advances in medical technology. Elderly people in the more developed nations have a better chance today of living without disabling conditions. Good health will stand them in good stead if, as predicted, they have to stay in the workforce longer. Welfare considerations aside, one of the effects of below-replacement fertility levels will be to push up the proportion of the workforce over 50 years old. Economically, this would reduce a country's investment costs—young people are expensive to train, though cheap to hire—and maintain consumption levels. Delaying retirement would also reduce dependence on welfare benefits and enable workers to save longer to fund their old age.

Impact on families

One of the more unpredictable impacts of aging and a drop in fertility levels is the effect it will have on the traditional idea of the family. Not only is the proportion of children declining, the general aging of the population is also decreasing the number of women of child-bearing age. Italy currently has the lowest total fertility rate in the world at 1.2 percent and one of the highest median ages at 40 years. If this pattern of mainly single-child families were to continue for two generations, by 2050 almost three-fifths of the children born would have no siblings, cousins, aunts, or uncles. In many countries, extended families provide many of the ingredients that socialize a people—interdependence, support, obligations, and sharing of resources. In many developed countries, the extended family has already been replaced by the nuclear family with its weaker links between related members.

◀ Natural disasters, such as droughts, can have a drastic effect on regional and local populations. Crop failures and lack of water often drive the inhabitants of rural villages or towns to seek sustainance elsewhere. The sudden influx of large numbers of refugees places a strain on local food and water supplies and frequently leads to deaths from starvation or diseases that arise from overcrowding and insanitary conditions.

Carried further, the burden of caring for increasingly elderly parents and grandparents will fall onto the only child. The problem will also arise of who will care for people without any family.

Some of the implications of single-child families can already be seen. China is the world's most populous country with over 1 billion people. For many years, it has had a policy of restricting parents to a single child to prevent the population from expanding beyond the limits the state could reasonably support in terms of food and labor. Fertility controls have been rigorously enforced, but an unforeseen consequence has been the shift in the ratio of males to females. In many countries, particularly where agriculture is the main method of feeding and supporting the family, male children are seen as vital in providing for parents in their old age. The effect in China has been that, if the first child is a girl rather than a boy, the unwanted female babies have been left to die or abandoned to orphanages. However, with fewer females available of breeding age, many young men are having difficulties finding a wife. It may be that as China industrializes there will be a shift in cultural thinking that begins to value girls as well as boys. Until this happens, however, many young Chinese men face growing old without siblings or ever having a family of their own.

SEE ALSO: ENVIRONMENTAL SCIENCE • EPIDEMIOLOGY • GERONTOLOGY • REPRODUCTION

Potential Energy

 This rock has a certain potential energy. If the rock fell, the potential energy would be turned into kinetic energy.

Potential energy is a concept used in the discussion of any field of force in which energy is conserved. Potential theory can apply to a mass in a gravitational field, a charge in an electric field, a pole in a magnetic field, and a nuclear particle in a nuclear field. These concepts are treated identically as far as potential energy is concerned, so it is only necessary to consider one of them, for example, gravitational potential. In moving an object through a gravitational field, the only energy gained or lost is through the change in potential energy. Another way of defining a conserved field is to say that the energy required to move an object in the field is independent of the path taken by the object.

Examples of objects with potential energy are a compressed spring and the monkey of a pile driver raised to a high level. If the compressed spring is allowed to expand, its potential energy is released as kinetic energy and heat. In the case of the monkey of a pile driver, work is done to raise it higher in Earth's gravitational field. When the monkey is at its highest point, it has maximum potential energy, and when the monkey is released, it moves to a lower energy level. The stored potential energy is then converted into the energy of movement, or kinetic energy, before it hits the pile and dissipates the difference by doing work on the pile—applying a force and causing it to move. Much of the energy is converted to heat and sound.

To obtain more work from the monkey at a given site, the engineers could increase the height

▶ Victoria Falls in Zimbabwe. At the top of the falls, the water has maximum potential. Hydroelectric plants harness this potential energy by channeling the water through turbines that convert it into electricity.

from which it is released or increase its weight. The gravitational potential energy in such circumstances may be found by multiplying the weight of the object by its height. A weight of 25 pound-force (100 newtons) at a height above ground of 3 ft. (1 m) would have a potential of 75 foot-pound-force (100 newton meters). That much energy will be released and that much work done, when the object falls. Hydroelectric dams convert gravitational potential energy to power turbines and thus generate electricity.

Potential is a relative term, as in electricity, where the term potential difference is used. True, or absolute, potential must be referred to a zero level and this is generally at an infinite distance from the source of the field. In practice, physicists and engineers choose an arbitrary zero reference level to suit their particular purpose. For gravitational potential, the zero reference level is often Earth's surface. Similarly, electricians refer to ground as the zero potential.

The concept of the potential at a point in a field is also commonly encountered. In a gravitational field, it is the work required to bring unit mass—one pound or one kilogram—to that point from an infinite distance. In electricity, it is the work or energy required to bring unit charge—one coulomb—from infinity to the point; the unit in which electric potential is measured is the volt.

SEE ALSO: Dynamics • Energy, mass, and weight • Gravity • Hydroelectric power • Potentiometer • Power

Potentiometer

A potentiometer is primarily a highly accurate instrument for measuring voltage and current. However, the word is also used to describe a totally different device—the three-terminal potential (voltage) divider, which is a form of rheostat and usually abbreviated to "pot."

Electric measurements

Potentiometers, as precision electric-measuring instruments, work on the principle of balancing one voltage against another. If, for example, two batteries are connected—positive to positive and negative to negative—then the net driving force, or emf, in the circuit is the difference in the two battery voltages. If a galvanometer is connected in this circuit, a reading on it indicates current flow and an imbalance of the two voltages. When the galvanometer shows no deflection, there is no current flow and the batteries are perfectly balanced, that is, they have the same voltage.

The sliding-wire potentiometer

In the sliding-wire potentiometer, a length of uniform cross-section wire, say 3 ft. (1 m), is kept taut between two terminals. Connected to these terminals is a battery in series with a variable resistor—usually a rheostat. The taut wire has uniform resistance, thus the voltage at any point along the wire (measured from one of the terminals) is proportional to the distance of that point from the terminal. The voltage of the battery and the value of the rheostat are of secondary importance to the fact that they must remain constant for the period of measurement.

The voltage to be measured can be either a battery or the voltage across a current-carrying resistor. Whichever it is, two leads are taken from this source; one is connected to an end terminal of the wire, and the other is taken via a galvanometer to a handheld pointer. Touching the wire with the pointer will generally produce a reading on the galvanometer indicating that there is an imbalance between the unknown voltage and the voltage of the wire at that point. The pointer position is then moved until a zero reading is obtained on the galvanometer, and the distance of this point from the terminal is accurately measured.

This method is repeated using a standard cell to replace the unknown voltage. A new balancing point is found and the new distance measured. Knowing the voltage of the standard cell and the two distance measurements enables the unknown voltage to be accurately determined, the ratio between the two distances being the ratio between the unknown voltage and the standard cell voltage.

Measuring large voltages

The sliding-wire potentiometer is limited to voltages roughly of the same order as the standard, or reference, cell. Some adjustment is possible, however, using the rheostat. Reducing its resistance increases the current flowing through the wire and consequently increases the voltage per unit length of the wire, enabling larger voltages to be balanced. Even so, inaccuracies creep in when the unknown voltage differs widely from the standard cell voltage.

To measure large voltages, a voltage divider is used. For example, if a voltage source in the region of 1,500 volts is to be measured, then a reduction of 1,000:1 is required, giving a measurable voltage in the region of 1.5 volts. A voltage divider consists of a series of resistances tapped at

▼ Left: A carbon-track potentiometer has a rotating shaft and a metal ring contact, which engages with the inner ring (connected to B) and the track (connected to A and C). Right: A rheostat works on the same principle but with slider B replacing the rotating shaft.

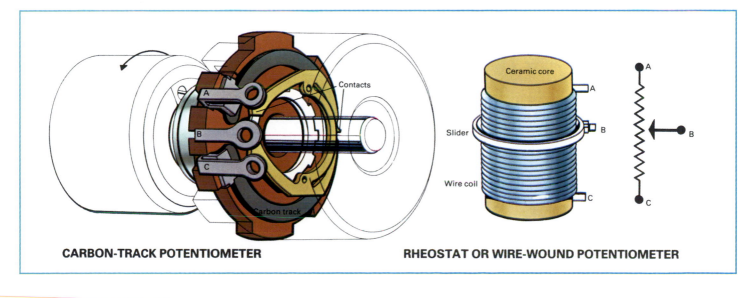

CARBON-TRACK POTENTIOMETER

RHEOSTAT OR WIRE-WOUND POTENTIOMETER

some point along its length. A 1,000:1 reduction could be achieved by applying the full voltage across, say, 100,000 ohms with a tapping point 100 ohms from one end—the voltage across this 100 ohms is then one-thousandth of the full voltage. This voltage can be measured using the potentiometer, and if the result is calculated to be 1.519 volts, then the full voltage is 1,519 volts.

The standard cell

In potentiometer measurements, the one important absolute standard is that of the standard cell. From this standard cell, all currents and voltages can be accurately determined.

Standard cells must be stable; that is, their voltage must remain unchanged for many years, they must be insensitive to temperature changes, and they must be commercially reproducible within close tolerances. This specification is provided by the standard Weston cell, which has a positive electrode of mercury and a negative electrode of cadmium amalgam. At room temperature (68°F, 20°C), its voltage is 1.01858 volts, and its temperature coefficient is less than 28 microvolts per °F change in temperature. With the purest materials, any two standard cells will have voltages within a few microvolts of each other and a lifetime of up to 20 years.

The rheostat

A rheostat is a device commonly found in laboratories and is used to provide variable resistance, current, and voltage for measurement and control purposes. It consists of a coil of finely spaced wire wrapped around a tube of insulating material. This device is mounted horizontally on a wooden base, and the ends of the coil are taken to two terminals. Above it is positioned a slide arrangement with metal brushes that make contact with the coil surface. The slide arrangement is made from a good conducting metal, and a third terminal is fitted to it. By moving the slider, the resistance between the third terminal and either of the coil terminals can be altered.

The pot

A pot is basically a small rheostat used in instrument panels and with electronic equipment in general—in fact, in all low-power applications where variable currents and voltages are required, such as for the volume, tone, and balance controls of an amplifier.

In a pot, a shaft is rotated that sweeps a contact (called the tap or wiper) in a circular path over a resistive material (called the track). Typically, the shaft can be rotated between 270 and 300 degrees between end stops. The end stops have three ter-

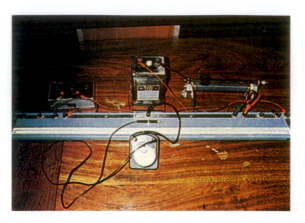

◀ A Wheatstone bridge— a precision instrument for measuring resistance— has a slide wire mounted on a graduated scale and a resistance box (on the left) of standard resistances.

minals, two connected to the ends of the track and the third connected to the wiper. The track can either be a toroidal-shaped coil of wire (wire-wound pot) or a surface deposit of carbon on an insulator (carbon pot). Another type of pot, the panoramic potentiometer, or pan pot, is used in audio mixing desks to control the position of a sound between a pair of stereo speakers.

Pots are described by the end-to-end resistance of the track and are manufactured in preferred values, such as 10 ohms (10 Ω), 1 kΩ, 5 kΩ, 10 kΩ, and so on. A second classification is by their response, which can be linear, logarithmic, or sine–cosine functions.

The rapid expansion of transistors and microelectronics in all sections of industry has brought a need for miniature potentiometers with highly accurate low-power applications. For use with printed circuit boards, a device used mainly as a variable voltage divider has been developed, made with a ceramic-metal resistive material called cermet. The miniature trimming potentiometer can set and/or control component applications in both analog and digital circuitry.

PRINCIPLE OF A WHEATSTONE BRIDGE

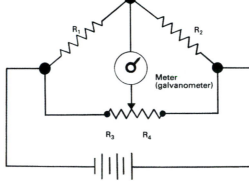

R_1

R_2

Meter (galvanometer)

R_3 R_4

The unknown resistance, R1, can be determined because the standard resistances, R2, R3, and R4, are known. A DC voltage is passed through the circuit, and the voltage is balanced by adjusting the value of one of the known resistors.

SEE ALSO: ELECTRICITY • METER, ELECTRICAL • RESISTOR

Powder Coating

Polymeric coatings have two principal functions: decoration and protection. As decoration, coatings add color and gloss, or other surface effects, to objects of value; for protection, they shield those objects from the rigors of their environments, such as humidity, pollution, chemical vapors, and the ultraviolet content of sunlight. Powder coatings are polymeric coatings that are applied in powder form and subsequently melted and formed into a film by oven curing.

Environmental benefits

Traditionally, polymeric coatings have been applied in the form of paints and varnishes. In such coatings, the materials that form the final coated film often account for less than half the weight of the paint or varnish: the rest is solvent that evaporates as the coating dries and hardens.

Many of the solvents in paints and varnishes are classified as VOCs (volatile organic compounds, or components). They include benzene and other aromatic compounds, nonaromatic hydrocarbons, and oxygenated organic solvents, such as alcohols, ethers, hydroxy ethers (glycol ethers), and ketones. Many VOCs are known to cause acute and long-term health damage.

While a typical person uses paints and varnishes only rarely and is therefore unlikely to come to harm from their solvents, the operators of industrial liquid-coating lines must be protected from solvent vapors. Furthermore, the paint-curing ovens associated with such lines vaporize considerable quantities of VOCs that must be incinerated or destroyed in some other way to prevent them from contaminating the environment. These measures add considerably to the cost of coating, and they generate carbon dioxide (CO_2), a gas thought by some experts to be responsible for global warming.

The advantages of powder coatings stem from their lack of solvent. Powder-coating lines are free of the pungent and harmful solvent vapors that can surround traditional paint lines, although operators must wear dust masks to prevent inhalation of finely powdered coating. Powders typically release less than 1 percent of their weight as VOCs, and such quantities can be dispersed directly through tall exhaust flues without causing significant environmental damage.

Powder coatings are more economical and convenient in use than are their liquid counterparts. Spray booths that operate continuously with one type (and one shade) of powder coating can be set up to reuse oversprayed powder so that

▲ Multiple spray heads apply powder coating to an automobile body on a production line. Afterwards, the body will pass through an oven, where heat will melt and cure the coating.

more than 95 percent of the powder ends up being applied. When changing from one type of powder to another, overspray is easily removed from the booth and overspray recovery system by use of a vacuum cleaner. Also, components that have received too much coating or the wrong type of coating can be cleaned in the same way.

Powder manufacture

A typical powder coating consists of one or more solid resins, pigments, and small quantities of additives, such as lubricants or flow modifiers. These solids are mixed in the required proportions and fed into a melt extruder—a heated horizontal cylinder in which an Archimedes' screw turns. The solids blend melts as the screw drives it through the heated cylinder, and its components become well dispersed. At the outlet of the melt extruder, a perforated disk and cutter turn the solidifying blend into a mass of granular chips whose composition is uniform.

Those chips are then reduced to powder in a jet-mill micronizer: air jets whirl the granules around a disk-shaped chamber, causing them to collide with themselves and with the chamber walls. The collisions gradually chip away at the granules, which progress toward the center of the disk as their dimensions shrink. When the particle size reaches around 0.002 in. (50 µm), the powdered coating is carried out from the center of the disk on a current of air. After quality-control checks, approved powder is bagged for sale.

Formulations

One major class of powder coatings is based on polyester resins. They can produce thermoplastic coatings, which soften on heating, or they can be thermosetting. In thermoplastic powder coatings, the molecules of a high-molecular-weight polyester diffuse into one another when the sprayed object is heated and the coating melts. The chain length of the polyester is so great that the entanglement of those chains produces a sufficiently tough and cohesive coating.

In a thermosetting polyester powder coating, cross-linkers, such as isophorone diisocyanate or melamine, react with functional groups on the polyester molecules to form cross-links (chemical bridges) between them. Cross-links increase the hardness and chemical resistance of the film.

Other powder coatings are based on epoxy resins, which form thermoset coatings by reacting with cross-linkers such as melamine and urea. They are more durable than polyester-based coatings but are prone to degradation by ultraviolet radiation on prolonged exposure to daylight, making them less suitable for outdoor use.

Applying powder coatings

The first step in applying a powder coating is surface preparation. Metal surfaces are prepared in a variety of ways, depending on the metal, but many steps are common to all preparation sequences. First, the metal is washed using alkaline or neutral detergents to remove all traces of oils and greases that would otherwise make the coating prone to detachment. An acid wash then removes corrosion, and a subsequent chromate or phosphate wash chemically modifies the surface of the metal to make it bond well with the applied coating. The metal is then rinsed and dried.

Most powder coating lines use spray guns to apply electrostatically charged paint particles. The charges draw opposing charges in the surface that is being coated, and the attraction between opposite charges draws the powder particles to the surface of workpieces and then holds them in place. The workpiece must be grounded, otherwise it could discharge to the walls of the spray booth, possibly triggering a powder explosion.

Polyester coatings tend to be negatively charged by using compressed air to blow them past an electrode at 80 kV within the spray gun. Epoxies can be charged tribostatically by blowing them through a Teflon barrel within the gun: friction between the paint particles and the Teflon generates the charge. Some components are coated by dipping them into a bed of fluidized powder through which ionized air passes to charge the particles and keep them "boiling."

Curing

The formation of a film from a powder coating occurs in stages when exposed to heat. First, the powder melts and its particles start to coalesce. The liquid then "flows" across the surface, that is,

it forms an even layer. Thermosetting coatings then start to cure as their cross-linking reactions proceed. Finally, the coating hardens as its temperature starts to fall.

The exact curing method depends on the articles being sprayed. Objects that have low heat capacities tend to be coated and then cured for 10 minutes at around 400°F (around 200°C). Heavier objects, including cast-metal valves and pipes, can be cured by heating before spraying. The heat content of such objects is sufficient to melt and cure the coating before the workpiece cools below the curing temperature.

Applications

The acceptance of powder coatings has increased greatly since the start of their use in the 1960s and has been boosted by increasingly rigorous emissions controls. Powder coatings are now used for electrical components, domestic appliances, car bodies, and concrete reinforcement bars (rebars); they are also used for wires, metal furniture, and metal cladding for buildings.

ELECTROSTATIC SPRAYING

In electrostatic spraying, compressed air blows charged powder particles toward the grounded conducting object to be sprayed. The charges of the particles induce opposing charges in the workpiece, and mutual attraction between opposite charges holds the coating in place until it is stoved in a tunnel oven. The coating particles acquire their charges in the spray gun either by rubbing along a barrel that charges by friction (tribostatically) or by the action of a high-voltage electrode (corona discharge).

The electrostatic attraction to the workpiece minimizes overspray—the proportion of coating that misses the target—and ensures the coating reaches even those parts of the surface that are obscured from the direct line of fire of the gun. Almost all overspray is collected in a cyclonic separator and returned to the feed hopper, so there is practically no waste of coating. Extracted air is purified by filters before discharge.

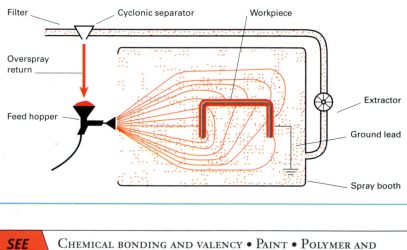

SEE ALSO: Chemical bonding and valency • Paint • Polymer and polymerization • Spray gun

Power

Power is the rate at which work is done. This concept is important in assessing the value of a machine or device. This rate, which is the same as rate of conversion of energy (such as from electricity to mechanical power in an electric motor), is frequently measured with a dynamometer, which measures the torque of a rotating shaft.

When used in a scientific context, the concept of power does not differ much from that met in everyday language. A powerful person can be expected to labor faster than a less well built one; a powerful computer can compute more steps in a second than a less powerful model.

Force, work, and power

Consider the example of a battery-driven motor used for raising loads up a cliff. The first consideration is the maximum load that the motor can lift. Load is force and is measured in such units as newtons (N) or pound-force (lbf.). Second, it is important to know how much work the motor can do before the battery is discharged. The work done is equal to the lifting force multiplied by the distance moved. Work is the same as energy and is measured in such units as newton meters (Nm) or foot-pound-force (ft. lbf.). The standard international unit of energy is the joule (J), defined as one newton meter.

For example, if the load to be raised is about 25 lbf. (about 100 N) in weight and the battery is exhausted after the load has been lifted 300 ft. (100 m), then the work done is 7,500 ft. lbf. (10,000 Nm), which is 10,000 J. This work done by the motor is the same as the energy gained by the load—in this case, potential energy. If the motor is 100 percent efficient in its conversions of

◀ A waterwheel derives power from the kinetic energy of the moving stream; power in this instance is the rate of flow of energy from the stream to the wheel. The stream has less energy after it has passed through the wheel.

electric energy to mechanical energy, then the total stored energy of the battery before lifting the load is 10,000 J.

In this example, no consideration has been given to the speed at which the load was lifted. The third important factor of a machine is how fast the machine can work—this factor is the power of the machine.

▼ Measuring horsepower using Regnier's dynamometer, which is a tension-measuring device.

The basic definition of power is

power = work done ÷ time taken

but work is equal to force exerted x distance moved so

power = force exerted x speed of movement.

Any of these formulas can be used for calculating power. If the load in the above example is raised in 5 minutes (300 seconds), then the power developed by the motor is about 33 joules per second (33 J/s).

FACT FILE

- *New cylinders for the Scottish engineer James Watt's experimental steam engines were bored by a cannon-boring machine powered by a waterwheel, invented by British industrialist John Wilkinson. Wilkinson went on to become the first user of a commercial Watt engine.*

- *Modern high-tech power-generating windmills have winglike vanes attached to the ends of the blades. The airfoil section of the vanes creates an airflow pattern that virtually doubles output efficiency in the same way that ducks flying in close formation fly faster with less effort, because of the effect of their wingtip airflow vortices.*

Electric power

Electric power is generally expressed in watts (W), and one watt equals one joule per second. In an electric component, such as a resistor, the power consumed, measured in watts, is the product of the voltage across the component and the current (I) flowing through it. The voltage (V) across a resistor is equal to the current multiplied by the resistance (R)—Ohm's law. So the power consumed by a resistor (this power is dissipated in the form of heat) is I^2R or V^2/R. A 12-ohm resistor will dissipate heat at a rate of about 1,000 watts (1 kW) when operating at 110 volts and consume a current of 9.2 amps.

A 1,000-megawatt (1,000 MW) power plant will ideally be able to supply enough electricity to power a million single-bar (1 kW) electric heaters while using enough fuel to give it energy at a rate of one billion joules per second. The total current supplied at supply voltage (110 volts) will be 9 million amps.

Horsepower

Horsepower (hp) is another frequently used unit of power and is equivalent to 550 ft. lbf. per sec. or 750 W (approximately). This unit of power was developed by the Scottish engineer James Watt, who used strong dray horses for short periods in his research a century ago. A 100-horsepower electric winding engine operating at 1 kV will require 75 amps when pulling 7.5 tons (6.8 tonnes) up a shaft at a speed of 3.3 ft. per sec. (1 m/s).

SEE ALSO: ELECTRICITY • ENERGY, MASS, AND WEIGHT • INTERNAL COMBUSTION ENGINE • PHYSICS • POTENTIAL ENERGY

▲ A Harrier aircraft, which is capable of taking off and landing vertically. The power in an engine is provided by the rapid burning of hot gases, which turn the turbine and compressor.

Power Plant

The first public electricity-generating plants in Europe and the United States started operating in 1882, in London and New York City, although smaller private generators had been built for many decades before. The electricity they produced was first used to power arc lamps for street lighting and lighthouses. Then, after the U.S. inventor Thomas Edison's introduction of the low-power incandescent lamp in 1879, electricity was also used for household lighting.

Early systems used reciprocating steam or gas engines to drive direct-current (DC) generators, called dynamos. The supply voltage varied from installation to installation, and each station supplied a small geographical area. In 1891, the first alternating-current (AC) generator, or alternator, started producing electricity at a power station in Frankfurt am Main, Germany. The voltage of AC electricity can be changed using transformers, which do not function on DC electricity. This possibility makes AC electricity more suitable for distribution over large networks, since its voltage can be increased for long-distance transmission, then reduced near the point of use. This property is desirable because high voltages reduce power loss, but low voltages require less insulation.

In 1884, the invention of the high-speed steam turbine by the British engineer Charles Parsons provided the generating industry with a new source of mechanical power. Whereas the back-and-forth piston movements of reciprocal engines are converted into rotary motion by cranks, turbines convert the kinetic energy of moving steam directly into rotational motion. Also, turbines produce power continuously, whereas reciprocal engines produce bursts of power that coincide with their piston strokes. These two differences make turbines better suited than reciprocating engines for driving generators. Consequently, turbines rapidly overtook reciprocating engines in power generation.

Other advances have occurred in the way that fuel is burned to provide energy for generating electricity. Early coal-fired power stations had hand-stoked furnaces that burned lump coal to boil water; modern coal-fired stations burn pulverized coal entrained in a stream of air—a combination that burns like a gas and is well suited to automated furnaces. Oil-fired power stations burn fine sprays of heavy heating oils in the same way, and in a nuclear power station, heat for boiling water is provided by a controlled chain fission

▼ The control room of the Dinorwic pumped-storage hydroelectric plant in the Snowdonia region of Wales. The upper and lower reservoirs are visible on the wall-mounted display panel at right. Dinorwic's turbine hall and water culverts were carved into a mountain, so the plant has little impact on the natural beauty of its surroundings.

▲ The Castle Peak Power Station (CPPS) in Hong Kong is one of the world's largest generating plants. CPPS "A" plant, built between 1982 and 1985, has four generating units rated at 350 MW each; CPPS "B" plant, completed in 1993, has four 677.5 MW units. Both plants can burn either pulverized coal or oil. In 1996, two of the "B" units were adapted so they can also burn gas.

reaction. Gas-fired power stations burn fuel gas—usually natural gas, which is mainly methane—and the expanding combustion gases drive a gas turbine directly, rather than giving up their heat to boil water for a steam turbine.

Meeting demand

Electricity suppliers are required, often by law, to provide customers with electricity whose voltage and frequency at the point of supply is within a narrow tolerance of the nominal values. Typical supply voltages are 110 V, 220 V, and 240 V; typical alternation frequencies are 50 Hz and 60 Hz. To meet these criteria, the generator output must match the demand for power at any time.

Demand varies considerably with the time of day, the day of the week, and the season. Peaks in demand occur at times of the day when many people are cooking; cold snaps can increase consumption in electrical heaters, and hot weather can increase demand where a large proportion of buildings have air conditioners.

Some electricity suppliers use pump-storage hydroelectric plants to cater for fluctuations in demand. They have an upper reservoir and a lower reservoir. At times of high demand, water runs from the upper reservoir, through turbines that drive generators, to the lower reservoir; when demand falls, powerful electric pumps return water from the lower reservoir to the

Base-load units provide the cheapest electricity in large, highly efficient thermal plants that use low-cost fuel, such as coal, oil, or nuclear fuel, to produce electrical power outputs of 1,300 MW or more. The high efficiency of such plants depends in part on fine running clearances between the turbine rotors and casings. Fine clearance means that load (output) changes must be undertaken very slowly, since variations in steam flow cause temperature changes and differential thermal expansion (and contraction). An attempt to increase load rapidly might cause the turbine rotor to expand at a greater rate than its casing, for example, forcing the rotor tips to gouge into the casing and causing permanent damage. For this reason, base-load generating units are designed to run at constant full capacity between infrequent closures for routine maintenance.

Intermediate-load plants are used to cater for predictable and slow load variations, such as the morning and evening peaks. They are generally older steam-powered plants with outputs of a few hundred megawatts, although some new plants are built to the same specifications. In either case, looser clearances make for more rapid load changes at some cost to efficiency.

Peak-load power plants are cheap to build and flexible to operate, but they are expensive to run. Gas turbines are good peak-load equipment, since their lightweight alloy casings can reach full operating temperature within three minutes of starting. Hydroelectric plants are used for base or peak load; they are expensive to build but have extremely low operating costs.

Alternators

Alternators are the common feature of all power plants. They developed from 60 MW after World War II to 660 MW and 1,300 MW. Alternating current at 60 Hz is standard in North America; some other countries use 50 Hz. These frequencies require respective rotational speeds of 3,600 rpm and 3,000 rpm for alternators whose rotors have two magnetic poles and half those rates for four-pole alternator units.

The power outputs of alternators are limited by the rate at which heat can be dissipated as it is produced by heavy currents flowing in their coils. In the case of an alternator with an output of 660 MW at 22 kV, for example, the stator current is 30,000 amps. Since overheating could damage the insulation and cause short circuits, developments in alternator output have occurred through improvements in cooling. In future, it might be possible to increase output considerably by using high-temperature superconducting coils, whose lack of resistance would remove the mechanism

upper reservoir. Another approach to meeting fluctuations in demand is to trade power with suppliers in neighboring states or countries. This approach is helpful if one supplier has an excess of generating capacity or if the neighboring generators have different demand patterns owing to cultural or climatic differences, for example.

In general, however, electricity suppliers strive to meet demand using their own primary generating capacity rather than by using pumped-storage or bought-in power. To be flexible yet economical, suppliers must have a range of different types of generating units in their networks. These units are classified as base-load, intermediate-load, and peak-load units.

by which heat is generated in the alternator. This improvement would allow the construction of more compact generators of high efficiency.

Most alternators have three sets of generating coils, each displaced by 120 degrees around the turbine shaft relative to the others. The outputs of the three coil circuits have equal maximum voltages, but they are 120 degrees out of phase with one another so that a given output reaches its peak one-third of a cycle after another output, and two-thirds of a cycle after the third. The three phases are distributed separately; they are sometimes united to drive heavy-duty three-phase motors with separate inputs for the three phases but are mostly used individually as single-phase commercial and residential supplies.

The output from the alternator is connected to two transformers. One, the unit transformer, provides a low-voltage supply for auxiliary equipment, such as pumps, associated with the turbine and boiler. The other, the generator transformer, steps up the voltage for the supply grid. For a typical 660 MW generator operating at 22 kV, the unit and generating transformers have outputs at 11 kV and 400 kV, respectively. A typical 60 MW set operating at 11 kV has unit and generator transformer outputs at 6.6 kV and 132 kV.

Conventional power plants

Conventional plants are thermal plants that use carbon-based fuels to heat water for steam turbines, as opposed to nuclear or gas-turbine plants. The technical details of all conventional plants are similar, the only significant difference being in the handling facilities for the particular fuel. Around 75 percent of U.S. electricity supply is produced by this type of plant.

Fuel releases heat as it burns in a furnace, and much of this heat passes to water contained in tubes around the boiler; the rest escapes in hot flue gases. Around 35 to 40 percent of the heat is absorbed in converting liquid water at its boiling point into steam. This energy—the latent heat of vaporization—is absorbed by cooling water in the condenser after the steam has passed through turbines. It does no useful work, so it represents a major loss of energy from the cycle.

The water first enters the economizer section, where it almost reaches its boiling point. It then passes into a steam drum at the top of the boiler. From there, the water circulates through evaporator tubes that line the furnace, it then returns to the drum. At this point, around 20 percent boils off as steam and leaves through pipes in the top of the drum, and the rest passes back through the evaporator. The steam then passes through superheater tubes in the hottest part of the boiler.

Superheated steam under pressure enters the turbine of a turbogenerator. It delivers energy to the turbine blades as it passes through them on the way to a condenser. In the condenser, the pressure drops rapidly as the steam turns to water, and this drop in pressure draws more steam through the turbine. The water that collects in the condenser passes to a pump that returns it to the boiler under pressure for another cycle.

To achieve the maximum rate of conversion of heat into electrical energy, the temperature and pressure of the superheated steam are made as high as possible within the safety limits of the boiler materials. With austenitic steel (iron with 18 percent manganese, 3 percent chromium, and 0.5 percent carbon), superheaters on 660 MW boilers generate steam at approximately 2,400 psi (165 bar) and 1051°F (566°C). Power plant boiler units are of massive construction—typically 60 ft. (18.3 m) wide, 130 ft. (40 m) deep and 200 ft. (61 m) high—and water circulates through tubes that completely line the sides of the boiler.

◄ Construction of the alternators of the Dinorwic hydroelectric power plant in Wales. The team in the foreground is preparing the stator—the stationary part of the alternator. The rotor—the gray cylindrical assembly visible in the background—will turn inside the stator under torque from the water turbines. Each side panel of the rotor is a magnetic pole, so this 12-pole rotor provides 50 Hz electricity when it turns at 500 rpm.

The turbine has at least three sections on a common shaft: the high-pressure turbine, the intermediate-pressure turbine, and one or more low-pressure turbines. Each turbine is designed to extract the optimum power from steam at the pressure prevailing in its section. Steam from the high-pressure section passes back to the boiler, where it is reheated to its original temperature. In this way, more energy is put into the cycle without requiring further latent heat, thus improving overall efficiency. From the reheater, the steam goes to the intermediate section, exhausts directly to the low-pressure section, and then passes to the condenser, which operates under a partial vacuum; this low pressure gives high efficiency.

The water in the circuit that passes from the boiler to the turbine and condenser is kept free of air and salts that could cause boiler corrosion and furring. It never comes into direct contact with the cooling water in the condenser. Any top-up water is passed through an ion-exchange resin that removes salts and then through a deaerator. Small amounts of corrosion-inhibiting chemicals are added, and regular samples of the condensate are analyzed for chemical composition.

The efficiency of the cycle is improved by the use of the feed heaters and air heaters. Feed heaters are fed with surplus steam from tapping points on the turbine and preheat the condensate before it enters the boiler. The latent heat in this steam is thus not lost from this cycle. Similarly, air heaters near the exhaust of the boiler use hot flue gases to warm the incoming air.

The fuel is burned with a controlled amount of air to ensure complete combustion and minimum pollution. Oil and natural gas burn readily in furnaces; coal must be ground to a fine powder, known as pulverized fuel, before it is burned. The burned coal forms a fine ash that is collected by electrostatic precipitators to prevent it from being deposited on land around the power plant. Pulverized fuel ash, or PFA, is a useful by-product whose applications range from use in land reclamation to making lightweight building blocks.

In recent years, environmental regulations in many countries have made it necessary to fit desulfurization units to remove sulfur dioxide—an acid-rain-forming gas—from the flue gases of power stations that burn high-sulfur fuels, such as coal. These units use water-based slurries of limestone to convert sulfur dioxide into solid calcium sulfate (gypsum), which is used in landfill.

A 2,000 MW coal-fired plant burns around 4 million tons (3.6 million tonnes) of coal each year. This coal comes from mines in trucks or in trains that can load and offload automatically while on the move. An equivalent oil plant burns

▲ The turbine hall of a 2,000 MW coal-fired power station, where four units produce up to 500 MW of electrical power each. The gray pipes carry steam, and the blue housing provides thermal insulation for the steam turbine. One end of the alternator of this unit is visible at left of the steam turbine.

around 2.5 million tons (2.3 million tonnes) of oil; these plants are usually situated near oil refineries or docks that handle petroleum products, and they are supplied by pipeline.

The cooling water in the condenser is contained within thousands of tubes and never comes in contact with water in the steam circuit. The cooling water temperature warms up by 14 to 18°F (8–10°C) while passing through the condenser. Where the cooling water is drawn from a large body of water such as a sea, estuary, or large river, it may be returned directly to the source, where its excess heat is dispersed by mixing and natural cooling. If the water resource is less abundant, as is the case for a small river, evaporative cooling towers remove some of the excess heat before the water is recirculated or returned to its source.

Nuclear power plants

Nuclear power plants use heat from nuclear fission reactions to generate steam for turbines. The steam passes through the boiler–turbine–condenser circuit as it does in a conventional plant.

Various types of nuclear fuels are in use, and all are based around uranium-235 and plutonium-239, which are fissile isotopes. These fuels are used as sintered pellets of their oxides or as rod-shaped "pins" of their alloys with zirconium. In either case, the fissile isotopes are accompanied by nonfissile nuclei, such as uranium-238, and the fuel is contained in alloy tubes that prevent it from having direct contact with coolant.

Control rods that contain neutron-absorbing elements, such as boron, can be lowered into the core to halt the chain reaction if necessary or simply slow the reaction in response to a decreasing load. The core must also contain a moderator, whose function is to slow neutrons to make them more efficient in causing fission reactions. In some reactors, the coolant is also the moderator. This is the case for AGRs (advanced gas-cooled reactors), where carbon dioxide cools and moderates, and for all reactors whose cores are cooled and moderated by normal (light) water.

In boiling-water reactors, or BWRs, cooling water that circulates around the fuel rods forms steam in the space above the reactor. This steam is used directly to drive turbines.

In other types of reactors, coolants circulate between the core and a boiler that produces high-pressure steam for the turbines. Such coolants include carbon dioxide (in AGRs) and liquid sodium metal or sodium–potassium alloy (in LMRs—liquid-metal reactors).

In pressurized-water reactors, or PWRs, high pressure prevents cooling water from boiling within the core, even though it exceeds its normal boiling temperature. This pressure is needed to maintain power output, since a safety feature of most reactor designs is that pockets of steam (voids) in the core tend to stop the reaction.

The reactors and boilers of PWRs are held in steel pressure vessels whose walls are around 12 in. (0.3 m) thick. Nevertheless, coolant temperature cannot reach that of the superheated steam used in conventional stations—if it did, the core pressure would have to be enormous to prevent boiling. A PWR therefore uses larger quantities of lower-grade steam than an equivalent conventional reactor. Its turbines are correspondingly larger and, in some cases, run at half the speed of a normal turbogenerator but with twice the number of poles in the alternator so as to maintain the required alternating frequency of the output.

Hydroelectric power

Hydroelectric power (HEP) systems supply around 10 percent of the U.S. electricity demand. In other countries, such as Brazil, they produce almost all the electricity supplied.

HEP plants generate power from the gravitational potential energy of water trapped behind a dam or barrage. Such water flows through turbines to generate electricity, and the head of water—the vertical distance between the surface of the trapped water and the point at which it leaves the turbine—determines the rate at which power can be extracted. For this reason, a high-head reservoir dammed into a mountain gorge uses much less water than a low-head river barrage in producing the same amount of energy.

Compared with steam turbines, water turbines rotate slowly—at 100 to 300 rpm—so their associated alternators have a large number of poles to generate at system frequency. HEP generation may be base load, peak load, or on a sea-

▼ Tarraleah hydroelectric power station in Tasmania, Australia. The pipes on the hillside carry water to the turbine hall below.

sonal basis, depending on water supply. Some HEP plants also have electrical pumping stations as part of a pumped-storage scheme for electricity supply management or for replenishing elevated water reservoirs for irrigation systems.

Gas turbines

A gas turbine is a combustion chamber that is fed on one side by fuel and air from a fan and that exhausts combustion gases through a turbine on the other side. The fan and turbine are mounted on a single shaft, and part of the energy of the expanding combustion gases is used to compress the intake gases. Some of the remaining energy can be harnessed to generate electricity, but most is lost in hot, fast-moving gases. Some gas turbines are custom designed for power generation; others are based on aviation jet engines but modified for function at sea level, internal temperatures—1100 to 1500°F (600–800°C) rather than 1600 to 2000°F (900–1100°C). Such turbines burn natural gas or refinery naphtha rather than high-grade aviation kerosene.

In simple gas turbine designs, the shaft that carries the compressor fan and the high-pressure power turbine also carries several turbine stages designed to extract energy from gases at intermediate and low pressures; the whole assembly rotates at around 10,000 rpm and drives a lower-speed alternator through a transmission. In more complex designs, a high-speed shaft carries the fan and first power turbine, and a lower-speed shaft carries the other power turbines and drives the alternator. In either case, the alternator drive turns at a constant speed, and load changes are catered for by modifying the fuel feed rate.

The maximum electrical power output of most gas-turbine generators is between 2 MW and 80 MW; some produce up to 200 MW. In some cases, multiple gas turbines drive a single alternator unit. These power outputs are obtained at less than 26 percent efficiency—around half the efficiency of a modern coal-fired power station—and at higher fuel costs.

However, gas-turbine generators are cheaper to build and occupy less space than equivalent coal-fired units. They can also reach full load in a few minutes rather than over several hours, making them particularly useful for peak-load use. Furthermore, the overall efficiency of a gas-turbine unit can be improved beyond 40 percent by using its exhaust heat to produce steam for heating buildings or for a steam turbogenerator.

SEE ALSO: Energy resources • Generator • Hydroelectric power • Nuclear reactor • Power supply • Turbine

Power Supply

The invention of the incandescent electric light-bulb in about 1879 initiated public demand for electric energy, and the new form of energy was soon being used to provide motive power and heat. Its cleanliness and flexibility of use, coupled with the simplicity of installations, rendered it popular with residential, commercial, and industrial users. In 1882, the first public power station in the world began operation in London, followed later the same year by a power station in New York. These systems both produced DC electricity, and it wasn't until the 1890s that the world's first AC power station opened near Frankfurt am Main in Germany.

The generation of electricity is essentially an energy-exchange process, requiring the release of energy stored as latent heat in fossil fuels such as coal or oil, the extraction of heat from nuclear reactions, or the conversion of potential energy in a head of water into hydropower. Today most electricity is produced by the burning of fossil fuels, but prior to the 1930s, most electricity was produced using hydropower. Increased efficiency in the production of electricity from heat, how-

ever, has resulted in hydroelectricity accounting for only 19 percent of today's world electricity output. Other methods of producing electricity include solar cells, magnetohydrodynamic generators, and wind turbines. Electricity is not a primary source of energy, neither is it directly usable, as it requires the consumers' apparatus to convert it to light, heat, or motive power. Its usefulness lies in the relative ease with which it can be manipulated and conveyed over long distances compared with other forms of energy.

To transfer energy from power plant to consumer, the electric transmission system has been developed from the earliest local distribution systems, working at about 200 V (volts), to the modern national networks, which generally operate at levels of up to 765 kV. These transmission systems also allow the interconnection of the power systems operated by different companies, or even by different countries. Such interconnections enable supplies to be maintained in emergencies—such as the breakdown of a generating plant—and also allow the sharing of capacity to give more even load requirements on the generating plants.

▲ Outside urban areas overhead cables connected by tall transmission towers are the cheapest means of distributing electricity to consumers.

◀ This model of an electric power plant designed by Nikola Tesla for installation in New York was never used. Tesla, the Croatian-born scientist and electrical engineer, was a champion of AC current, as opposed to DC current, for electric power systems. Westinghouse Electric supported Tesla's view and, in 1893, installed all AC power and lighting equipment at the Chicago World's Fair. The General Electric Company, headed by Thomas Edison, preferred and installed DC current systems. In later years, it was the AC proponents who won out in the United States.

Power losses

The basic circuit for transferring electric power from source to load comprises two conductors, one providing the forward path and the other the return path, enabling the current to pass through the load and thus do work. The function of the source is to provide a voltage or electric pressure to establish and sustain the current in the circuit.

If the source provides a steady DC voltage, the magnitude of the current will be determined not only by the resistance of the load but also marginally by the resistance of the conductors and the source, in accordance with Ohm's law. The total power in the circuit will be the product of the voltage and the current or the sum of the power delivered to the load and the circuit power losses.

The power losses in the conductors are proportional both to their resistance and to the square of the current. That is, if the conductor cross-sectional area is halved (doubling the resistance), the losses are doubled, and if the current is doubled, the losses are increased fourfold. As power is equal to current times voltage, for the same power, doubling the voltage enables the current to be halved, thus quartering the losses and improving transmission efficiency fourfold.

In an AC circuit, the current and voltage waveforms are sinusoidal, and their effective values are 0.707 times their peak values. Theoretically an AC two-wire system requires twice the conductor material of an equivalent DC circuit to transmit the same power to a resistive load at the same efficiency.

A further phenomenon associated with AC circuits is that the circuit components, particularly reactive (capacitive or reductive) loads, such as those from electric motors, exhibit additional characteristics owing to the current creating magnetic and electrostatic fields that temporarily store and then release energy throughout the cycle. The effect is to displace in time the voltage and current waveforms from each other, and the effective power in the circuit is reduced by a power factor that is proportional to this displacement.

The total circuit power may therefore be expressed as the power delivered to the load plus circuit losses:

$$0.707 \, V_{max} \times 0.707 \, I_{max} \times \text{power factor}$$

$$= 0.5 \, V_{max} \times I_{max} \times \text{power factor}$$

V_{max} and I_{max} are the peak voltage and current values, respectively. As a result of this phenomenon, some current flows in the circuit without doing any useful work.

The conductors of the supply cable must be insulated both from each other and from their surroundings, and the insulation must be able to withstand the maximum voltage of the system, which under abnormal transient conditions may rise to a value higher than the maximum working voltage.

AC systems

The standard AC power systems adopted throughout the world are three-phase three-wire and three-phase four-wire. The three-wire system is used mainly for high-voltage distribution, the four-wire system being found predominantly in low-voltage distribution, where both three-phase and single-phase loads have to be supplied.

One of the most useful features of AC systems is the ability to manipulate the voltages by means of transformers, something that cannot be done with a DC system. Thus, a ready means is available for attaining the high transmission voltages required for the efficient bulk transmission of AC power. In addition, the transformer is equally able to reduce the voltage at the receiving end down through the various distribution voltage levels to safer working voltages.

The development of solid-state converters has made the use of DC for bulk transmission of power more attractive by making it easier and less expensive to step DC voltage up to suitable levels for transmission. Such DC systems offer lower construction costs and reduced transmission losses and are being used for both overland and undersea applications.

Distribution

The voltages used in electricity supply systems vary somewhat from one country to another, but in general, the basic distribution principles are similar. The following description is a general account of a typical modern system.

Large modern generating sets generate electricity at about 22 kV and are typically grouped in plants, each having a total capacity of 2,000 MW or more. Because this voltage is too low for the economic transmission of large quantities of power over long distances, the voltage is raised to 400 kV by means of a transformer connected to each generator. The transformers are linked via high-voltage circuit breakers to the switching station from which overhead or underground cables connect the supply to the power system's high-voltage network.

Transmission line voltages vary with the distance to be covered and the amount of power to be carried. For example, in the United States, the voltages used range from 69 kV to 765 kV. These

▼ A simplified diagram to show the way in which power is brought from the electric plant to the user, with typical voltage levels used at each stage. The 22 kV from the generator is stepped up to 400 kV for transmission to the national supply network and stepped down at successive substations to the final consumers' level of 415/110 V.

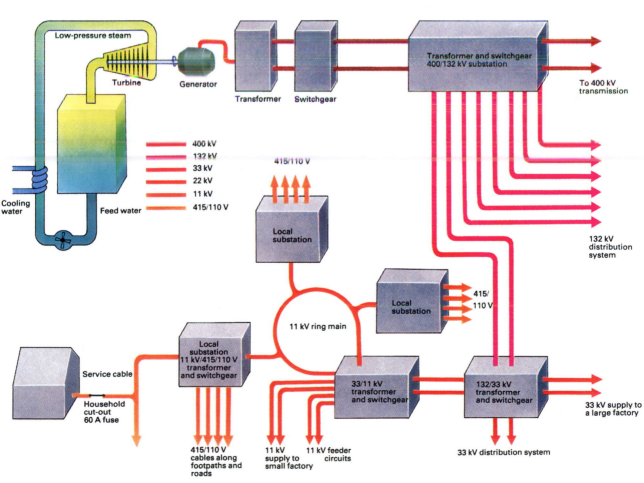

voltages are measured between any two of the three three-phase conductors.

Frequently the power plant is remotely sited, and the high-voltage system conveys power efficiently over long distances to tapping points where there are large demands for it. At these points, a large substation is established, comprising more high-voltage switchgear, transformers to step down the voltage (to 110 kV or 132 kV), and a lower-voltage switching station. To this switching station are connected the lines of the lower-voltage system.

If the substation is required to serve more than one town, the low-voltage system may consist of several overhead lines to carry the power to the small and medium-sized towns in the area. If it is within or close to a large city, the lower-voltage system may be of comparatively short underground cable circuits.

The power is transformed successively via numerous distribution networks (from around 5 to 30 kV), which individually handle power levels appropriate to the demand in the areas they serve until it reaches the low-voltage system (110 or 240 volts single phase), to which ordinary domestic consumers are connected. Large consumers, such as factories, are connected at one of the intermediate voltages; the greater the power required, the higher the voltage at which they are connected.

It would be possible to supply all loads on a single circuit, and residential consumers usually have a single-circuit supply. As the size and importance of the load increases, however, it is considered necessary to have at least a duplicate supply so that, if a fault develops or maintenance to equipment is required, power can still be supplied to the consumers. This system gives a high degree of security of supply.

Cables and overhead lines

Where possible, electricity is transmitted by overhead lines, which are cheaper and technically simpler than underground cables. For these reasons, power is carried by overhead lines in rural areas, but in urban areas, it is frequently impossible to obtain a route for an overhead line, and the increased costs and technical problems of underground cables have to be faced.

Power lines are usually made of aluminum, copper, or steel-covered aluminum. The towers themselves are made of a lattice of steel. Because the towers are tall, the cables do not need to be tensioned, so few are needed to carry the cables great distances. Many people, however, find these power lines unsightly, and in Italy in 2000, the National Electricity Company responded to pub-

◄ A 330 kV outdoor cable termination in southeast Australia. It is part of the Snowy Mountains hydroelectric program that includes 16 major dams and 7 power stations.

lic criticism by holding a competition for designers to create more attractive towers. Two of the winning designs are planned to go into production. In environments that are particularly sensitive, however, there may be pressure for electricity suppliers to use underground cables despite the added costs.

At the lower voltages (about 30 kV and below) employed in distribution systems, cost differentials are much smaller, and the technical difficulties do not arise. Underground cables are therefore common at these voltages even in quite small towns. At higher voltages, underground cables may be contained within pipes filled with pressurized oil. The oil provides the cables with some protection from water in the event of a cable developing a leak. In some instances, power lines may also be carried on tall wooden poles.

Substations

The purpose of a substation is to connect a higher-voltage network to a lower-voltage network by means of transformers, and the main items of equipment at a substation are switch gear and transformers.

Switch gear consists of bus bars to carry the current, circuit breakers, and isolators. A circuit breaker must be capable of interrupting the abnormally heavy currents that flow in a short-circuit fault and of closing or opening a circuit on load. An isolator, except at the lower voltage, is an off-load device used to isolate a circuit (or part of a circuit), or a selector switch used to connect a circuit breaker to one bus bar or another.

Protection

All systems are liable to faults, whether caused by natural factors, such as the salty atmosphere in coastal regions or lightning storms, or by accidental damage such as a crane jib striking an overhead line. Usually one conductor is short-circuited to another conductor or to ground. Under these circumstances, the circuit must be de-energized as quickly as possible, and the job is done automatically by protection equipment.

The simplest protection of all is the fuse, which both detects and interrupts a fault when the heavy current melts the fuse wire. Fuses are used at voltages up to about 11 kV. Where circuit breakers are installed, other protective devices detect the faulty current and send a signal to the tripping coil of the circuit breaker, which then opens to interrupt the flow of current in the faulty circuit.

In some cases, the protection operates when a preset current level is exceeded. The protection can incorporate a time delay or be almost instantaneous in operation. If several sets of this type of protection are installed to protect various sections of a circuit, the ones at the remote end would operate very quickly, and those nearer to the main substation would have progressively longer time delays. This method ensures that a fault at the end of the circuit results in only that part of the circuit being switched off.

More complex systems measure the current entering and leaving a circuit and operate only when there is a difference in these values. Thus, faulty current flowing right through a healthy circuit into a faulty circuit will not cause the healthy circuit to be opened. Another system measures both current and voltage to determine the distance from the circuit breaker to the fault. It will not operate immediately if the fault lies beyond the circuit it is protecting. Solid-state electronics and microprocessor systems are widely used, especially in automatic designs.

Synchronism

In general, power systems are three-phase AC operating on a frequency of 50 or 60 Hz. Therefore, when a generator is run up to speed to go on load, it must be switched into the system only when it is running in synchronism with the other generators in the system.

The voltage of each phase of the generator must reach its peak at the same time as the corresponding phase of the rest of the system, otherwise unacceptable fluctuations would occur until the generator was tripped out again. To synchronize the generator, its speed is adjusted very slightly up or down as necessary until the voltage peaks match. At that precise moment, the circuit breaker controlling the generator is closed, and the set is synchronized to the system.

Stabilization

The stability of a power system is its ability to withstand abnormal disturbances without violent fluctuations in voltage, frequency, or loss of synchronism. Over the length of a circuit, owing to the effects of induced magnetism in the conductors (reactance), the voltage peaks gradually become displaced relative to the sending end volt-

▼ Welding a joint on an aluminum conductor of an electric cable consisting of three oil-filled cores.

age. The power transmitted along that circuit is determined by a mathematical function known as the power-angle rule. As the angle between the voltage peaks increases, the power transmitted increases to a maximum at an angle of 90 degrees and then decreases.

The same mathematical function determines the power output of a generator, but here it is the rotor angle that is involved, that is, the angle between the pole of the field winding on the rotor with the corresponding voltage peak on the stator winding. As the steam supply to the turbine is increased, the rotor tends to accelerate, thus increasing its angle relative to the stator voltage peak and developing more power. This operation would be quite stable until the critical 90 degrees angle was approached, when a small increase in steam input to the turbine would cause the rotor to pass the 90 degrees point and develop less power. The rotor would then accelerate rapidly and lose synchronism with the system.

In normal operation, the reactance of a system would be low enough to permit maximum output from the generator at an angle well below 90 degrees, in fact, at an angle not exceeding about 30 degrees, from where a 100 percent increase in turbine power would be necessary to reach the critical 90 degrees angle.

When a fault occurs close to a generator, however, the voltage drops to nearly zero, and consequently, the power output of the generator is also nearly zero (although a heavy current flows, it is not in phase with the voltage and does not represent useful power). At that instant, the steam power input to the turbine greatly exceeds the nearly zero power output of the stator, and the rotor accelerates for the whole of the duration of the fault. It is therefore essential for the fault to be cleared as quickly as possible so that the voltage may return to normal.

Because of the high rotor speed when the fault has cleared, the generator attempts to develop more power than is being applied to the turbine. As a result, the rotor is slowed down until it settles at a new angle where power input and output are matched. As the faulty circuit has been switched out, the reactance between the generator and the system will be higher than before the fault.

Today faults are cleared in about 120 milliseconds (ms), but efforts are being made to improve this time to about 80 ms, 40 ms each for protection operation and circuit breaker operation.

Control

The demand for electricity varies throughout the day and the year, but electricity cannot be stored in large quantities and made available when

required. The amount generated at any time must equal the amount demanded by the consumers, and if more power is needed, more power must be generated at that instant. Small changes are taken up by minor changes in supply frequency and voltage. The rotational inertia of the generating station acts as a power reserve.

At the control centers, the control engineers have to forecast continually electricity demand for several hours ahead, for the next few days, and for the following week and, from these forecasts, plan which power plants will be required to run at any time and approximately how much output will be required.

As the demand varies, more generators are started up or closed down. Which ones are started up first and which left until last depends on the cost of generating power at the particular plant: generally it is cheaper to generate at large new plants than at smaller, older ones.

System voltage is controlled by changing the tappings on transformers to alter their voltage ratios slightly, by varying the rotor field strength of the generators, or by switching in or out devices known as shunt reactors associated with the cable systems. System frequency is controlled by adjusting the steam supply to the turbines.

▲ A 400/275 kV three-phase transformer at a large grid substation. Voltages are stepped up or down at such stations to connect a higher-voltage electric system to a lower-voltage network, or vice versa. Transformers are one of the two main pieces of equipment for stepping voltages; the other is the switch gear.

SEE ALSO: Cable, power • Electricity • Fuse and circuit breaker • Power • Power plant • Switch • Transformer • Turbine • Voltage regulator

Pressure

▲ Balloons are kept inflated by the force of rising hot air pressing against the inner surface of the balloon. The balloon rises because the hot air is less dense than the colder air outside.

The ability of any material to resist penetration depends not on the force applied but on the force exerted on unit area. The force per unit area is pressure, and it is measured in such units as pounds per square inch (psi), kilograms per square meter (kg/m²), newtons per square meter (N/m², also called the pascal, Pa, the official SI unit) and in the special unit of pressure, the bar (often used in atmospheric pressure measurements). The measurement of pressure is always taken with the force perpendicular to and equally distributed across the surface.

Pressure and force

Consider two people of the same weight—say, 180 pound-force, which is 800 newtons—trying to walk across mudflats. One, wearing ordinary shoes, starts to sink; the other has strapped short boards under his feet and has no problem. The weight of the first was spread over only about 155 sq. in. (0.1 m²), while the second person using mud shoes distributed his weight over perhaps 1,550 sq. in. (1 m²).

A measure of the pressure exerted by a force is obtained by dividing this force by the total area over which it is applied:

pressure = force ÷ area

Use of this relationship shows that the first man was pressing on the mud with a pressure of 1.2 psi (8,000 N/m²) while his colleague was pressing with a pressure of only 0.12 psi (800 N/m²)—one-tenth the pressure of the first man and sufficiently lower to prevent the second man from sinking into the mud.

Many other examples may be used to demonstrate that it is pressure rather than force that determines ease of penetration into a surface. Thumb tacks have a large head to spread the force over the thumb. A sharp knife cuts better than a blunt one, because the pressure of contact is greater. Camels have large soles to their feet to prevent them from sinking into desert sands. A woman in stiletto heels would do more damage to flooring than an elephant. Tracked vehicles, such as tanks, can readily cross terrain impassable to wheeled vehicles, and a hovercraft can cover ground impassable to tanks.

Pressure in fluids

Fluids (liquids and gases) behave differently from solids. Disregarding the weight of a fluid, if it is under compression (say, in a vessel), then at all points in the fluid, the pressure will be the same, because of the freedom that molecules in a fluid have to move about. If there were two points of different pressure, there would be a net force and consequently net motion of the molecules until the difference in pressure was eliminated.

Using this principle in the case of a fluid with weight shows that pressure is related to the height of fluid above the point of measurement and its density (mass per unit volume). Consider a small volume within a fluid. If there were any net forces on this volume, it would move, and so in a stationary fluid, there are no net forces. Thus, the difference in the vertical component of force between top and bottom of the volume (this is upward force—the pressure being greater at the lowest point) is exactly balanced by the weight

weight of the volume. This weight is in turn determined from the height and density of the volume under consideration.

Similar reasoning shows that the ability of a storage tank to resist leaks depends on the pressure exerted on its structure by the liquid inside rather than on the total weight of the contents. The force exerted on unit area of the tank bottom will, however, be a weight—the weight of the liquid column resting on that area. Yet because pressure acts equally in all directions, the pressure on the walls is also related to the height of liquid above that point on the wall. If this situation were otherwise, the tank walls could be made of paper. Indeed, the liquid causes a pressure at every point inside itself as well as its container owing to the mechanics of the molecules.

Pressures can be easily determined from the multiplication of height and density. A submarine moving at a depth of 1,000 ft. (300 m) in seawater of average density 65 lbf. per ft.^{3} (10,400 N/m^3) has a pressure on its surface of 65,000 lbf. per ft.^{2} (3,120,000 N/m^2).

▲ In windsurfing, the pressure of the wind on the sail causes the board to move.

◀ A jackhammer is driven by pressurized air supplied by air motors.

In the discussion of pressures in fluids, we have so far assumed that the fluid is incompressible—density does not change with the pressure on the fluid. This assumption works for liquids (such as water) where the molecules are densely packed, but with gases, the situation is different.

Pressure in gases

A gas in a container also exerts a pressure, owing to the rapid motion of a huge number of individual gas atoms or molecules, which continually bombard the wall of the container. The pressure is the combined result of all these collisions. Unless the container is very large, however, there is no depth effect because the density of gases is so small. However, where there is a depth effect, density will change because of the much greater mobility of the molecules.

In one important case, there is a variation with depth. The pressure exerted by the atmosphere—a gas enclosed by Earth's gravitational field—is comparable with that of the liquid in the tank: its density is far less, but its dimensions are very large. The atmospheric pressure at a point is found by multiplying the height of air above by the average density. This is not an easy calculation, but in practice, we are not often interested in the absolute (actual) atmospheric pressure but in how it varies from time to time. This information is provided by barometers.

This absolute pressure is very large—about 14.7 lb. per sq. in. (100,000 N/m^2)—and it is only because we are used to it that it is not noticed; we could not survive without it. This pressure, which is also known as 1 atmosphere (1 atm), is equivalent on a mercury barometer to about 30 in. (760 mm) of mercury.

As well as the mercury barometer, other methods of measuring atmospheric pressure include the U-tube manometer, suitable for measuring small pressure differences, and the Bourdon gauge, suitable for measuring large differences. In addition, the measurement of rapidly changing pressures may be carried out using piezoelectric or electrostatic devices.

SEE ALSO: BALLOON • BAROMETER • GAS LAWS • PRESSURE COOKER • PRESSURE GAUGE • VAPOR PRESSURE

Pressure Cooker

A pressure cooker is a container with an airtight seal that traps the steam that would otherwise escape during normal cooking. Such a device was invented by Denis Papin, a French physicist, who in 1679 published a description of his "digester." He proudly demonstrated its capabilities of reducing bones to an edible jelly. Today the container may be a saucepan for home cooking, an elaborate digester used in processing wood pulp for paper manufacture, an autoclave used for sterilizing medical supplies, or a stainless steel vat used in the canning industry. The principle is always the same.

All liquids exert a vapor pressure regardless of the temperature. As the temperature is raised, the vapor pressure increases, because the molecules gain enough energy to overcome the intermolecular forces that bind them together. When the vapor pressure reaches or exceeds the atmospheric pressure or the pressure from an object in contact with the liquid, the liquid boils.

Water boils at standard atmospheric pressure at a temperature of 212°F (100°C). In a pressure cooker, the temperature must be increased before the vapor pressure equals that of the surrounding pressure; therefore, water under pressure boils at a higher temperature. When the surrounding pressure is lower, a lower temperature is needed to make the water boil. The pressure cooker is especially useful at high altitudes where, because

▲ Domestic pressure cookers are made of heavy steel with a locking lid to prevent it from blowing off during cooking. A safety pressure valve (below) is fitted to prevent over-pressurization. It operates automatically to vent enough steam to maintain a set temperature.

of the lower atmospheric pressure, the boiling temperature of liquids is lower, and therefore a higher temperature is needed to speed up the cooking process. At sea level, a pressure of 15 psi (103 kN/m²) above normal atmospheric pressure will produce a cooking temperature of 250°F (121°C). The higher temperature of the pressure cooker penetrates food more quickly and reduces the loss of minerals and vitamins that occurs with long cooking times. Pressure cookers can also be used to fry foods under pressure, the method making food cooked in this way more moist and less greasy than conventional fried food.

In the catering industry, pressure cooking is necessary because it shortens the cooking periods. However, safety factors dictate a maximum size for pressure cookers, which may not be large enough for the needs of the industry. The new generation of steam cookers uses the same basic cooking principles as the device invented in 1679; the main difference is that steam cookers now operate under higher temperatures without the pressure buildup of domestic models. Pressureless units are easier and safer to operate, and more even steaming of a variety of foods is achieved.

Industrial pressure cookers

Steam digesters are used in making wood pulp. Pressure in the digester of 75 to 110 psi (520–760 kN/m²) allows the wood chips to be cooked until the fibers are loosened. At the end of the cooking time, the pressure is released rapidly, causing the ligno-cellulosic bonds in the wood fibers to break apart into cellulose, hemicellulose, and lignin.

Autoclaves are pressure vessels used for medical purposes and in some manufacturing industries. Higher temperatures in the autoclave mean more dependable sterilization; killing bacteria is also of extreme importance in food preservation, where pressure cooking methods are highly recommended for preventing botulism.

Pressure cookers of all types must have their lid fitted with safety pressure valves to prevent explosion of the container.

SEE ALSO: AUTOCLAVE • CANNING AND BOTTLING • FOOD PRESERVATION AND PACKAGING • PRESSURE • VAPOR PRESSURE • WATER

Pressure Gauge

A pressure gauge is an instrument designed to indicate the pressure within a fluid—a gas or a liquid—or the pressure that a solid object exerts on a sensor. Analog gauges are usually mechanical transducers: an analog gauge contains a pressure-sensing element mechanically coupled to an indicating pointer, whose shape depends on pressure. As the pressure-sensing element changes shape in response to pressure changes, the pointer rotates around a central pivot to a maximum angle of deflection of around 270 degrees. As it does so, the pointer, indicates pressure against a calibrated dial. Sometimes, two or three pointers are geared together to give a more precise indication. The complete instrument is usually housed within a flat circular case fitted with pipe connections.

Digital pressure gauges are usually based on piezoelectric transducers that produce a voltage in proportion to the pressure that acts on them. Circuitry then interprets that voltage as a numerical pressure value for the display of the device.

In both analog and digital pressure gauges, pressure-sensing elements undergo an elastic deformation in response to pressure. For a given pressure, the extent of deformation depends on the shape, strength, and elasticity of the element.

Some pressure gauges measure differential pressure from the deformation of a membrane that separates gases at two different pressures, for

▲ The power output of this high-performance motorcycle engine is boosted by a supercharger, driven by chain from the crankshaft, which forces air into the cylinders. The condition of the engine is monitored by pressure gauges—the two white dial-faced instruments.

example. Another type of gauge measures absolute pressure this type of gauge includes piezoelectric devices. A third type measures the pressure of a fluid relative to atmospheric pressure—gauge pressure—and must be corrected for variations in atmospheric pressure in order to obtain a true pressure reading.

Bourdon tube gauges

A simple but widely used type of pressure gauge was patented in 1849 by the French watchmaker and inventor Eugène Bourdon. Its pressure-sensing element is a C-shaped tube, with an oval cross section, that is sealed at one end. When fluid pressure acts on the inside of the tube, the tube tends to straighten out, producing the mechanical displacement required to drive the pointer. Other shapes—spirals, helixes, and twists, for example—are also used in similar pressure gauges, but in all cases, the tube is flattened into an oval cross section, this shape being a major factor in determining the sensitivity and linearity: a round tube would be too resistant to distortion.

Diaphragm gauges

A basic pressure-sensing diaphragm takes the form of a thin membrane, which is usually circular and made from metal. The pressure to be measured acts against one face of the diaphragm, causing it to bulge and produce the displacement that can be communicated to the indicator by a mechanical magnifying linkage, for example.

To preserve linearity of reading, the displacement due to the bulging must be kept extremely small—about one-third of the thickness of the membrane. For this reason, this type of system is best used in conjunction with sensitive displacement-sensing transducers that respond accurately to motion on such a small scale.

Capsules and bellows

The sensitivity of a diaphragm can be improved on by sealing together two curved and corrugated diaphragms to form a capsule and evacuating the space between them. As the external pressure increases, the two membranes get closer together. One diaphragm is fixed, and the other is connected to an indicator so that its position relative to the other diaphragm is displayed as a pressure reading. This type of pressure-sensing element is at the core of aneroid barometers.

Sensitivity to pressure can be further increased by joining several capsules in a cascade. This type of pressure-sensing element commonly combines up to ten capsules, giving the assembly the appearance of a set of bellows. True bellows are in effect cylinders with corrugated sides, but they are not commonly used in pressure gauges.

Magnifying mechanisms

A magnifying mechanism is a geared or levered linkage that transmits the displacement of the sensor to the pointer. It performs two functions: it magnifies the small displacements to provide readable movements of the pointer, and it corrects discrepancies to produce a linear reading.

Materials

Sensor materials must be chosen both for their mechanical performance and for their resistance to the fluids to which they will be exposed. Examples include alloys of bronze, beryllium, nickel, and stainless steel. Quartz crystals, which are used in piezoelectric pressure sensors, are notable for their excellent mechanical strength and resistance to most types of chemicals.

Linkages are made from corrosion-resistant materials, sometimes with jeweled or ball bearings. The case may be of metal or plastic but traditionally has been brass.

Uses

Most common gauges, such as car oil-pressure gauges, are based on the Bourdon tube, which is rugged, reliable, and easy to manufacture. More

▲ The pressure gauge at top right indicates the depth of this diving bell. The internal pressure is kept near atmospheric pressure to obviate the need for decompression.

◄ The gauges on this anesthetics cart indicate the pressures of anesthetic gases and oxygen. A drop in pressure indicates that a cylinder is almost empty and must be replaced.

sensitive instruments, such as barometers, use diaphragms, capsules, or bellows. The usual range of the Bourdon tube is from about 5 psi (34 kPa) to about 100,000 psi (690 MPa), whereas the bellows gauges can be sensitive to pressures as low as 0.01 psi (69 Pa). (For comparison, standard atmospheric pressure is 14.7 psi, or 101 Pa.)

Piezoelectric pressure transducers are used to measure fluid pressures in chemical reactors and pipelines. They have sufficient chemical resistance, and their output signal can be communicated by wire to a distant control room.

Some common measurements, such as engine oil pressures or gas supply pressures, are gauge pressures corrected assuming standard atmospheric pressure. This method is sufficiently accurate for most purposes, since the deviation of atmospheric pressure around its standard value is slight compared with the typical pressure reading.

Barometric measurements are absolute, and differential pressures are used mainly in physical experiments and pitot tubes, which measure the flow rate of a fluid (or the airspeed of a plane) from the difference between pressures measured parallel and perpendicular to the line of flow.

Accuracy varies from around ±5 percent for a crude gauge to ±0.1 percent for a precision instrument. A typical general-purpose gauge has an accuracy of around ±1 percent.

SEE ALSO:	Barometer • Manometer • Pressure • Sphygmomanometer • Transducer and sensor

Printed Circuit

Printed circuits consist of conducting strips applied in films on the surfaces of insulating boards. Passive circuits—circuits that have no internal source of power or amplification—were printed as early as 1945. These circuits are similar to modern thick-film circuits, where the circuit is deposited as a film onto an insulating substrate.

Rigid printed circuits in the form in which they are known today had their beginnings in the 1950s, with the introduction of printed wiring boards. The insulating board substrate had a laminated construction and was clad on one side with copper from which the conductor pattern was chemically etched. Components were mounted on the uncoppered side, and their leads were passed through holes for soldering to the printed circuit conductors that connected them.

Boards clad only on one side with a conductor pattern were soon followed by those having interconnected conductor patterns on both sides. In more recent years, the increasing complexity of circuits, chiefly in the aerospace and computer industries, has meant that not even double-sided boards could accommodate the more complicated circuits and has led to the development of multilayer printed wiring, in which layers of conducting circuits are separated by insulating layers.

Flexible printed wiring, which consists of circuit layers sandwiched between a flexible insulating base and a top protective layer of the same material, appeared in around 1960. Flexible printed wiring does not rival rigid printed wiring but is complementary to it in that it can be used to replace bulky wiring harnesses used to make connections to complicated printed-circuit boards or to allow completed circuits to be folded into restricted spaces. Printed circuits are also being applied to surfaces other than special circuit boards, for example, on the cases of radios and telephones. All that is required is for the surface to be firm enough for printing on and sufficiently heat resistant to allow the components to be soldered into place. This development is complemented by the increasing use of surface-mounting components, which are bonded to the surface of the circuit by soldered connections so that mounting holes are unnecessary for support.

Although the term *printed circuit* strictly refers to circuits that have both conductors and circuit components—resistors, capacitors, and inductors—printed on the same board, it is also used interchangeably with the term *printed wiring*, which applies to circuits in which only the conductor pattern is printed. Assemblies of discrete

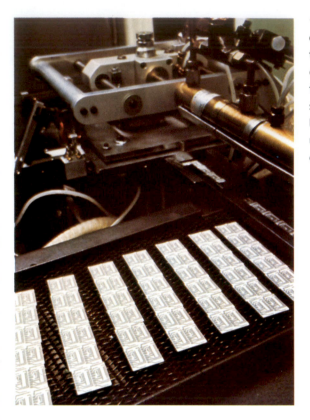

◄ Each of these strips will eventually be split into twelve identical printed circuits. Manufacture of thick-film printed circuits starts with formation of leading grooves. Gold is usually printed on a ceramic or plastic base.

components mounted on a laminated board and interconnected by printed circuits are referred to as printed-circuit boards, or PCBs.

Design and layout

Many applications require custom-designed printed-circuit boards. The shape, material, method of mounting, and form of external connections are decided by the design and operating environment of the equipment it is intended for.

Board materials include paper bonded with phenolic resin and glass fibers bonded with epoxy resin—the two most extensively used materials. Bonded glass-fiber materials have superior characteristics to those of phenolic-bonded paper, but their cost is greater. Ceramic bases, made with materials such as alumina, are also used.

Circuit design is done on a magnified scale on films that are then reduced by photographic methods to the scale required for determining the position of etch-resistant materials on boards. These materials trace paths on circuit boards prior to the processing that forms the circuits.

Depending on circuit complexity, drafting the layout of conductors and components for a printed-circuit board can be time-consuming. The process has been much aided by the introduction of specialist software packages that allow circuits to be designed on screen, sometimes with the help of a light pen, and then printed on film.

The conductor pattern is reproduced in black ink from the master layout of board conductors and components at two or four times the actual size on a dimensionally stable white or translucent material. When the conductor pattern is particularly intricate, printed layouts are made 8 or 16 times actual circuit size in order to obtain adequate definition and accuracy.

The width of the conductors is determined with regard to such factors as current level and the voltage drop and temperature rise caused by the resistance of the printed conductor. The physical sizes and terminal positions of the components must be taken into consideration when choosing the spacing of conductors, as must the possibility of current leakage, voltage breakdown, and capacitance between conductors. The routing must be chosen so as to avoid conductor crossovers, while keeping conductor length to a minimum. If conductor crossovers cannot be avoided, double-sided or multilayer boards are generally used, although it is possible to cross conductors in flexible printed wiring.

Capacitors and inductor coils can be made an integral part of the conductor pattern if their values are not too high. Printed resistors, however, cannot, since they must be formed from different materials, such as nickel–chromium alloys. Soldered or wire-wrapped joints, edge contacts, or plug assemblies form the board's connections.

Manufacture of etched copper PCBs

The manufacture of the commonly used phenolic-bonded paper and epoxy-bonded glass-fiber boards begins by impregnating rolls of reinforcing material—paper or glass fiber—with bonding resin. The impregnated material passes through rollers that remove any excess resin. The remaining resin is then cured in a long drying oven. The cured material is cut into sheets and stacked with alternating sheets of adhesive-backed copper foil. The stack is then placed in a press, where it is subjected to temperatures around 340°F (170°C) and pressures around 1,500 psi (10 MPa) for an hour or more.

In the screen-printing process, the film of the circuit layout is converted into a negative stencil, whose holes correspond to the positions of copper in the final printed-circuit boards. This stencil is then used to print an etch-resistant ink onto the copper surface of the board, where it cures to form a hard, coherent film.

In the photoetching process, the copper surface is coated with a photosensitive material that is exposed to light through a negative image of the circuit. Where the photosensitive material is exposed to light, it hardens to form an etch-resistant coating. A subsequent wash removes the unexposed photosensitive material, leaving an etch-resistant film in the pattern of the circuit. An advantage of this process over screen printing is that it is more faithful to fine circuit detail.

Once the conductor areas have been marked out in etch resistant film by screen printing or the light-exposure method, the sheet is immersed in an etching solution until the unwanted areas of copper have been removed. A typical etchant is a solution of copper (II) chloride in hydrochloric acid. The reaction is as follows:

$$Cu + CuCl_2 \rightarrow 2CuCl$$

The product, copper (I) chloride, is usually insoluble in water, but the hydrochloric acid converts it into a soluble complex that dissolves away from the surface of the board. The etching solution can be regenerated by the addition of chlorine gas, which converts copper (I) chloride to copper (II) chloride in an oxidation reaction:

$$2CuCl + Cl_2 \rightarrow 2CuCl_2$$

When the unprotected copper has been removed, the etching solution is neutralized and the etch-resistant film is removed in an alkaline bath. The film consists of an acid-functional polymer that forms a soluble salt with bases, such as choline $(CH_2(OH)CH_2(CH_3)_3N^+OH^-)$, whose organic nature helps it dissolve in the film. The sheet is then washed in acid to remove any tarnishing, which is an insulating copper oxide that forms on the surface of the copper metal. Finally, a lacquer or lacquer-and-metal coating is applied to the conductors to serve as environmental protection, a soldering aid, or a solder resist.

In a slight variant on this process, the areas of copper that are to be removed are protected using a photosensitive coating and a positive mask of

◀ A circuit designer checks the accuracy of an outline of a circuit on film that will be used for photoetching. Stray black spots can be scratched away using a sharp knife. The film is several times larger than the printed circuit will be, so even fine detail can be seen with the aid of a magnifying lens.

◄ Once a printed circuit has been coated with an insulating layer, additional components, such as resistors, capacitors, and even integrated memory and processing circuits, can be fixed in place and connected electrically by welding their contacts to conductors on the board.

in place by hand. On large runs, automatic assembly machines are employed in which the leads of components are cut to the correct length, formed into a staple shape, inserted into the appropriate holes, and finally bent beneath the board to hold the component rigidly in position. The flow-soldering technique is usually employed for mass soldering of the leads to the printed conductors. Soldering irons mounted on robotic arms introduce solder to the joints, and the machines are calibrated so that the amount of heat transfer is insufficient to cause damage to components.

The circuit boards are then given a lacquer or varnish coating to protect them from corrosion. Finished circuit boards are then inserted into a tailor-made mounting inside the casing of a piece of electrical equipment or embedded in foam or encapsulated as protection against moisture, mechanical damage, thermal shock, or vibration on their way to an assembly line.

the circuit layout. The board is then electroplated with tin or a mixture of tin and lead, forming a layer of relatively inert metal over the copper that will form the conductors; other parts are insulated by the protective coating, so they are immune to electrodeposition. The protective film is then removed as before, and an etching solution removes the copper that it concealed. Tin and tin–lead mixtures resist the etchant but are subsequently removed by other chemicals that leave copper intact—a process called tin stripping.

Finishing

Any of the above techniques can be used to make single-sided or double-sided boards on which conductors are present as copper strips. Multilayer boards are made by interleaving the required number of double-sided boards with insulating bonding material and fusing the whole assembly together in a heated press.

Each etched sheet carries many identical sets of printed conductor patterns, and these must be separated using mechanical saws before further processing. The separate units are then drilled and pierced using machine tools to form holes into which components can be slotted and soldered or where copper can be deposited to make electrical connections between circuits in different layers. The positions of such holes and the circuits are designed such that only the layers that are meant to connect are brought into contact, and those that are not meant to connect have no copper at that point in their layouts.

For small quantities of printed-circuit boards, discrete components are assembled and soldered

Other technologies

Whereas conventional thick-film printed-circuit boards are made by removing excess copper from insulating boards, alternative technologies apply conducting strips to insulators. One advantage of such techniques is that they apply no more than the required amount of conductor.

Circuits may also be produced by direct printing using metallic inks and stencils or from paper-backed transfers. These inks are generally fired at high temperature to form the conductor; however, some metallic inks require no firing. In some cases, copper foil is embossed directly onto insulating substrates in the form of the circuit and then bonded into place on the board.

High-precision component fabrication is possible with thin-film circuits. They are made by depositing the conducting metal from its vapor in an otherwise high vacuum.

► A circuit of gold conductors and metal oxides printed onto a white ceramic board.

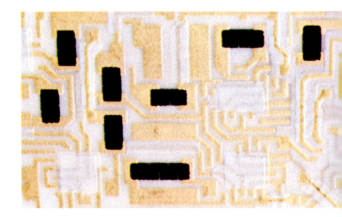

SEE ALSO: Capacitor • Computer • Computer graphics • Engraving and etching • Resistor

Printing

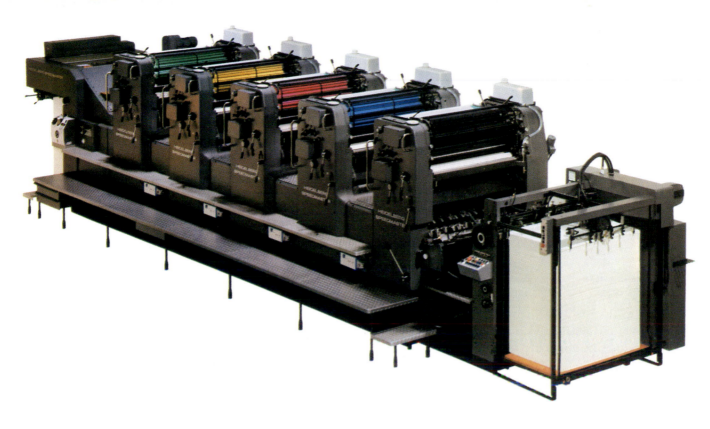

▲ An offset machine with five color-printing units. It uses zinc, aluminum, or multimetal litho plates and can produce 10,000 sheets, 28.75 x 40.13 in. (730 x 1,020 mm) in size, in one hour.

Printing provides many familiar ingredients in our lives. Apart from the more obvious books and newspapers, the products of the printing industry are many and diverse. They include posters, fabrics, banknotes, telephone books, stamps, postcards, brochures, magazines, labels, wallpapers, income tax forms, cartons, plastic containers, candy wrappers, and many other forms of packaging. Today, even electronic circuits and working surfaces in kitchens are printed.

History

The history of printing is closely linked with the general history of civilization. As the main vehicle for the conveyance of ideas during the past 500 years, the printing press has had its influence on every sphere of human activity: on politics and government, on literature and education, on business and economic affairs and on the development of society as a whole. In turn, the demand for printed matter in new forms and in greatly increasing quantities has led to revolutionary changes in the technology of printing.

Although the modern printing industry is generally considered to have been born out of the invention of movable-type letters from metal by Gutenberg and his followers in the mid-15th century, the Chinese had been printing on paper many hundreds of years earlier. Paper originated in China in about 105 C.E., when papyrus and parchment were being used in Mediterranean countries. Printing from wood blocks was practiced in China and Japan from the sixth century onward, and in 767 C.E., the Empress Shiyautoku is said to have ordered a million copies of a Sanskrit charm in Chinese characters for distribution to her people. The invention of movable type has also been traced back to China, where in 1042 C.E., Pi Sheng used clay for molding type. Later, in 1314, Wang Chen introduced wooden type, which was less easily broken. These types could not be widely used, however, because the 40,000 or so characters in the Chinese language made typesetting too involved. The fact that there are only 26 characters in the Roman alphabet simplified the task for European languages.

The art of papermaking did not spread to Europe until about 1157, when Jean Montgolfier escaped from the Saracens and returned to France to set up a paper mill. It is said that he learned the art while working as a slave in a paper mill during the Second Crusade. For three centuries after paper became known in Europe, it was used only as a material for handwriting. Books were laboriously produced in very small numbers, and their use was confined to the churches and monasteries. It was only in the 15th century that the invention of methods of printing books allowed the spread of knowledge to pave the way for learning and culture.

The birth of the industry

In 1440 Johann Gutenberg, a Mainz (Germany) goldsmith, began experimenting with printing when he was a political refugee in Strasbourg. He later returned to Mainz, and by 1450 he had developed his invention to the point where it could be exploited commercially. In partnership with a lawyer called Johannes Fust, who advanced the money, he commenced casting metal type, which was to be used in printing his famous Bible. Gutenberg soon ran into serious financial trouble, and in 1455 Fust terminated the agreement, the bulk of Gutenberg's type and presses going to Peter Schöffer, who was in Fust's service and later married his daughter. There are rival claims for the invention of printing on behalf of a Dutchman, Laurens Coster, but details of his life are very scarce, and none of his work remains.

The only major work that can confidently be called a product of Gutenberg's own workshop was the 42-line Bible published in 1456. It was printed a page at a time in an edition of 200 copies, of which about 30 were printed on vellum. Its quality was such as to rival the best manuscripts. Gutenberg's achievement lies not merely in his invention of a practical method of printing books but in the standards of technical perfection established in his workshop, not surpassed until the 19th century. In today's world of specialization, it is also worth noting that these early printers turned their hands to all the arts: punch cutting (making the patterns), matrix fitting (making molds from the punches), type founding, ink making, printing, and publishing.

Within 15 years of Gutenberg's death in 1468, printing presses had been set up in every country in western Europe, most of the printers being

A four-color offset press uses three special printing colors—cyan (a light blue), magenta (a purplish-red), and yellow—that can be added with black to give the impression of a full range of colors.

▼ Two-color presses are the workhorses of printing, providing cheap and quick reproduction of posters, flyers, handbills, and newsletters in one or two colors.

German nationals. William Caxton, the first English printer, learned the trade in Cologne, and after a period of printing in Bruges, he returned to England in 1476 to set up his own press. He published many important literary works written in English, including *The Canterbury Tales*.

The early printing presses of the 15th century were of the wooden-screw type and were little more than adaptations of the wine presses and bookbinding presses of that time, printing one sheet at a time. They were levered by hand and demanded a great deal of muscle power. The area of the form, in which the type is held in the press, was very small because of the limited force applied, and repeated readjustments of the sheets were necessary. In the early 16th century, a metal screw was introduced, and the press improved by the use of a sliding bed (on which the form lay, face up, to be inked and then slid under the platen, which was the plate that applied the pressure), but no basic changes in the technique of printing took place for 300 years. The beginning of the 19th century brought a period of technical advance that has continued to the present day.

Technical advances

In 1800, Earl Stanhope invented an all-iron press with a screw and a system of levers that produced an improved impression on a larger platen area. This method made it possible to print a large form in one pull, whereas the wooden press required two pulls, each one covering only half the area. Hand presses with further improvements over the Stanhope press were later introduced,

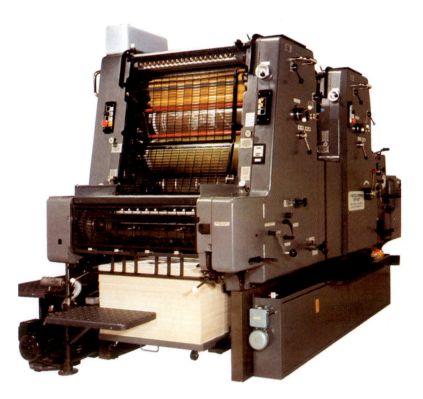

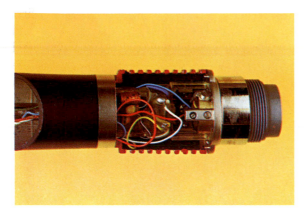

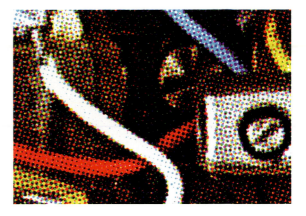

This photograph has been reproduced in four colors with a screen of 150 dots per inch. In the enlarged view of the picture (right) the separate yellow, cyan, magenta, and black dots can be seen. Each color screen is set at a different angle, with black at 45 degrees.

including George Clymers's Columbian Press (Philadelphia 1816), which was the first iron press without a screw, and Copes's Albion Press (1830).

A German named Friedrich König, intrigued by Watt's invention of the steam engine, set out to design a printing press powered by steam. Unable to find support for the idea on the continent, he went to England in 1806, and with the backing of Thomas Bensley, König developed the first mechanized platen press, capable of 400 impressions an hour. In 1811, König patented a steam-powered cylinder press, in which a horizontal printing form moved back and forth under a revolving cylinder, printing over 800 sheets an hour. Two of these presses were ordered by *The Times* newspaper. In the first paper produced on the new press on November 29, 1814, John Walter wrote of this "greatest improvement connected with printing since the discovery of the art itself, relieving the human frame of its most laborious efforts in printing." Two years later König produced the first perfecting press, which allowed both sides of a sheet of paper to be printed in one pass of the machine.

Another important step was made when curved stereotyped printing plates were fixed to cylinders for printing a continuous reel or web of paper on rotary letterpress machines. (A stereotype is a plate duplicated from an original form so that either several copies of the same thing can be made at once, using the capacity of a large press, or so that a curved plate, for use on a cylinder press, can be made from a flat original.) This principle is still employed in printing newspapers today. Folding systems were incorporated so that newspapers were folded as fast as they were printed, and machine speeds steadily increased until large metropolitan newspapers were using presses that could produce an average of 50,000 copies an hour.

Developments in presses have had to be matched by similar progress in typesetting in order to meet the demand for faster composition. Until the late 19th century, each letter of a word had to be selected individually by a compositor. Although experiments began much earlier, the first practical automatic typecasting machine, the Linotype, was introduced in 1885. On these machines, the words to be printed are tapped out on a keyboard, causing the appropriate brass matrices to be gathered to form a mold, which is then used to cast a solid line of type, or slug, from molten alloy. Linotype and Intertype line-casting machines are still sometimes used today. Three years after Linotype was invented, the Monotype system of automatic typecasting was patented. This system involves two machines: a keyboard produces a punched paper spool, which is fed to a unit casting individual type characters from molten alloy. The Ludlow system of typecasting introduced in 1905 provided a combination of hand and mechanical composition. Matrices of type characters are set in a special composing stick, and the line is inserted into a casting device that will then produce one or more slugs.

In recent years, the trend has been away from hot-metal typesetting to photographic composition and phototypesetting. In this process, letters are assembled on photographic film or paper at high speeds, and the resulting photographic image is then used to make printing plates.

Much of the history of printing is the history of letterpress printing, the process in which ink is applied to paper from a relief surface. Letterpress is not only the oldest process, but until comparatively recently, it was used to produce the major proportion of all printed work. During the past 50 years, however, the balance has swung strongly toward offset lithography.

Lithography

The process of lithography, which is based on the fact that grease and water do not readily mix, was discovered by Alois Senefelder in about 1798, apparently by accident. The image is made to retain ink, while the rest of the plate is ink-repelling. The printing surface in his original process was a polished slab of a special form of

◀ Copies of the *New York Times* roll off the presses at the printing plant in Carlstadt, New Jersey. Completed pages are produced by a laser scanner, which produces film to make lightweight metal plates. These plates are then used for printing by offset lithography.

machines, with between one and six color printing units on the press for full-color reproduction.

Web offset, which prints on reels of paper that pass through the press cylinder, has developed rapidly and is now widely used in the production of illustrated books, magazines, and newspapers incorporating color.

Heat-set web offset, which incorporates drying ovens, enables good-quality color to be printed at speed on a variety of papers. A modern web offset press can print up to 64 pages of the size of this book at one pass, printing on both sides at once and producing around 30,000 copies per hour.

Gravure printing

Compared with letterpress and lithography, gravure printing is a recent process. It was first developed in about 1895 by the Rembrandt Company of Lancaster, England, from a process invented by Karl Klic, a Bohemian. Ink is transferred from very small cells recessed in a copper surface. Traditionally gravure cylinders have been chemically etched through a gelatine protective layer, but the current trend is for the cells to be engraved electromechanically, electronically, or by carbon dioxide laser.

Printing illustrations

Until the 19th century, illustrations were either drawn and illuminated by hand or printed from wood blocks. The invention of lithography made it possible for drawings on litho stones to be printed. It was the invention of photography and its marriage with printing, however, that made it possible for illustrations to be reproduced cheaply and in large quantity. Since the discovery of photoengraving by Niépce, in 1829, and the application of the halftone principle by Fox Talbot in 1852, there has been a succession of technical advances in photomechanical methods of producing printing surfaces for various qualities of reproduction by letterpress, lithography, and gravure printing.

The halftone process involves breaking up the continuous tones, which have varying shades of gray or color, into fine dots of varying size, which fuse optically to give the illusion of light and

limestone found in Bavaria, Germany. Senefelder patented the process and wrote a comprehensive account of this method of reproduction. The process was later to be exploited by artists such as Goya, Degas, Lautrec, Matisse, and Picasso. It is only since the 1950s, however, that lithography has acquired commercial importance, to the extent of replacing letterpress as the major process of printing.

The first powered flatbed litho press dates from about 1850. Later, metal plates began to replace the cumbersome litho stones, and in 1900, the first rotary litho machine appeared in the United States, printing directly from aluminum plates. Three years later, the first offset rotary presses were introduced for printing on tinplate. In offset printing, the ink is first applied onto a rubber-covered cylinder and then transferred onto the tinplate.

In 1905, this same offset principle was used for printing on paper, and now the term *offset* has become synonymous with lithography. The rapid growth of the lithographic process has been firmly based on the use of zinc, aluminum, or multimetal litho plates, run on rotary offset

▼ Left: In letterpress printing, the ink is coated onto the raised surface of the printing plate, and the paper is applied directly to the plate. Letterpress is the oldest of the printing processes. Center: In lithography, the image is ink retaining, while the rest of the plate is ink-repelling. Lithography has overtaken letterpress in the last 50 years to become the most popular method. Right: Gravure printing traps ink in impressions recessed in the plate surface—the amount of ink in each cell dictates the color and tone.

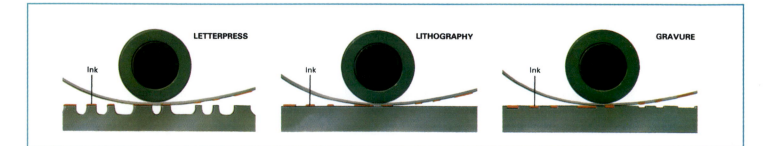

shade. In this way, and printing only in black, blue, red, and yellow ink, it is possible to print color pictures that appear to contain all the colors in the visual spectrum (full-color reproduction).

Print identification

The identification of the printing process used to produce a given sample of print can be very difficult, but there are a number of points that can provide clues. This task can be made lighter with the use of a high-quality magnifying glass.

A letterpress print may show a slightly embossed effect on the reverse of the sheet, ink squash may have caused the thickening of the ink film around the edges of a letter or a halftone dot, and the general effect is of crisp, bright, and sharp detail. Litho prints tend to be less contrasting, the halftone dots have fuzzy rather than sharp edges, there is no ink squash or embossing effect, and very small highlight dots can be seen even on fairly rough paper. Prints produced by the conventional gravure process show a pattern of square cells of equal surface area but varying ink film thickness, type matter may have a sawtooth edge, and solid areas may show a pattern of white spots or lines where ink has failed to flow sufficiently to eliminate the cell pattern. Gravure printing is also expensive.

Selecting the printing process

The three major processes of printing in use today are letterpress, lithography, and gravure. In letterpress, ink is transferred from a raised surface; in gravure, the ink flows out from small cells in the printing plate; and in lithography, printing takes place from a flat surface on which image areas attract ink and nonimage areas repel it. Printing presses range in size from the small offset machines used in many offices to the huge web-fed installations producing newspapers and magazines. Letterpress machines may be based on the platen, flatbed cylinder, or rotary principle. Gravure and litho presses all use the rotary principle, which allows higher printing speeds. The most suitable method of production and type of press for a particular printing job depends on

▲ A color picture is printed using four colors. First, the cyan separation is printed (top left), then the magenta is added (top right), and then the yellow (bottom left). The black is printed last to give a full range of tones. Extra "spot" colors can be printed on some machines, but the cost of doing so on a standard four-color machine would be expensive, as the machine would have to be cleaned and set up for a new print run.

many factors: the quality required, length of run, whether illustrations are involved, the number of colors, and the paper used.

Offset lithography is the most versatile process, and the quality of reproduction can reach a high standard. The fact that ink is applied to the base by a soft and resilient rubber-covered cylin-

▲ Inside the drum of a laser scanning machine. The original photograph or artwork is fitted to the drum, which then spins around a fixed laser. The laser reads the picture and converts the information into digital form, which is then electronically manipulated so as to produce four sets of screened color film.

der means that a wide variety of papers, cardboard, and even tinplate can be printed by offset litho. This is not the case in letterpress, which demands the smooth surface of a coated paper for printing fine-screen halftones. Machine speeds are normally higher in litho than in letterpress printing, although machine stoppages tend to be more frequent, and more waste sheets are printed. The litho process is particularly suitable for jobs involving a large number of illustrations, since the litho printing plate is always made via a photographic negative or positive. On the other hand, as type and blocks are movable within a form, the letterpress process allows changes to be made at the last minute or even during the course of a printing run. Its disadvantage is that metal type is heavy, bulky, and expensive to store and has now been superseded by the assembly of letters on photographic film using computer-based photocomposition equipment.

Photogravure is an excellent process for the reproduction of illustrations in monochrome or color, giving good depth of tone in shadow areas and a delicacy and softness in the middle and lighter tones. The costs of plate and cylinder making are very high, however, so the process is best suited to very long runs on web-fed rotary presses, hence its use in the printing of large-circulation color magazines, catalogs, and stamps.

Other printing methods

Small-scale or specialist printing may require different techniques. Serigraphy, or screen printing, is largely done by hand, although it can be automated. Screens are made from silk or synthetic gauzes, and the design is transferred onto it by spreading glue across it and then dissolving it from the areas to be printed. Ink is forced through the screen using a squeegee, and then the frame is lifted and repositioned over the next item to be printed.

Collotype printing is used for high-quality reproduction of photographs or illustrations. It uses a glass or cellophane plate, which has been coated with a photosensitive material and exposed under a negative. In the areas where it receives light, the material hardens and loses its hydrophilic properties in proportion to the intensity of the light. Like lithography, it uses the principles of mutual repulsion of ink and water, but it is also similar to rotogravure in that the thickness of the ink film is not uniform but is in proportion to the tones in the original image.

FACT FILE

■ *Crosfield Laser Gravure uses hundreds of watts of carbon dioxide laser power to engrave a groove of variable depth on a gravure cylinder. Printing runs in excess of a million copies can be made with these cylinders.*

■ *Reprographic printing of images developed on a screen has been achieved over the vast distance between Earth and the far reaches of the Solar System. Pictures of Jupiter and Saturn sent back by Voyager and Pioneer spacecraft were printed via screens, digital scanners, and printing terminals.*

■ *Some of the earliest texts to be printed on paper were made in China in the second century by applying damp paper to carved marble Buddhist scriptures and wiping ink over the relief formed on the paper.*

SEE ALSO: Engraving and etching • Ink • Lithography • Newspaper production • Paper manufacture

Prism

Since antiquity, humans have been fascinated by the ability of clear crystals and cut glass to produce colors from white light. The first scientific study of this phenomenon was undertaken in 1666, when the British physicist Sir Isaac Newton turned his attention to optics, and in his experiments, he used a triangular block of glass—a prism. Sunlight from a hole in a window shutter was deviated by the prism and spread out into a spectrum of colors: red, orange, yellow, green, blue, indigo, and violet. A second prism placed in contact with the first, but reversed, recombined the colors to give white light again, demonstrating that the prism was not generating the colors itself but merely spreading out the components of sunlight.

Newton's experiment showed that the different colors of light are deviated to different extents by a prism, violet being deviated the most and red the least. In 1621, the Dutch mathematician Willebrord Snell had shown that the amount of refraction at a boundary depends on a property of the solid called the refraction index, and the prism experiment proved that the refractive index of glass varies with the color of the light, which we now know to be a measure of its wavelength. When a beam of light passes obliquely through a parallel-sided glass block, each wavelength is deviated through a slightly different angle at the first face and is refracted back through the same angle as it emerges through the opposite face, thus reconstituting white light. If the sides of the two faces are not parallel, however, the dispersals of the two faces do not cancel out, and a spectrum is formed. In optics, any block of this kind is called a prism, although the most commonly used prism has the cross section of an equilateral triangle (having sides equal in length) so that any pair of faces may be used.

Newton's arrangement is not the best for the study of the spectrum, because the wavelengths overlap considerably, and a modern spectroscope uses a slit and a collimating lens to throw parallel light on the prism and a telescope to view the spectrum. Glass is not transparent to ultraviolet and infrared wavelengths, and thus, alternative materials are used for studying them. Quartz is transparent over a greater wavelength range and is the most common alternative. For very short ultraviolet wavelengths, calcium fluoride (fluorite) is used; sodium chloride (rock salt) prisms are suitable for long infrared wavelengths.

Refraction by a long prism has a major disadvantage for spectroscope use in that the dispersion of the spectrum is nonlinear; the wavelengths

◄ Two glass prisms. Light passing through one prism is separated into a spectrum of colors. The second prism recombines the spectrum.

at the red end are closer together than at the violet end. Many spectroscopes use a diffraction grating at the dispersive element because it is linear; in the case of the reflection grating, the transparency of the material is irrelevant.

Reflecting prisms

There is a completely distinct use for prisms whose section is a right-angled triangle with 45 degree base angles: to reflect light through 90 or 180 degrees, without causing dispersion. A beam of light passing perpendicularly through one of the short faces is neither deviated nor dispersed and strikes the hypotenuse (long) face at 45 degrees inside the prism. The critical angle for glass is about 42 degrees, so the beam is totally internally reflected and emerges through the other small face, having been reflected through 90 degrees. Such prisms are used in periscopes, where metal mirrors would corrode with use.

The prisms in prismatic binoculars are used rather differently. Light enters by the hypotenuse face, is totally internally reflected off each of the small faces in turn, and reemerges through the hypotenuse. The beam has been reflected through 180 degrees and the image reversed in the process. By using both a vertical and a horizontal prism, the inverted image that would be seen through a refracting astronomical telescope is righted, an essential requirement for binoculars and telescopes intended for terrestrial use.

SEE ALSO: BINOCULARS • DIFFRACTION • GLASS • LIGHT AND OPTICS • PERISCOPE • RAINBOW • SPECTROSCOPY • TELESCOPE, OPTICAL

Projector, Movie and Slide

A projector is a device that uses light to produce an image on a reflective or translucent screen. Movie projectors produce rapid sequences of images from the frames of films; slide projectors cast single images from individually packaged frames of developed film, called slides.

The earliest form of projector was the Victorian magic lantern, a 19th-century device that used candles or oil lamps to cast light through scenes or figures painted on glass, projecting those images onto a wall or screen. Later, transparent positive photographs were projected, and lantern-slide lectures became popular educational and entertaining events, often relating the adventures of explorers of the time.

In the latter half of the 20th century, the home slide show became the modern equivalent of the lantern-slide lecture, with vacation snapshots being a popular subject. It was made possible by the availability of compact automatic cameras, color-reversal films that could be developed directly as slides, and affordable slide projectors.

▲ An old-fashioned reel-to-reel movie projector. Early films were made of celluloid, which ran the risk of catching fire with the heat of the lamps needed to project the image. More energy-efficient lamps using quartz–halogen bulbs are used in modern projectors as they produce much less heat.

With time, slides were superseded by the home video, taken by portable camcorder and shown on a television screen using a video-cassette player.

Movie projection started on December 28, 1895, when the French industrialists and inventors, brothers Auguste and Jean Lumière, used their newly invented *cinématographe* to show a film of workers leaving their factory. A movie projector has components similar to those of slide projectors, augmented by a mechanism that holds each image still for an instant of projection and then moves the film on to the next frame.

Recent developments in projection technology include systems that project digital images. They range from movies recorded on digital versatile discs (DVDs) and played on dedicated DVD players, to graphics and moving images generated and played on computers.

Slide projection

A slide projector holds a mounted frame of developed film (a positive image) in a position called the object plane. A condenser system uses lenses or mirrors to collect light from an electric lamp and concentrate it on the object plane. The slide filters the appropriate frequencies of light to produce a color image that is projected and focused onto a screen by a projection lens.

Light source. The earliest projectors used candles or oil lamps to provide light for projection. They were replaced by tungsten-filament incandescent electric lamps rated at up to 1,000 watts, depending on the size of image to be projected. Such lamps produce a great amount of heat as well as light, and blowers are necessary to prevent overheating, which could damage slides and the plastic components and casing of the projector.

Most modern projectors use quartz–halogen lamps, which produce much less heat than incandescent lamps of equivalent light outputs. Apart from being more energy efficient than tungsten-filament lamps, quartz–halogen lamps require little or no cooling, and they usually have integral dichroic reflectors that direct visible light toward the object plane while allowing infrared light to pass through. Since the balance of frequencies in their output is similar to that of daylight, quartz–halogen lamps give a more faithful reproduction of original colors than is obtained with tungsten-filament light sources.

Condenser. The condenser system of a slide projector consists of a convex lens between the light source and object plane and, in the case of filament-lamp projectors, a concave spherical or parabolic mirror behind the lamp to reflect light that would otherwise shine away from the object plane. Heat-absorbing glass protects slides from overheating by filtering out infrared light, which is invisible but carries heat energy.

Projection lens. The focal length of the projection lens determines the throw of the projector—the relationship between the distance between the screen and projector and the size of the projected image. A short focal length, for example, is suitable for use in a small room to give a large picture, while a longer focal length lens produces the same size picture at a greater distance, making it more suitable for use in lecture rooms. Zoom lenses of variable focal length are available and are particularly suitable for portable projectors that are able to be used in a variety of locations with different throws.

Since it is easier to make lenses with long focal length, the curvatures required being less, these lenses are generally more satisfactory from the point of view of giving sharp coverage all over the screen with freedom from false color and distortions. Compound lenses can be used to minimize such distortions, but the heat generated by the light source means that the components of such systems cannot be cemented together, and any lens coatings must be able to withstand high temperatures without becoming discolored.

Slide transport. Early slide projectors had a simple carrier that moved back and forth across the projection lens, allowing for slides to be changed manually when out of the object plane. They were replaced by devices that have moving magazines with slots for 36 or 50 slides. Motorized or solenoid-operated rams push slides sideways into and out of the object plane. Such machines operate by remote control; the operator pushes a single button to start a sequence whereby the current slide is pushed out of the object field, the magazine advances by one slot, and the next slide is pushed into the object plane. The focal length of the projection lens may be adjusted by a remote-operated servomotor.

In a variation on this system, as many as 80 slides are stored in a circular carousel that rotates above the object plane. To change slides, a ram clears the object plane by pushing any slide up into the carousel. The carousel then rotates,

▲ This anamorphic lens expands images horizontally to project wide-screen images of slides. The slides must be taken using a lens that compresses the image horizontally in the frame.

▼ The Kodak Carousel projector. Multiple-slide projectors such as this are useful for presentations, since they permit smooth progress through a preset sequence of slides.

taking the first slide in while the next slide drops into place under gravity alone.

Screen. The typical screen is a sheet of fabric covered on one side with a matte white coating that reflects the projected image. Often the screen is attached on one side to a spring-loaded roller that holds it under tension when extended and draws it back into a cylindrical carrying case after use. The free side of the screen has a rod sewn into its edge that holds it straight and some means of attaching it to a fixed point when the screen is extended.

Variations. Variations on the standard projection mechanism include rear projection and reflective projection. Rear projection uses a translucent white screen, and the projector illuminates the screen from the opposite side to the viewers. Reflective projection is a means of projecting images of opaque objects, such as paintings and book pages. Rather than shining through a slide, the light source in reflective projection shines light onto objects, and the reflected light then passes to the projection lens. Light intensity must be moderated to avoid scorching the object, so reflective projection produces dim images.

Liquid-crystal projectors. A recent development in the projection of static images is the LCD (liquid crystal display) projector. In this device, the LCD acts as a transparent slide, and the image displayed is under the control of a computer. A powerful quartz–halogen lamp provides the back illumination. This type of device is ideally suited to presenting material direct from computer files.

Overhead projector

Overhead projectors are widely used in education and in business settings to project images printed or hand written on transparent plastic sheets. An overhead projector consists of a light box and an adjustable overhead lens-and-mirror system.

The condenser is a Fresnel lens that has a flat side and a ridged side. The flat side serves as the top of the light box and the object plane. The ridged side has the same optical effect as a much thicker convex lens. Light passes upward through any transparency on the object plane and is reflected and focused by an angled mirror and a lens in the overhead assembly. Throw is adjusted by altering the height of the overhead assembly.

Movie projection

Although the principles of projection are the same for moving images as they are for static images, there are significant differences between the technical details of slide and movie projectors. Some of these differences stem from the requirement of more powerful light sources, particularly when projecting huge images in movie theaters.

For many years, the carbon-arc lamp was the only means of producing light of sufficient power for a large movie theater. In such a lamp, an electrical arc is struck between two carbon electrodes, which incandesce as they slowly burn away. The arc is at the focus of a parabolic mirror, which directs all its light in a parallel beam. The electrodes are kept at this focus by an automatic feed mechanism. Even the largest carbon-arc electrodes, which may be over 0.5 in. (13 mm) in diameter and take 250 amps of current, do not last more than an hour before they burn away.

Modern movie projectors use quartz–xenon lamps, in which the arc is formed between tungsten electrodes within a quartz bulb filled with pure xenon gas. Such lamps give a steady bright light that is similar in color to daylight. They run for up to 2,000 hours without replacement.

Both carbon-arc and quartz–xenon lamps run on direct-current rather than alternating-current supplies, because the variation in light intensity as the arc reversed would cause flicker if an alternating current were used.

A pair of condenser lenses concentrates the light beam on the object plane, and the heat generated here is so intense that it can melt a film if it becomes stuck. A projection lens then focuses the image on the movie theater screen.

Film transport

The film-transport mechanism of a movie projector ensures that the moving images run smoothly and without flicker. It requires each frame to remain perfectly still and in place while being projected and then moves the film on by one frame while the light source is cut off. This sequence is repeated 24 times per second to give an impression of continuous motion.

▶ The Maltese cross is a device for converting a constant rotational motion into the intermittent motion required in the film transport of a movie camera. A pin on the rotating pulley catches an arm of the Maltese cross with each rotation, taking it around through a quarter turn before releasing it.

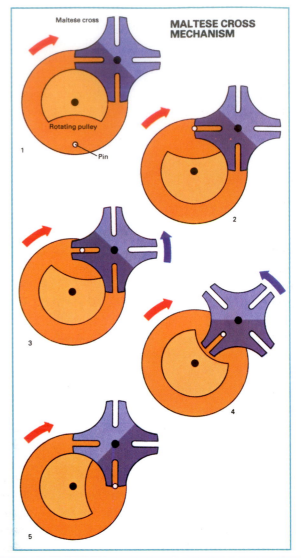

MALTESE CROSS MECHANISM

▼ A rotating shutter wheel allows light to pass when the film has stopped with a frame lined up with the aperture gate (left). The shutter blocks light when the film moves (center) and allows it to pass again when the next frame is in place in the gate (right).

Of the various mechanisms used to provide intermittent film motion, the simplest is the claw, a mechanical arm with pins whose spacings match the sprocket holes along the film. A cam mechanism engages the claw with the film, draws the claw down, withdraws it from the film, and moves it up again by a suitable number of sprocket holes ready for the next frames. Claws are mostly found in small projectors for home use.

The 35 mm and 70 mm gauge projectors for movie theaters use the Maltese cross mechanism, so called because it has a four-pointed star wheel with slits in each point, the slits corresponding to

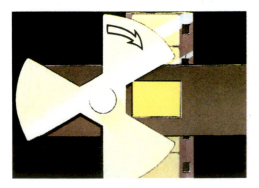

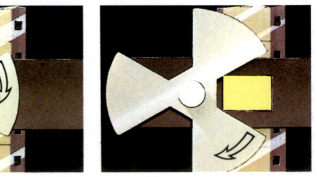

the gaps between the arms of a Maltese cross. A wheel with a pin projecting from one side rotates next to the cross in such a way that the pin engages in one of the slits for each rotation, moving the cross through 90 degrees. The Maltese cross drives a sprocket wheel that advances the film by a frame for each quarter turn.

The mechanism that controls the passage of light through the film to eliminate flicker consists of a shutter and an aperture gate. The shutter is a wheel that rotates eight times in one second and has three open segments that allow light to the film while it is stationary. Some projectors have two shutter wheels that rotate in opposite directions so as to close the light path from the top and bottom of the frame simultaneously. The aperture gate has a rectangular opening that screens off the film that surrounds each frame.

The film transport also leads the film through the soundtrack player, where the optical or magnetic soundtrack is read by appropriate devices and converted into an electrical sound signal. The motion through this device must be smooth, otherwise the sound will be distorted. For this reason, the sound head is located well away from sources of vibrations, such as the gate. This solution is possible because the soundtrack and corresponding images are separated by a length of film. The film passes through rollers and then around a heavy drum—the sound drum—whose inertia practically eliminates speed variations.

Film storage

At 24 frames per second—1,440 frames per minute—each minute of a movie corresponds to 90 ft. (27.4 m) of 35 mm film stock, which has 16 frames per ft. (52.5 frames per m). At that rate, one mile (1.6 km) of film corresponds to just under one hour of movie. Consequently, vast quantities of film have to be handled whenever a full-length feature film is shown, and these quantities are greater still for 70 mm films.

At first, celluloid films were shown in reels up to 1,000 ft. (300 m) of 35 mm; reel lengths were kept short and films stored in metal cans between screenings because of the fire risk associated with celluloid. With the introduction of less flammable safety film, it became established practice to run 35 mm reels of 2,000 ft. (600 m). Each reel ran just over 20 minutes, and a typical feature film would require five or six reels of film and two projectors. Near the end of one reel, the projectionist would thread the next reel through the idle projector in preparation for changeover; at changeover, the projectionist would follow cue marks on the film, pressing a pedal to start the second projector and switch the optics without breaking the flow of the movie. This procedure required the undivided attention of the projectionist; missed changeovers were not uncommon. Modern multiplex cinemas use film platters to eliminate the need for changeovers and reduce demands on projection staff.

Video and digital projection

A number of options exist for projecting movies recorded in video or digital format. The oldest and simplest of these systems is simply a high-intensity television screen whose image is projected through lenses. Since the image from a single screen tends to be rather dim, even for projecting in a small room, it is common practice to have three such screens—one each for the red, green, and blue components of the image—and use lenses to merge the images on the screen.

With digital movies, each frame is encoded as a gridlike array of picture elements, or pixels. This information can be used to drive an LCD display in a transmission projector or to drive the micromirrors in a reflective display. Each micromirror measures 4 x 4 μm and has two tilt positions. In the "on" position, it reflects light to the projection lens, contributing to the image.

PLATTER SYSTEM

When a film is due to start a screening run, its individual reels are spliced together to form a continuous strip and wound onto a horizontal disk, or platter. For each screening, the start of the film is taken from the center of the reel, threaded through a guide system to the projector and back, and then wound onto a takeup platter. The platters rotate as the film plays, and after each screening the film is ready for the next showing. Using the platter system, a single operator can project films for several viewing rooms.

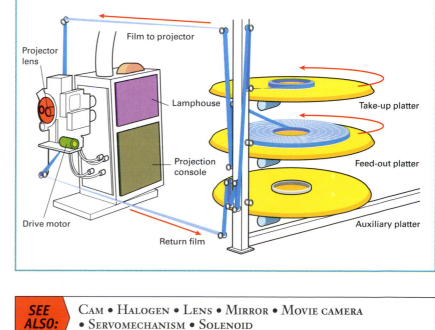

Film to projector

Projector lens

Lamphouse

Take-up platter

Projection console

Feed-out platter

Drive motor

Return film

Auxiliary platter

SEE ALSO: CAM • HALOGEN • LENS • MIRROR • MOVIE CAMERA • SERVOMECHANISM • SOLENOID

Propeller

Aircraft propellers and marine propellers operate according to the same principles: they both consist of a number of angled blades attached to a central rotating hub. The rotation of the blades produces thrust, but in order to give useful thrust in air (which has a density about 1/800 that of water), the size and speed of an aircraft propeller must be considerably greater than that of a marine propeller.

Aircraft propeller

A typical aircraft propeller may have three blades, each about 4 ft. (1.2 m) long, that rotate at about 1,500 rpm. The blades have an airfoil section, similar to that in aircraft wings, and the thrust is produced by the lift effect given by the passage of the blade through the air. Components of both thrust (lift) and drag are present, and in order to give high thrust and low drag, both the airfoil section and the angle of attack have to be carefully designed. The angle of attack is the angle at which the blade cuts into the airstream and is affected by two factors: the speed of the aircraft through the air and the speed of rotation of the blade.

Unlike aircraft wings, all parts of the surface of a propeller do not travel at the same speed; the outer areas move much faster than those near the hub. Blades are made with a characteristic twist and tapering airfoil section to compensate for the speed differences along their lengths.

Small, single-engined aircraft generally have fixed-pitch propellers, and their speed is controlled by varying the engine speed. Larger aircraft, however, usually need variable-pitch propellers to match the demands put on them by aircraft speed, altitude, and engine speed.

Large aircraft generally have over 100 degrees of pitch control. At one extreme, the blades are edge-on into the airstream (that is, feathered), giving least drag if, for example, an engine should fail. Coarse pitch is used for higher speeds and altitudes, fine pitch for takeoff, disking (zero thrust), windmilling, and finally, reverse thrust to assist braking. The control may be purely mechanical (by cams and levers), electromechanical, or electrohydraulic.

Thrust and balance

The physical and aerodynamic features of the blades are closely related. For example, if the diameter of the propeller is increased, the speed of rotation must often be decreased—otherwise the tips of the blades may cut the air at supersonic speeds, with undesirable effects. Supersonic propellers are used, but their efficiency is generally poor, and they make a whining sound, often heard from light-aircraft propellers during takeoff.

The mechanical loads on the blades are due to direct centrifugal force and also, because of the twist along their lengths, to a centrifugal twisting moment (CTM). Similarly, the aerodynamic loads are due to thrust and to an aerodynamic twisting moment (ATM). The complete propeller must therefore be balanced dynamically and aerodynamically. Weights are built into the hub to counterbalance both conditions. In addition, the

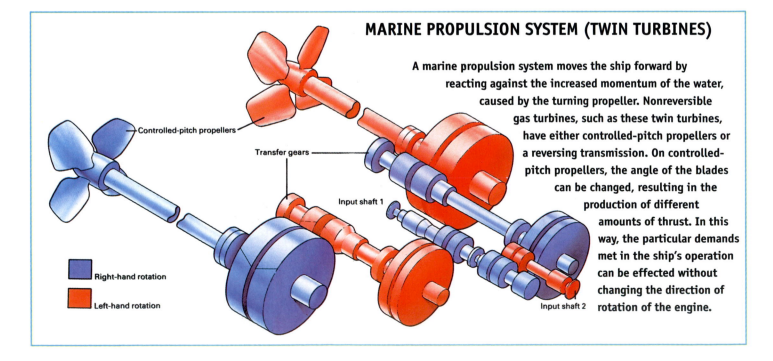

MARINE PROPULSION SYSTEM (TWIN TURBINES)

A marine propulsion system moves the ship forward by reacting against the increased momentum of the water, caused by the turning propeller. Nonreversible gas turbines, such as these twin turbines, have either controlled-pitch propellers or a reversing transmission. On controlled-pitch propellers, the angle of the blades can be changed, resulting in the production of different amounts of thrust. In this way, the particular demands met in the ship's operation can be effected without changing the direction of rotation of the engine.

Controlled-pitch propellers

Transfer gears

Input shaft 1

Input shaft 2

Right-hand rotation

Left-hand rotation

aerodynamic angle of each blade is trimmed to within a few seconds of arc to compensate for manufacturing tolerances.

Materials

The first blades were made from solid hardwood, and they were followed by the laminated wood blades, that are still in use for both airplanes and helicopters. Most modern blades are made from cast or forged alloys, although other materials in current use include fabricated sheet steel blades with a honeycomb inner structure and several types of plastic materials.

A variety of protective coatings are used, particularly along the leading edge, and although the drag creates a lot of heat, electric deicing elements are frequently fitted along the leading edge of the blade.

Marine propeller

The marine propeller has been employed in the propulsion of ships since about 1850. In its various forms, the propeller remains the most efficient instrument for converting the power developed by a ship's machinery into the necessary thrust to push the ship through the water.

The propeller works by accelerating the water passing through it, exerting a forward thrust by the reaction from the increase in momentum of the accelerated flow. This momentum increase is achieved by giving either a low increase in speed to a large mass of water (large, slow-running propellers) or a high increase in speed to a small mass of water (small, fast-running propellers). The former represents the most efficient means of propulsion; the latter corresponds to what is commonly understood as jet propulsion.

The flow of water into the propeller is very significantly affected by the shape of the hull immediately ahead of it. In moving forward, the ship drags along some of the surrounding water so that the relative speed of advance of the propeller through the water is actually less than the ship's speed. This field of flow affected by the ship is called the wake field.

In addition, the axial speed of the water varies across the propeller disk so that each rotating blade alternately passes through regions of high- and low-speed water. In general, when the blade is in the top of the aperture (at the 12 o'clock position), the relative water speed is at its lowest, and when the blade is in the bottom of the aperture, the water speed is at its highest. As a result, the forces developed by the blades are cyclic in nature, fluctuating about the mean value and giving rise to problems with vibration, strength, and cavitation.

Cavitation

A propeller blade acts in a way similar to an aircraft wing in that a section through a blade has an airfoil shape. The passage of the water sets up a pressure reduction on the forward side of the blades and a pressure increase on the aft side of the blades. The largest contribution to the propeller thrust comes from the pressure reduction, and if the pressure at any point falls to the pressure at which water vaporizes, cavities of vapor are created in the water. This phenomenon is termed cavitation and can be harmful to the efficient operation of the propeller. The subsequent collapse of the cavities can cause noise, erosion of the blade surfaces, and increased vibration.

The risk of cavitation is the main reason that a marine propeller differs from its airscrew equivalent in that it has much wider blades. A wide blade helps to restrict the level of the pressure reduction and thus reduce the amount of cavitation. Nevertheless, because of the variations in water speed into the propeller, it is often impossible to eliminate it completely.

Types of marine propellers

All types of propellers operate on the same basic principle of accelerating the water behind the ship. The conventional propeller is a single-piece casting with two or more blades (commonly four to six) designed specifically to operate at best efficiency under the ship's normal operating conditions. Considerable effort is made to machine and finish these usually nonferrous castings to the high degree of accuracy that is required.

The controllable pitch propeller has its blades mounted separately on the hub so that, if different levels of thrust are required, the propellers can be swiveled by a mechanism inside the hub.

The ducted propeller is either a conventional or a controllable pitch propeller fitted inside a nozzle. Because of its airfoil shape, the nozzle helps to accelerate the water flow into the propeller as well as producing a certain amount of thrust itself. This type of propeller has proved very efficient in special applications, such as tugs and trawlers, and is now being used on large bulk carriers.

▲ This propeller plane is used to ferry cargo, such as large aircraft components. If the ability to lift heavy or bulky loads is more important than speed, as in this case, propellers are more economical than jet engines. Large aircraft such as these require powerful engines and, as engine powers increase, greater thrust is achieved by increasing the number of blades up to as many as five. The chord (blade width) may also be increased. In practice, increasing the number or size of blades gives diminishing returns owing to increased weight and poor acceleration.

SEE ALSO: AERODYNAMICS • AIRCRAFT DESIGN • AIRCRAFT ENGINE • HYDRODYNAMICS • MARINE PROPULSION • OUTBOARD MOTOR

Protective Clothing

◄ Protective clothing is not only worn to protect people against harm from their environment—it is also used in manufacturing to prevent items such as silicon chips from becoming contaminated. Clean-room clothing is made from materials that do not shed fibers or allow particles of skin or hair to pass through the fabric.

Protective clothing is necessary in a wide variety of different situations to protect against injury caused, for example, by fire, chemicals, insect bites, and offensive weapons. Protective clothing is worn by people working in the armed forces, law enforcement agencies, and a variety of different industries, such as chemical and manufacturing industries, as well as people practicing dangerous sports, such as motor racing, ice hockey, and boxing.

Some of the earliest forms of protective clothing include body armor, such as helmets and shields. Some of the earliest examples include helmets made of rhinoceros skin, used by Chinese warriors in the 11th century B.C.E., and helmets made of beaten copper, which were in use by 3000 B.C.E. in Sumeria. The medieval period saw the development of full body armor to protect every vulnerable surface from attack. Other early forms of protective clothing include the gloves worn by blacksmiths to prevent burns and also the gloves worn in falconry to avoid being cut by the falcons' talons.

The development of new forms of protective clothing received much impetus from the Industrial Revolution. Factories using chemicals or heavy equipment are potentially dangerous environments, and so new types of clothing were devised in response to these new requirements. The improvement of firefighting techniques dur-ing the 19th century also led to the development of fire-resistant clothing. More recent developments include clothes designed to protect the armed forces from the effects of chemical weapons, the space suits worn by astronauts, and the protective clothing worn by people working in the nuclear industries.

Materials

Apart from natural materials such as rubber and leather, many of the materials used in protective clothing are synthetic. Nomex, for example, is an aramid fiber that is resistant to high temperatures, and it is therefore useful in firefighting applications. Tyvek is made of submicron denier high-density polyethylene filaments that are formed into a nonwoven structure that provides breathability while still forming a barrier to fiberglass, asbestos, pesticides, and radioactive dust. Kevlar is another aramid fiber that is extremely strong and resistant to heat and is commonly made into bulletproof vests. Indura is a form of cotton that is treated with phosphorus-based chemicals, making it resistant to flame. Many materials, including Rayon and Kevlar fiber, can be aluminized to give protection against radiant heat. Natural materials can also be altered in various ways to improve their protective qualities. Leather, for example, may be specially tanned and treated to reduce the tendency to harden when in contact with extreme heat.

In applications where water resistance and thermal insulation are required, Gore-Tex may be used in combination with Thinsulate to provide these qualities. Gore-Tex consists of a thin membrane of microporous polytetrafluoroethylene, which allows water vapor, but not water droplets, to pass through. Gore-Tex is waterproof and windproof but still breathes freely. Thinsulate is made of a dense layer of microfibers that traps air, forming a layer of insulation. A layer of Thinsulate provides up to twice the level of insulation as the same thickness of down.

Protective clothing in industry

The many dangers resulting from the manufacture and use of strong chemicals require workers to protect themselves using overalls that may be made of rubberlike synthetics or other chemical-resistant materials. In situations where serious contamination is likely, such as in the pesticide industry, disposable overalls may be used. Other items of clothing, such as hats and gloves, must be made in such a way that they do not absorb chem-icals. Therefore, gloves should not contain fabric lining, and hats must be made of plastics or other nonabsorbant materials. Again, disposable items may be used, but where nondisposable gloves are used, it is necessary to wash the gloves thoroughly before removing them. Boots may be designed to protect against chemicals or crushing by heavy objects—steel toecaps are common in heavy industry and in the construction industries. Where there is a danger of inhaling poisonous gases, masks with respirators that filter the air must be worn. In situations where splashing of irritant chemicals is possible, goggles must be worn to protect the eyes. Goggles or face shields must also be worn to protect against splinters of flying debris or particles of molten metal, such as might be found in the steelmaking industry.

Fishing and diving

The sou'wester is a hat originally made of oilskin and used by people in the fishing industry to protect against driving rain at sea. These hats are recognizable by their broad brim and the long back

▼ A racing driver, protected by his fireproof suit and inner helmet, makes last-minute checks just before a Grand Prix.

that protects the neck. Today these hats are usually made of synthetic materials, as are other articles of clothing called oilskins that are worn at sea. Oilskin overalls are now available with an integral slimline lifejacket. This feature is especially useful since bulky lifejackets are often donned only in very rough weather and statistics show that most drownings occur in rather mild conditions.

The first diving suit was invented in 1819 by a German inventor, August Siebe. It consisted of a copper helmet attached to a suit made of canvas and leather. The helmet contained glass portholes and was connected to the surface via a tube that pumped air into the helmet. The pressure of the air prevented water from entering the helmet as well as providing the diver with air to breathe. This simple design has since developed into complex articulated metal suits used in deep sea conditions. Because the diver is completely protected from the huge pressures of the water outside the suit, it is not necessary to undergo the complex and slow procedure of decompression carried out by scuba divers.

Divers lose body heat 60 times more quickly underwater than on land, so rubber suits are worn to insulate the diver from heat loss. In warm waters, divers wear wet suits made of neoprene, which traps a layer of water between the diver and the suit. This layer is warmed by the diver's body and then acts as an insulator. In colder conditions, a dry suit is used that is completely waterproof. In very cold conditions, added insulating materials may be worn under the suit.

Space suits

Astronauts must be protected against the extreme conditions found in space, such as high levels of radiation from cosmic rays, zero air pressure, and

◀ This diver's wet suit, made from foam neoprene, effectively protects him from the cold.

▼ These workers in a bronze factory have to wear special clothing to protect them from the heat and any splashes of molten metal. Their suits are made of Proban, which is a specially-treated cotton. Unlike materials made from synthetic fiber or synthetic and cotton blends, cotton does not melt away to form a hole through which the flame or molten metal can penetrate, nor does it melt to form a residue that sticks to the skin of the wearer.

micrometeoroids—small pieces of microscopic debris traveling at high speed. Space suits are therefore internally pressurized and are made of materials that block radiation and that are resistant to damage by micrometeoroids.

The current space suit used by astronauts in the space shuttle is called the Extravehicular Mobility Unit (EMU). This suit is designed to be used for space walks and is made from a wide variety of protective materials, including Gore-Tex, Nomex, Nylon tricot, and Kevlar.

Sports clothing

Participants in many sports can avoid serious injury through the use of protective clothing, much of which today takes advantage of the latest plastics and fiberglass technology.

Items of protection that are general to many sports include mouth guards and helmets. Mouth guards are valuable in that they reduce intercranial pressure after a strong blow to the chin. Helmets, in addition to their obvious use in motorcycle and car racing, protect against skull deformation, intercranial pressure, and rotational motion, which can result in neck injuries.

Football players wear shoulder pads of double cantilever construction projecting some distance from the body and helmets with face guards. Helmets are of three different types—padded, air (or fluid), and suspension—and the face guard extends in front for more than 3 in. (7.5 cm).

Basketball players wear protective knee pads and lightly padded shorts to protect the ileum (the highly vulnerable lower part of the small intestine) from injury. In baseball, by contrast, it is generally only the catcher who is properly pro-

◄ The cold at high altitudes would kill these mountaineers if they were not wearing special lightweight suits. The suits are made of a mixture of down, Gore-Tex, and Thinsulate.

tected by means of face guard, chest guard, shin guards, and a padded glove on the catching hand.

In soccer, the shins are particularly vulnerable, and ankle injuries keep many players out of the game. The shoes are sometimes paired with separate ankle guards, worn under the socks. Shin guards of lightweight polystyrene with foam backing give some protection to the shinbone.

Some goalkeepers wear knee pads as well as the more familiar gloves. One of the new types of gloves has a palm surface that is textured like a table tennis bat to give an improved grip on the ball. Even more remarkable is an alternative enhanced-grip glove, made of suede with the palm surface sprayed with a tacky plastic coating. Although these gloves are very effective in dry conditions, they are virtually useless in the wet.

Ice hockey and boxing

An ice hockey goalkeeper wears padded shorts, a knee-length sandwich of nylon-foam-plastic-foam-nylon; goalies' "sleeves" (a one-piece foam and nylon garment covering both arms and the collar-bones); a body pad (a nylon-covered rubber breastplate overlapping the goalies' sleeves); leg pads made of 4 in. (10 cm) thick stuffed leather stretching wide on either side of the leg; a hard plastic groin cup with extra rubber reinforcement; a catching glove (padded leather with a gauntlet stretching up the forearm); a stick glove with a pad nearly 2 in. (5 cm) thick on the back for blocking the puck; a foam-lined plastic helmet with an integral wire mask set well away from the face; long socks (anchored to a suspender belt); and skates covered by an unbreakable plastic shell, padded to protect the ankles. Finally, inside the skating boot itself, there is a removable foam rubber liner.

In contrast, boxers wear little protective clothing. Boxers' gloves, however, are well padded and not only protect the hands but soften the impact of a blow. Fighting gloves weigh 8 oz. (230 g) for welter- to heavyweights and 6 oz. (170 g) below welterweight. The boxer's hands are also bandaged beneath the gloves during a fight. Heavier, more padded gloves are used for sparring. Gum shields protect the teeth and gums by reducing the impact from punches and head clashes and padded head guards are worn during training.

SEE ALSO: ARMOR • CHEMICAL AND BIOLOGICAL WARFARE • DIVING SUIT • FIBER, SYNTHETIC • FIREFIGHTING • POLYAMIDE • RUBBER, NATURAL • RUBBER, SYNTHETIC • SPORTS EQUIPMENT

Protein

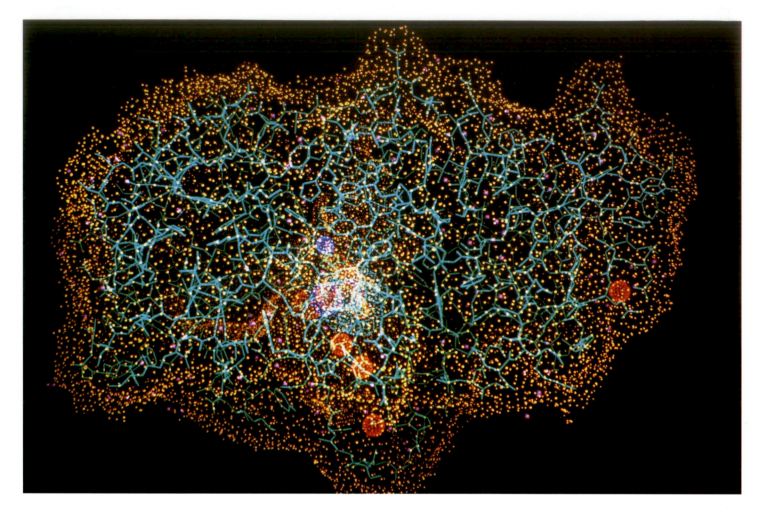

Proteins are major constituents of all living organisms, from the single-celled bacterium and the submicroscopic virus to complex animals like ourselves. There are thousands of different proteins known to exist, and an advanced animal or plant may be capable of producing as many as 10,000 distinct protein types during its lifetime. Biochemically, proteins are large molecules that are formed by the biological polymerization of amino acids. Each protein produced has a specific structure and a particular function, and proteins by their action enable the living cell to grow and perform all the activities necessary for its survival.

Structure

A protein consists of one or more chains of amino acids linked together by means of peptide bonds, and each protein has a unique structure that is determined at the molecular level by the particular amino acids in the chain and their sequence. There are only 20 common amino acids, and all proteins are assembled from these basic building blocks. Plants are able to form all of the amino acids they need, but animals must obtain some of them from food. A peptide bond is formed as a

▲ A computer graphics representation of the protein thermolysin. This protein is an enzyme found in the bacteria *Bacillus thermoproteolyticus* and is responsible for hydrolizing specific peptide bonds.

result of a condensation reaction between the amino group, $-NH_2$, of one amino acid and the carboxylic acid group, $-COOH$, of another amino acid:

$$-COOH + -NH_2 \rightarrow -CO-NH- + H_2O$$

| carboxylic acid group | amino group | peptide bond | water |

Chains of amino acids linked together by means of peptide bonds are sometimes called polypeptides. The peptide bond is the only type of covalent bond found between amino acid units in proteins, apart from the disulfide bridge, $-S-S-$, which sometimes occurs between two units of the sulfur-containing amino acid cysteine, $HSCH_2CH(NH_2)-COOH$, to link together different parts of a protein chain. Weaker ionic and hydrogen bonds may also occur between atoms in the chain. It is the order, or sequence, in which the amino acids are arranged in the chain that confers three-dimensional structure, and therefore a particular function, on a given protein. Theoretically, the number of ways a polypeptide chain could fold up is enormous. However, X-ray crystallography has shown that, for a given protein, only one particular folded shape, or conformation, is preferred. Certain sequences seem to specify coils, or α-helices, or so-called β-pleated sheets, while others commonly produce sharp bends in the polypeptide chain. Most of the protein's structure is, however, unique to that particular molecule, and the mechanisms that stabilize these complex conformations are incompletely understood. One thing is certain, though, and that is that certain amino acids (the hydrophobic, or water-repelling, amino acids) prefer to be near the center of the protein molecule, and some amino acids (the hydrophilic, or water-attracting, amino acids) prefer the outside of the molecule. In all known protein structures, the polypeptide chain folds so that hydrophilic amino acids tend to be on the outside, while the center of the molecule forms a hydrophobic core. Two main types of protein—fibrous and globular—result from the chemical bonds linking the protein chains. Fibrous proteins form long chains that may run parallel to one another and are connected by cross-links. These types of protein are very stable and often physically strong. Globular proteins, as their name suggests, are folded in such a way that they form globules. These proteins have irregular amino acid sequences and are relatively unstable.

Functions

Most proteins serve either a purely structural role, or more important, they interact with other molecules to bring about all sorts of essential changes. Because of their strength, fibrous proteins are structural. Connective tissues, such as collagen, for example, are fibrous proteins. Enzymes, the very efficient catalysts whose job it is to speed up the different chemical reactions that constitute the metabolism of the cell, are principally globular proteins. Each distinct enzyme speeds up a particular type of chemical reaction. Some enzymes may work on only one substrate, while other may work on several. All enzymes, however, work by binding the substrates (the molecules to be reacted) in a pocket on the surface of the protein, called the active site. These substrates are bound in such a way that the products of the reaction form more easily than if the enzyme were absent. Enzymes commonly speed up chemical reactions by a factor of one million to one trillion times. Without enzymes, many chemical reactions would be so slow that life would not be possible.

Other proteins have the specificity of enzymes but do not necessarily bring about straightforward chemical changes. For example, the two muscle proteins actin and myosin interact to produce a rapid shortening in their length and thus form the basis of animal movement. Hemoglobin in the blood specifically carries oxygen, and some proteins, for example, the cytochromes, carry electrons from one specific donor to an acceptor. This process of electron transport to other enzyme systems forms an important method of storing and releasing chemical energy. Antibodies are blood proteins that form chemical complexes with foreign compounds in the body, thus enabling us to protect ourselves against disease.

Uses of proteins

Although protein in one form or another, for example, wool or leather, has been used for centuries as something other than just a food source, the use of the chemical specificity of pure proteins has become possible only relatively recently. Enzymes that degrade other proteins are now added to detergents to increase their efficiency. Enzymes are employed for large-scale synthesis in the chemical and pharmaceutical industries, and "enzyme reactors" have been designed for energy production. In the medical field, protein

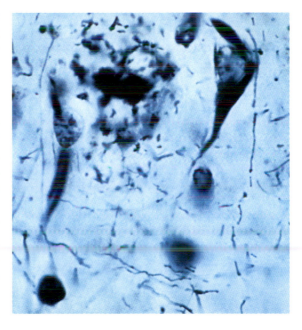

◄ An abnormal tangle of protein fibers can be detected in and around the brain cells of a patient suffering from Alzheimer's disease, which causes progressive senility.

► A particle of a protein food spun from a soybean base. The soybean is one of the best and cheapest sources of protein, containing about 4 percent crude protein—twice as much as beef or fish—and more soybeans are grown by farmers in the United States, with the exception of corn and wheat, than any other cultivated crop.

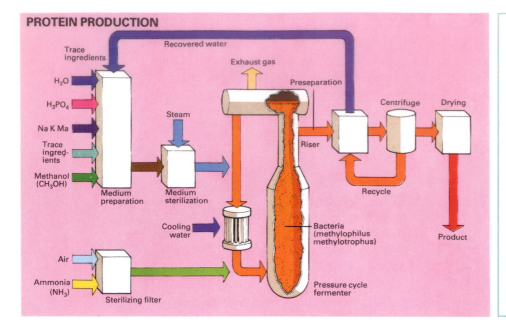

PROTEIN PRODUCTION

Trace ingredients
Recovered water
Exhaust gas
Preseparation
H_2O
H_3PO_4
Na K Ma
Trace ingredients
Methanol (CH_3OH)
Steam
Centrifuge
Drying
Riser
Medium preparation
Medium sterilization
Recycle
Cooling water
Product
Bacteria (methylophilus methylotrophus)
Air
Ammonia (NH_3)
Sterilizing filter
Pressure cycle fermenter

AMINO ACIDS

Amino acids are made of a basic amino group ($-NH_2$), a carboxylic acid group ($-COOH$), and an organic group (R) that is different in each type of amino acid. Proteins contain up to 20 different kinds of amino acids. Plants are capable of manufacturing all of these, but animals must obtain some of them from food. Those that humans must obtain from their diet are called essential amino acids and include the following: lysine, phenylalanine, leucine, theonine, tryptophan, isoleucine, methionine, and valine.

chemistry has already had a considerable impact. Many people suffer from incurable diseases because they are unable to make a certain type of protein; diabetics, for example, cannot produce insulin. By producing these proteins on a large scale and treating people with them, the deficiency can be remedied completely. A treatment for leukemia depends on the intravenous injection of the enzyme asparaginase. Certain diseases are treated by the injection of antibodies or antiserum derived from other animals, which neutralizes the virulent agent by forming chemical complexes.

▲ Fermentation, familiar for thousands of years as the process that turns grapes into wine, is now a leading target of biotechnology research. It can yield bacterial protein as an end product when yeasts grown on methanol pass through an oxygen-rich fermenter vessel. After drying, a protein-rich animal food results.

FACT FILE

■ *Injuries such as burns, traumas, and infections cause acute-phase proteins in the body to multiply significantly. They are one of the most important elements in our blood. C-reactive protein, for instance, has survived hundreds of millions of years of evolution. It is synthesized by the liver and increases up to 1,000 times in higher vertebrates when they are injured.*

■ *Complex computer graphics of protein molecular structures are delivering new information on proteins. Color coding of certain residues, for instance, can reveal the pH of the protein's normal environment by indicating a dominant color shading. Consecutive molecular graphics also show movements, such as the waving action of some molecular chains.*

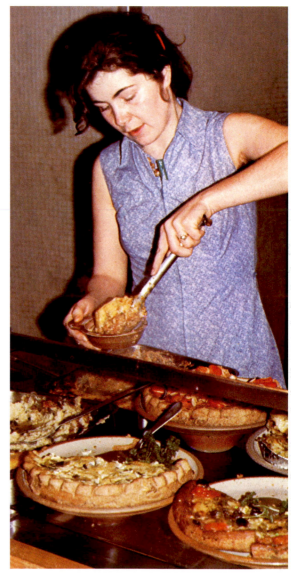

▶ Protein is vital for the growth and repair of the human body. The main food sources include meat, fish, eggs, cheese, and milk. In a vegetarian diet, a complete protein may be obtained from combining two or more foods with incomplete proteins, beans and rice, for example.

 SEE ALSO: AMINO ACID • BIOCHEMISTRY • ENZYME • FAT • METABOLISM • NUTRITION AND FOOD SCIENCE • VITAMIN

Psychiatry

Psychiatry is a branch of medicine concerned with mental health and disorders of the human mind. One of its pioneers was the Austrian neurologist Sigmund Freud, who in the late-19th and early-20th centuries developed psychoanalysis as a treatment for mental disorders. Freud proposed that many such conditions were rooted in traumatic events experienced by individuals. He and his followers used techniques such as hypnosis and word association as tools in identifying life crises obscured to the conscious mind but fundamental to its lack of well-being. Psychoanalysts still use Freud's techniques to bring the underlying causes of mental distress into the conscious mind of the patient, with the intention of making it more easy to resolve.

During the 20th century, increasing attention was paid to the biochemical processes that occur in a healthy human brain and the psychological disturbances that occur when these processes go wrong. With this understanding and advances in pharmacology, it became possible to use drugs to treat many types of psychological disorders.

Psychoactive drugs are not always free from side effects, however, and many patients prefer to follow a psychoanalytic approach rather than use drug therapy. In recent years, the tendency has been to combine increasingly specific drug therapies, using medications that have slight or insignificant side effects, with counselling.

Diagnosis

A complicating factor in psychiatry is that no physical changes need be present, and diagnosis must be made on the basis of changes in behavior or mood or differences from accepted behavioral norms. Such changes are prone to being judged subjectively—according to the preconceptions of the person performing the diagnosis—and in the past, many mental disorders were grouped together inappropriately or simply overlooked.

Since 1952, the American Psychiatric Association has published the *Diagnostic and Statistical Manual of Mental Disorders*—known as the *DSM*—as an aid in identifying specific disorders in patients. The *DSM* is now in the text revision of its fourth version—*DSM-IV-TR*, published in 2000. For each definition of a disorder, the *DSM* has strict diagnostic criteria—often including measures of the severity and frequency of episodes of the disorder. These criteria are a great help in diagnosis, in comparing the efficacies of different treatment regimes on a well characterized condition, and in studying its prevalence.

◀ Thomas Sutherland (left) was released from years of captivity in Lebanon in 1991. In common with the other released hostages, he was treated for post-traumatic stress disorder, which often follows long after stressful experiences.

New disorders

One advantage of the *DSM* approach to classifying mental illness is that many new disorders have come to light. Such disorders may have blighted people's lives for years, but the creation of closely defined diagnoses for them provides a reference point for research into new treatments.

One such condition is post-traumatic stress disorder (PTSD): a collection of anxiety-related symptoms brought on by a psychologically distressing event outside the normal range of human experience. Trigger events include being held hostage, raped, tortured, and held in a death camp and being present at a major fire or conflict. In some cases, the symptoms appear long after the trigger event. Since many of these occurrences have occurred throughout human history, it is likely that countless individuals have suffered PTSD without ever understanding their condition.

Some conditions are at least partly attributable to recent changes in society. Bulimia nervosa is one such condition, consisting of regular eating binges (at least twice a week) counteracted by exercise, vomiting, and the taking of purgatives in an attempt to maintain the sufferer's perception of "normal" weight. Some experts believe that the fashion industry has contributed to the increasing incidence of bulimia nervosa in recent decades by its preoccupation with underweight models, which can distort a susceptible person's perception of what ideal weight should be.

Somatoform disorder is becoming increasingly common. It consists of multiple physical symptoms and complaints without any apparent physical basis in apparently healthy people who may be genuinely disabled by their symptoms. Although chronic fatigue syndrome has become increasingly prevalent since the mid-1980s, psychiatrists have observed that patients suffering from somatoform disorder and chronic fatigue tend to refuse psychiatric help in the belief that a psychiatric diagnosis would cause their complaint to be dismissed as "all in the mind."

Not all forms of mental disorder are increasing: schizophrenia, for example, is decreasing in incidence. This seems to be a real phenomenon, and not just a changing fashion in diagnosis. Hysteria—neurological symptoms without neurological cause, often after trauma—has decreased considerably over several decades.

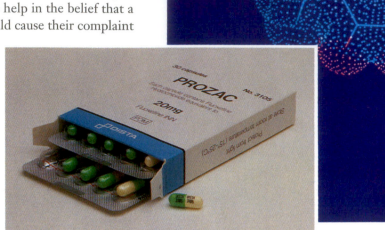

New drug treatments

The treatment of depression and anxiety is a notable example of how improved drugs have contributed to better therapy and quality of life for sufferers of mental disorders. Until the 1970s, the only treatment available for severe depression was electroconvulsive therapy (ECT)—seizures of the body induced by passing an electrical current through the brain. It is believed that ECT is so effective because it boosts the brain's levels of monoamines, such as seratonin—a neurotransmitter responsible for a feeling of well-being.

In the 1970s, low monoamine levels started to be treated using a class of drugs called monoamine oxidase inhibitors (MAOIs). They worked by blocking the action of monoamine oxidase, an enzyme that destroys monoamines. However, MAOIs interact with some other drugs and a variety of foods, including cheese and yeast extract, causing, in high doses, blackouts.

In the 1980s, MAOIs were replaced by tricyclic antidepressants, which cause a dry mouth and other minor side effects but did not interact with foods. Since the late 1980s, the tricyclics have also been superseded by selective seratonin-reuptake inhibitors (SSRIs). This class of drugs includes fluoxetine (Prozac) and fluvoxamine (Faverin). Like MAOIs and tricyclics, they act by boosting seratonin levels, but their side effects are milder than those of tricyclics. The SSRIs have also been found to be useful in the treatment of panic attacks and obsessive–compulsive disorder (OCD), irrational repetitive behavior.

▲ Fluoxetine, sold under the trade name Prozac, is an example of an SSRI (selective seratonin-reuptake inhibitor). This class of drugs has greatly helped sufferers of anxiety, depression, and obsessive-compulsive disorder since its introduction in the 1980s. The shape of the fluoxetine molecule, shown at top right, is the key to its interaction with receptors in the brain.

Some new psychoactive drugs have unprecedented therapeutic potency, but they are also more liable to cause side effects. Clozapine, for example, relieves the symptoms of schizophrenia in many patients who do not respond to other drugs or cannot tolerate them. However, it can cause destruction of white blood cells, and patients who take it must first undergo weekly blood tests to determine their extent of susceptibility to this particular side effect.

Behavior therapy

An important advance in therapy that does not rely on drugs has been the development of cognitive behavior therapy. It is a form of self-help given under the supervision of psychiatrists and psychologists. Its popularity is due to its relative low costs, long-term effectiveness and speed, and absence of drug-induced side effects.

Cognitive therapy combines behavioral retraining with a form of reinterpreting thoughts. For example, people who suffer from chronic fatigue typically avoid exercise because it makes them feel worse. For this reason, their physical fitness may deteriorate as they avoid exercise, and their decline continues. A cognitive therapist breaks this cycle by showing that much of their fatigue is due to lack of exercise. A small effort brings symptoms back, but daily exercise soon becomes tolerable and then causes marked improvements in health, revealing the link between fatigue and lack of fitness.

SEE ALSO: BRAIN • ELECTRONICS IN MEDICINE • MEDICINE • PHARMACEUTICALS • PHARMACOLOGY

Pulley

The origins of the pulley are not precisely known, but it was in use in Greece some time between the sixth and fourth centuries B.C.E. Basically a pulley is a wheel, the periphery of which may be flat to take a belt, may have a V groove to take a V belt, or may have a U groove to take a rope. The principle is that a belt is wrapped around the pulley tightly, and the friction forces between the two allow a drive to be established.

Pulleys can be divided into two broad categories: drive pulleys, which transfer power between two shafts via a belt, and pulleys that change the direction of or magnify a force, as in the case of a block and tackle.

Drive pulleys

In the transfer of power, a belt system has certain distinct advantages over other methods. If the driving and driven shafts are physically far apart, a belt and pulley system provides the most economic form of coupling. Furthermore, it has an inbuilt power limit, as the belt merely starts slipping under overload conditions. The disadvantage is that accurate speeds are impossible to achieve. The elasticity of the belt precludes this and there is no positive interlock, as there is, for example, between two gears.

A belt tends to travel faster than its drive pulley by up to 2 percent, owing to the change in the belt tension going around the pulley, giving rise to a phenomenon known as creep. The maximum speed at which belts can be driven are limited to about 5,000 ft. per sec. (1,524 m/s) for normal materials, as above this speed, the very large centrifugal forces generated jeopardize the integrity of the belt itself. The flat belt has now been largely superseded by the V belt because not only does the latter take up less space, but it can also be made considerably stronger and therefore able to transmit much more power. The fan belt of a car engine is a common example of a V belt.

One of the modern developments in pulley design has been to use them in conjunction with toothed belts to provide a positive interlock. Such a system overcomes one of the main disadvantages of the belt and pulley, namely the lack of an accurate phase (timing) and speed relationship between two shafts.

Lifting pulleys

A pulley and rope can be used to change the direction of an available force, or when force magnification is required, pulleys can be compounded into the configuration known as a block

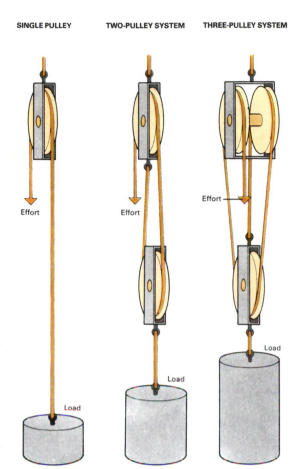

SINGLE PULLEY   TWO-PULLEY SYSTEM   THREE-PULLEY SYSTEM

Effort

Effort

Effort

Load

Load

Load

◀ Three simple sets of pulleys. The drive pulley turns at a speed relative to the size of the driven pulley. Altering their relative sizes would give an increase or reduction in the speed of the driven pulley. For example, if the drive pulley had twice the diameter of the driven pulley, the speed of the latter would be twice that of the former. Similarly, increasing the number of pulleys increases the lifting force the pulley can exert on an object. In practice, however, it is very rarely worth compounding the block and tackle beyond three pulleys in each case, as above this number, the force magnification starts to decrease. The limit is a theoretical magnification of six, which in practice is reduced 10 to 15 percent by friction. The magnification ratio (load divided by effort) is normally termed the mechanical advantage.

and tackle, which consists of a fixed part and a moving part. The fixed part contains a set of two or three pulleys freewheeling on a shaft that is carried in a cage. The moving part of the tackle consists of another set of pulleys on a shaft, mounted in a cage to which is attached a lifting hook. The rope then runs from the hand, around each fixed pulley and moving pulley in turn, and the other end is attached to the cage of either half of the tackle.

In the case of a block and tackle consisting of three pulleys, when an object is attached to the hook the weight of that object is shared between the four pieces of rope joining the two halves of the tackle. If we ignore friction, the tension throughout the rope must be the same and equal to a quarter of the imposed load. Thus, the part of the rope in the hand must be pulled with a force (the effort) equal to at least a quarter of the load in order to lift it, and the device has multiplied the force available by four.

SEE ALSO: CRANE • ENERGY, MASS, AND WEIGHT • FRICTION

Pyramid

◀ The Great Pyramid of Cheops, on the plateau of Giza, near Cairo, is a royal burial chamber built by King Cheops in the 26th century B.C.E.

Egyptian pyramids were the dominant features in complexes of buildings intended to serve the needs of important persons after death. They are of two kinds: step pyramids, in which all four sides are built in steps from the base to the summit, and true pyramids, in which the sides slope continuously (normally at an angle of about 52 degrees) from bottom to top. Step pyramids are the older: the first was built for King Zoser of the Third Dynasty (ca. 2660 B.C.E.) under the direction of his famous architect Imhotep. True pyramids superseded step pyramids at the beginning of the Fourth Dynasty (ca. 2600 B.C.E.), and the main period of pyramid building lasted for around another 500 years. Over 70 different pyramids have been identified, though many of them are in a ruinous condition.

Site preparation in Egypt

Four important considerations governed the choice of a site for building a pyramid. It had to be located near the royal residence, on the west side of the Nile, out of reach of the annual flooding, and at a place where the rock was firm and fairly level. Surface irregularities were probably removed by a laborious process that consisted of

erecting a low wall around the perimeter of the site, flooding the whole of the enclosure thus formed to a depth of a few inches, and cutting a network of trenches with their floors at an even depth beneath the surface of the water. The wall

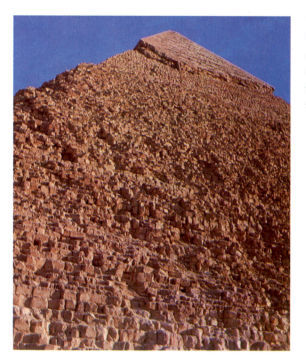

◀ The pyramid of Chephren at Giza. Although stripped of its outer covering, some of the Tura limestone mantle is still visible.

would then be dismantled, releasing most of the water immediately, and the remainder would soon evaporate. Last, the uncut rock within the network would be reduced to the level of the floors of the trenches. In the Great Pyramid, apparently an exception, a knoll of rock in the center of the site was left standing and eventually embodied in the building. Nevertheless, the rest of the bed of the pyramid deviates from a perfectly level plane by little more than half an inch.

Orientation

Immense care was taken to orientate the pyramid so that each side would directly face one of the four cardinal points. This end was probably achieved by sighting the rising and setting points of a star using a rod mounted vertically and an artificial horizon formed by a circular or semicircular wall leveled at the top. A line drawn to the rod from the midpoint between those two positions would run directly north–south. The east–west axis could easily have been determined by using a set-square, an instrument that the ancient Egyptians are known to have possessed. Recent research has suggested that the alignment could also have been achieved by using a plumb line and two opposing stars, at 10 degrees either side of true north, to intersect it. The sight line to the horizon point directly below the plumb line would then point directly north.

Composition

Pyramids that are sufficiently damaged to enable their composition to be examined show that the inner core was built in upright layers around a central nucleus. Each layer in a true pyramid normally consisted of horizontal courses of local stone faced with an outer skin of fine quality limestone obtained from the quarries at Tura in the Maqattam Hills, on the east side of the Nile opposite Giza and Saqqara. The outer sides of the nucleus and of the surrounding layers inclined inward at an angle of 75 degrees and thereby greatly reduced the risk of any tendency from the weight of masonry for outward pressure. Nothing was done to smooth the inner and the outer surfaces of the blocks of Tura limestone used in the core.

Chambers and corridors, if they were located in the superstructure, were built as the monument was being erected, and large objects, such as sarcophaghi (stone caskets), if they were of larger dimensions than the corridors, were placed in position before the roofs were built over the chambers. Subterranean corridors and chambers were tunneled in the rock before any masonry was laid.

◄ The grand gallery leading up to the king's chamber in the Great Pyramid of Giza. Why there should be chambers high in the structure as well as in the rock below is one of the unsolved mysteries of the pyramids.

At the same time as the construction of the core, whose upright layers diminished in height from the center outward and thus resembled a step pyramid, the whole pyramid was encased with an outer skin of Tura limestone. Each casing block was cut before laying to the pyramid angle of about 52 degrees. The Great Pyramid slopes at an angle of 51° 51′, an angle that would have resulted from a plan to make the height equal to the radius of a circle whose circumference was equal to the perimeter of the pyramid at the base. Egyptian mathematical texts provide no evidence for supposing that the true nature of π was understood—it is impossible to represent by a fraction. The last stone to be put in position, the capstone, was a miniature replica of the complete pyramid itself, generally made of granite and sometimes overlaid with gold. It was held firmly in place by a tenon projecting from its base, which fitted comfortably into a matching socket cut in the uppermost course of the masonry.

Handling the material

It has been estimated that the Great Pyramid consists of about 2.3 million limestone blocks of an average weight of 2½ tons (2.25 tonnes) and reaching a maximum of 15 tons (13.5 tonnes). In addition, much granite from Aswan, 500 miles (800 km) south of Giza, has been used in its interior; the nine slabs forming the ceiling of the king's chamber alone weigh nearly 45 tons (40.5 tonnes) each. A large number of these blocks were loaded on ships and brought to a quay near the site by river, and many of the blocks quarried locally also had to be moved on land to the pyramid.

Transport was by means of wooden sleds, pulled manually over temporary roadways paved with balks of timber. There is no positive evidence of the use of rollers, but it is possible that they were used both under sleds and under the blocks when they were not mounted on the sleds. Only one method of lifting stones in building was practiced by the ancient Egyptians before the introduction of the pulley in Roman times, and that was by hauling the block (on its sled) up a brick and earth ramp, the upper end of which leaned against the part of the building already finished. As the pyramid grew in height, the ramp would be raised and extended in length so that the same slope could be maintained. The other sides of the pyramid would have had brick embankments wide enough to allow the builders to stand on them and lay the outermost stones. One of the many striking features in the building of the pyramids is the perfection achieved in laying the stones of the outer casing. The British archaeologist Sir Flinders Petrie estimated that the mean thickness of the joints in the Great Pyramid was 0.02 in. (0.5 mm). Mortar was used mainly as a lubricant to maneuver the stones during laying.

Central American pyramids

Unlike Egyptian pyramids, Central American pyramids do not seem to have been built as funerary monuments; they were built as flat-topped platforms carrying temples, with steps running up. The pyramids consisted of a clay or sun-dried brick core faced with stone slabs and stucco.

Putting pyramid power to use

In the early 1940s, a French hardware dealer and practitioner of radiesthesia (divination by pendulum), Antoine Bovis, was visiting the Great Pyramid of Cheops at Giza, Egypt. Inside the royal chamber, in the center of the pyramid at exactly one-third the height of the pyramid from its base, he claimed to have spotted some small dead animals, completely mummified, with no sign of decomposition. He intuitively deduced that the pyramid shape was responsible. Ever since, the proponents of "pyramid power" have been trying to prove their strange proposal is true.

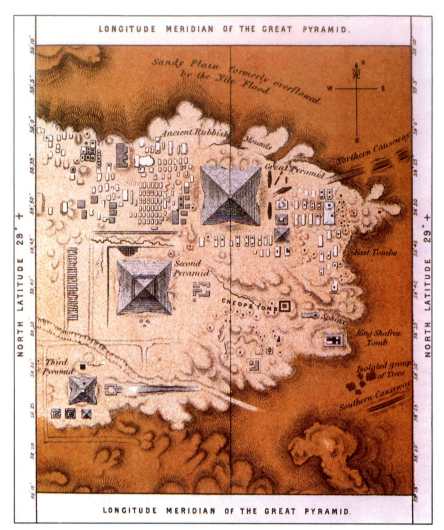

Attempts to mummify dead organic matter under small cardboard pyramids led researchers to believe there is a concentration of energy within the pyramid, focused at one-third its height.

A Czech radio engineer, Karl Drbal, is said to have conducted a series of experiments in which he placed a brand-new razor blade inside a 1:1,000 scale model of the Cheops pyramid at exactly one-third its height. He then aligned the pyramid in the same way as the original in Egypt and laid the razor blade longitudinally on a north-south axis. Drbal assumed that the energy concentrated at one-third the height of the pyramid would blunt the blade, but after getting 50 shaves from the razor, he was forced to accept the fact that exactly the opposite was happening.

This discovery led Drbal to apply for a patent from the Czech Patent Examination Commission in 1949. It took him ten years to persuade the commission, who eventually granted him Patent No. 91304 for his strange "device for maintaining the sharpness of razor blades and razors."

▲ At Giza, each main pyramid had subsidiary pyramids for the king's queens. Pyramids were situated on the west bank of the Nile, the side of the setting Sun, and as near to the water as possible. Most of the stone was transported along the river.

SEE ALSO: Building techniques • Pulley • Quarrying • Stone monument • Surveying

Index

Page numbers in **bold** refer to main articles; those in *italics* refer to picture captions.

A

ABS (acrylonitrile-butadiene-styrene) rubber 1772
accretion 1759
acid rain 1798
acids, poisoning from 1791
acrylamide (propenamide) 1771
acrylics 1771
acrylonitrile (propenonitrile) 1771
aerodynamic twisting moment (ATM) 1858
aircraft, pilotless **1747–8**
air hammers 1746
algae, uses of 1803
alkaloids *1790*
alternators *see* generators, alternating-current
aluminum, pipes and tubes 1751, 1752
Alzheimer's disease *1865*
amino acids 1864, 1866
ammonium dihydrogen phosphate (ADP) 1744–5
anesthetics, pressure measurement 1843
annealing *1786*
Antarctic, pollution monitoring *1800*
antidepressants 1868
aqua regia 1782
aramids 1805, 1806
Arctic, pollution monitoring *1800*
armor, body 1860
arms, reattachment 1765–6
asparginase 1866
assembly lines, hand tools 1789
asteroids *1761*
atropine 1792
autoclaves 1841
autogiros (gyroplanes), pilotless *1747*
automobiles
    catalytic converters 1782, 1802
    powder coatings *1823*

B

bacteria, and waste management 1802–3
bags, plastic 1774
Bakelite 1770, 1773
balloons *1839*
barbiturates, poisoning 1791
bar codes *1803*
barium titanate 1745
barometers 1840
bars 1839
baseball, equipment 1862
basketball, clothing 1862
bathrooms, plumbing *1787*
Bayer, Adolf von 1770
behavior therapy 1868
bellows 1843
benzoyl peroxide 1771, 1810
bezoar stones 1792
Bible, printing 1848
binoculars
    binocular microscopes *1743*
    prisms 1853
bioremediation 1802–3
birefringence 1794
bisphenol 1772
black smokers 1780
bleaches, ingested 1791
block and tackle 1869
blood
    circulation discovered 1733
    substitutes *1733*
blow molding, thermoplastic 1774–5
blowtorches *1786*

boiling water reactors (BWRs) 1832
bone, grafts *1766*
Bourdon gauges 1840, 1842
boxing, clothing 1863
brain, Alzheimer's disease *1865*
breasts, cosmetic surgery 1764–5
Brewster angle 1796
British Aerospace Harrier *1826*
Buna rubbers 1771
but-1-ene 1770
butadiene 1771

C

cables, power *1833*, 1836–7
cadmium, poisoning 1801
cancer 1767
    treatment 1783
capillary tubes, manufacture 1752
caprolactam 1804, 1811
carbon dioxide, from ice-cores *1800*
carbonic acid 1786
carbon monoxide, poisoning 1792
carbonyl chloride (phosgene) 1772
Carothers, Wallace 1804
catalytic converters 1782, 1802
cathodic protection 1754
cavitation 1745, 1859
Caxton, William 1848
cellophane 1769
Celluloid 1768
cellulose 1768–9
cement, pipes 1750
centrifugal twisting moment (CTM) 1858
ceramics, piezoelectric 1745
CFCs (chlorofluorocarbons) 1798
charcoal, activated 1791
Cheops, Great Pyramid of 1870, 1871–2
China, ancient, printing 1852
chlorofluorocarbons (CFCs) 1798
chloroform, poisoning 1791
chronic fatigue syndrome 1868
cinématographes 1854
circuit breakers (CBs) 1837
clavichords 1735
clay, pipes *1750*, 1751
clean-room technology, clothing 1860
cleft lip and palate 1766–7
climatology, global warming *1800*
clothing, protective 1806, **1860–3**
clozapine 1868
cognitive therapy 1868
combustion, flame-retarding agents 1771
compression molding 1775
computer graphics, of protein structure 1864, 1866
computer voice-stress analyzers (CVSAs) 1808
Concorde (aircraft) 1806
concrete 1750
condoms 1818
continental drift 1777
contraceptives 1818
control question tests (CQTs) 1808
converter matte *1781*
convulsants, poisoning 1791
cooperite (platinum sulfide) 1781
copal 1741, 1742–3
copolymers 1812
    vinyl acetate 1771
copper
    etched circuit boards 1845–6
    pipes 1751
        scale 1787

corrosion prevention, in pipelines 1754
cosmetic surgery 1764–5
cotton, flame-resistant *1862*
cracking, thermal 1776
craniofacial surgery 1767
C-reactive protein 1866
Crosfield Lasar Gravure 1852
crystals
    birefringence of 1794
    unit cells 1744
curare *1791*
Curie point 1745
cyanide poisoning 1792
cysteine 1864
cytochromes 1865

D

Dacron 1772
dammar 1741, 1742–3
Deep Sea Drilling Project 1777
dendrimers 1812
dentistry *1782*
dermabrasion 1767
diabetes, recent developments in research 1733–4
1,6-diaminohexane 1806
diamonds, diamond coatings 1763
diazepam (Valium) 1791
dichroism 1794–5
Digistar digital projectors 1756
diisooctyl phthalate (DOP) 1771
diving suits 1862
drawing (metalworking), tube 1751–2
drills, pneumatic *1788*, *1789*
drones, target 1747–8
drop hammers 1746
drought *1819*
DSM (Diagnostic and Statistical Manual of Mental Disorders) 1867
dyeing, plastics *1775*
dynamometers, Regnier's *1825*
dynamos 1827

E

Earth 1757
    age 1757–8
    light pollution *1803*
    source of water on 1761
earthquakes, plate tectonics and 1777, 1780
E. coli see Escherichia coli
ECT (electroconvulsive therapy) 1868
Eden Project *1768*
electroconvulsive therapy (ECT) 1868
electromechanical coupling constant 1744
electrostatic precipitators 1800
electrostatic spraying 1824
energy
    kinetic 1820
    pumped storage *1827*
energy breakeven 1763
enzymes, are catalysts 1865
epidemics 1816
erosion, tectonic 1778
Escherichia coli (E. coli) 1733
ethylene (ethene), polymerization 1810
Extravehicular Mobility Units (EMUs) 1862
extrusion
    pipes produced by 1752
    thermoplastic *1773*, 1774

eyes
    plastic surgery *1764*
    prosthetic 1767

F

fans *1745*
faults, geological, transform faults 1780
Faverin (fluvoxamine) 1868
fermentation, for protein production 1866
Fermilab, Tevatron particle accelerator 1763
fibers, synthetic, cellulose-derived 1768–9
fish, puffer fish poison 1792
fishing industry, clothing for 1861–2
fission, nuclear 1832
flame retarding agents 1771
flames and ignition 1745
fluids, pressure in 1839–40
fluvoxamine 1868
flying boats 1747
foam, plastic 1772, 1776
food, synthetic, from single-cell proteins 1866
football, clothing 1862
force(s) 1825
    pressure and 1839
forensic science, and poisons 1792
frequency 1745
frescoes 1743
Freud, Sigmund 1867
frogs, curare from *1791*
fuses and circuit breakers 1837
fusion, nuclear 1758, *1762–3*

G

galvanic skin response (GSR) 1807
galvanographs 1807
gases, and pressure 1840
gasoline, tetraethyl lead additive 1802
gastric lavage *1791*
gas turbines 1828, 1832, 1858
generators
    alternating current (alternators) 1827, 1829–30
    direct-current (dynamos) 1827
genetic engineering
    for blood substitutes *1733*
    for insulin 1733–4
    and transplants 1734
global positioning systems (GPSs) 1780
global warming *1800*
glucagon 1792
go devils (pigs) 1754
goggles, industrial 1861
Gore-Tex 1861, *1863*
GPSs *see* global positioning systems
graphics, computer *see* computer graphics
Great Pyramid of Cheops 1870, 1871–2
guitars, pickup 1739–40
gum shields 1863
Gutenberg, Johann 1847, 1848
gyroplanes *see* autogiros

H

halftone process 1850–1
hammers, riveting 1789
harpsichords 1735–6
Harvey, William 1733
helicopters 1748
helmets, sports 1862

hemoglobin 1865
  synthetic *1733*
hex-1-ene 1770
hi-fi systems 1739
hollow bar 1752
horsepower *1825*, 1826
hulls, Kevlar *1771*, *1804*
hydroelectric power (HEP) 1820, 1827
  pumped-storage schemes *1827*
hydrogen, isotopes 1763
hydrogenation 1782
hydrothermal vents 1780
Hyper-X hypersonic flight development program 1748
hypnotics, poisoning 1791
hysteria 1868

I

ice cores *1800*
ice hockey, clothing 1863
injection molding
  acrylic *1794*
  reaction (RIM) 1776
  thermoplastic *1773*, 1774
  for thermosets 1775
insulin, from genetic engineering 1733–4
integrated circuits (silicon chips; microchips), manufacture 1763
Intertype machines 1849
intrauterine devices (IUDs) 1818
ionization, of gases 1762–3
iridium 1781, 1782
iron and steel
  iron, pipes 1749
  steel
    austenitic 1830
    high-tensile 1749
    mild 1749
    pipes 1749, *1751*, 1753, 1754
isolators 1837
isomerism, polarimeters and 1793
isopentane 1776

J

jackhammers *1840*
jewelry, platinum and palladium 1783
joints (mechanical), in plumbing pipework 1786, 1787
Jupiter 1757, 1758, 1760

K

Kevlar 1805, 1806
  uses *1771*, *1804*, *1805*, 1806, 1860
Kuiper Belt 1761

L

Langerhans, islets of 1734
lasers
  used in printing *1850*, *1852*
  used for surgery 1767
Last Supper (da Vinci) 1741, 1742, 1743
lead, used in pipes 1751, 1787
lead zirconate titanate (PZT) 1745
leather 1806
Leeuwenhoek, Antonie van 1733
lenses
  anamorphic *1855*
  slide projector 1855
Leonardo da Vinci, Last Supper, restored 1741, 1742, 1743
leukemia, treatment 1866
LIDAR (light detection and ranging) 1797
lie detection 1807–8
life expectancy 1819
light
  pollution *1803*
  white 1853
limbs, reattachment 1765–6

Linotype machines 1849
liposuction 1767
lips, cleft lip and palate 1766–7
liquid crystal displays (LCDs) 1855
lithium-6, in stars 1761
lithography 1849–50, 1851–2
  offset *1847*, *1848*, 1850, 1852
  web offset 1850
  heat-set 1850
lithosphere 1777, 1778–9
liver transplants, from animals 1734
load 1825
Lumière, Auguste and Jean 1854

M

magic lanterns 1854
magnetism, Earth's 1777
magnifying mechanisms 1843
mannequins *1772*
Mannesmann process *1751*
manometers 1840
marine propulsion, propellers 1858, 1859
Mars 1757
mastic 1742–3
melamine-formaldehyde polymers 1773
mercuric chloride 1801
mercuric sulfate 1801
Mercury (planet) 1757
mercury (metal)
  toxicity 1801
  uses 1801
metals, heavy 1801
metalworking, tube drawing 1751–2
methacrylate esters 1771
methacrylic acid (2-methylpropenoic acid) 1771
methane, and the ozone layer 1798
methanolysis 1776
microchips *see* integrated circuits
microphones 1745
microscopes, for picture restoration 1743
microsurgery 1765–6
midair recovery system (MARS) 1748
Minamata disease 1801
minerals, at tectonic plate boundaries 1779
minimum torque indication (MTI) system 1789
modacrylics 1771
molding 1774–5
monoamine-oxidase inhibitors (MAOIs) 1868
Montgolfier, Jean 1847
motor neurone disease 1734
motors 1788
mountaineering, clothing *1863*
mouth guards 1862
movie film 1856–7
movie projectors 1854, 1856–7
MTI (minimum torque indication) system 1789
murals 1743
myosin 1865

N

narcotics, poisoning 1791
needles, hypodermic, manufacture 1752
neoprene 1771–2, 1862
Neptune 1757, 1758, 1761
newspapers, production 1849
Newton, Isaac, and light 1853
Nicol prisms 1795
nightshade, deadly *1790*
nitric acid *1783*
nitrocellulose 1768
Nomex 1806, 1860
nose, plastic surgery 1764, *1765*
nuclear fusion *see* fusion, nuclear

nuclear reactors
  boiling water reactors (BWRs) 1832
  nuclear fission 1832
  pressurized-water reactors (PWRs) 1832
nylons *1769*, 1804–5, 1811, *1812*

O

ocean floor
  hydrothermal vents 1780
  spreading 1777
Ohm's law 1826
oil pipelines 1753, *1754*
oil refining, and pollution *1798*
oilskins 1862
operating rooms, polygraphs *1808*
opium 1791
organs, musical, Hammond 1740
Orion nebula 1760
orreries, projection 1756
osmium 1781, 1782
ozone layer, depletion 1798

P

paintings
  oil 1741
  restoration 1741–3
paints, solvents 1823
paleomagnetism 1777
palladium 1781, 1783
pancreas
  artificial 1734
  transplants, cells 1734
pan pots 1822
paper, manufacture 1847
Parafil rope 1806
particle accelerators 1763
pascals 1840
peptide bonds 1864
Perlon U 1772
Perspex 1770
PET (polyethylene terephthalate) 1772
phenylethene (styrene) 1770, 1771, 1772
phosgene (carbonyl chloride) 1772
photoelastic analysis 1796
photoetching process 1845–6
photographic films, movie film 1856–7
photogravure 1852
physiology **1733–4**
Pianolas 1738
pianos **1735–8**
pickup, acoustic **1739–40**
picture restoration **1741–3**
piezoelectric constant 1744
piezoelectric effect 1744
piezoelectric material **1744–5**
  ceramics 1745
  quartz 1744, 1745
  as transducers 1745, 1843
pigs (go devils) 1754
pile drivers **1746**
piles, sheet and bearing 1746
pill, contraceptive 1734, 1818
pilotless aircraft **1747–8**
pipelines **1753–4**
  control systems 1754
  corrosion control and testing 1754
  gas 1754
  oil 1753, *1754*
pipes
  domestic plumbing *1786*
  scale 1787
pipe and tube manufacture 1749–52, 1754
pistons, reciprocating 1789
pituitary gland, cell culture 1733–4
planetarium projectors **1755–6**
planetars 1760

planetary science **1757–61**
planets
  age 1757–8
  chaotic bombardment of 1759
  extrasolar 1759–60
  formation 1758–9
  free-floating 1760
  gaseous (gas giants; outer planets) 1757, 1758, 1760–1
  habitable 1761
  migration 1761
  orbits 1761
  and planetarium projectors 1755–6
  terrestrial (inner planets) 1757, 1759
planetesimals 1758, 1759
plasma physics **1762–3**
  and nuclear fusion, in the Sun 1762
  plasma beat-wave accelerators 1763
  plasma deposition 1763
plastics **1768–72**
  cellulosic 1768–9
  epoxies 1772
  glass-reinforced (GRPs)
    for mannequins *1772*
    for pipes 1750, 1751
  polyalkenes 1770–1
  polycarbonates *1768*, 1772
  processing **1773–6**
  recycling 1776
  synthetic 1769–70
  thermosets 1750
  uses, pipes 1750–1, 1787
plastic surgery **1764–7**
plate tectonics **1777–80**
  and earthquakes 1777, *1780*
platinum 1781
  as a catalyst 1782
platinum diarsenide (sperrylite) 1781
platinum metals **1781–3**
platinum sulfide (cooperite) 1781
Plexiglas 1770
plumbing **1784–7**
Pluto, orbit 1761
plutonium, and nuclear fission 1831
pneumatic tools **1788–9**
  jackhammers *1840*
pneumographs 1807
poisons **1790–2**
polarimeters *1793*, 1796
polarization (light) **1794–6**
  circular 1796
  dichroic polarizers 1794–5
  elliptical 1796
  uses 1796
    polarimetry 1793, 1796
poling 1745
pollution
  acid rain 1798
  atmospheric 1797–8
    emission control 1800–2
  light 1802, *1803*
  monitoring and control **1797–803**
    from automobiles 1802
    natural remedies 1802–3
    using LIDAR 1797
  noise 1802
  water 1798, *1799*, *1802*
polyacrylonitrile (PAN; Acrilan) 1771
polyalkenes (polyolefins) 1770
polyamides 1772, **1804–6**, 1811
  Nomex 1806, 1860
  polyimides 1804, 1806
polycarbonates *1768*, 1772
polychloroethene (polyvinyl chloride; PVC) 1769–70, 1771
  plasticized 1770, 1771
polyesters 1772
  for powder coatings 1823–4

production 1811
recycling 1776
polyethylene (polyethene; polythene) 1770, 1773
formation 1810
low- and high-density 1770–1
uses 1770–1
polyethylene terephthalate (PET) 1772
polygraphs **1807–8**
polyimides 1804, 1806
polyisoprene 1771
polymers and polymerization 1809–12
polymethylmethacrylate 1770
polypeptides 1864–5
polypropylene (polypropene) 1770, 1809
uses *1769*
polystyrene 1770, 1772, *1775*
expanded (Styrofoam) 1776
polytetrafluoroethylene (PTFE; polytetrafluoroethene; Teflon) 1752, 1769, 1771, 1813–15
polythene *see* polyethylene
polyurethanes (PUs) 1772, *1776*
polyvinyl chloride see polychloroethene
polyvinylidene chloride 1744
population **1816–19**
post-traumatic stress disorder (PTSD) 1867
potassium sodium tartrate (Rochelle salt) 1744–5
potential energy **1820**
potentiometers **1821–2**
pots (rheostats) 1821, 1822
pan 1822
powder coatings **1823–4**
power **1825–6**
power plants 1826, **1827–32**, *1834*
alternators 1827, 1829–30
first public 1827, 1833
gas turbines 1832
natural gas-powered 1828
nuclear (nuclear fission) 1827–8, 1831–2
using carbon-based fuels 1830–1
coal 1827, 1831
power supply **1833–8**
pressure **1839–40**
atmospheric 1840
in fluids 1839–40
gases 1840
and force 1839
pressure cookers **1841**
pressure gauges **1842–3**
pressurized-water reactors (PWRs) 1832
printed circuits **1844–6**
printing **1847–52**
collotype 1852
gravure 1850, 1851–2
Crosfield Lasar Gravure 1852
history 1847–50
illustrations 1850–1
letterpress 1849, *1850*, 1851, 1852
newspapers 1849
print identification 1851
reprographic 1852
screen 1852
for circuit boards 1845
prisms **1853**
Nicol 1795
projectors
movie and slide **1854–7**
overhead 1855
planetarium **1755–6**
propellers **1858–9**
aircraft 1858–9
marine-propulsion 1858, 1859
propenamide (acrylamide) 1771

propene (propylene), polymers 1812
propenoic acid (acrylic acid) 1771
proplyds (protoplanetary disks) 1759–60
prostheses 1764, *1767*
protective clothing 1806, **1860–3**
proteins **1864–6**
dietary *1866*
fibrous 1865
functions 1865
globular 1865
structure *1864–5*, 1866
uses 1865–6
protoplanetary disks (proplyds) 1759–60
Prozac (fluoxetine) 1868
psychiatry **1867–8**
psychoanalysis 1867
pulleys **1869**, 1872
pulverised fuel ash (PFA) 1831
pumped-storage schemes *1827*
pumping stations, gas 1754
pumps, peristaltic 1752
PVC *see* polychloroethene
pyramids **1870–2**
pyrolysis 1776

Q
quartz, piezoelectric 1744, 1745

R
rain, acid 1798
rayon 1860
reconnaissance, by remotely piloted vehicles (RPVs) 1747
record players 1739
recycling, plastics 1776
refraction
double 1794
index of 1853
remotely piloted vehicles (RPVs) 1747–8
reservoirs, and pumped-storage schemes 1827
resins
epoxy 1772
natural, for varnishes 1742–3
phenolic 1775
polyester 1823
synthetic 1743
thermosetting 1773, 1775
resistance, electrical, and Ohm's law 1826
resonance, and piezoelectric ultrasound sensors 1745
resonance (planetary orbits) 1761
restoration, picture **1741–3**
rheostats 1822
rhinoplasty *1765*
rhodium 1781, 1782, 1783
ricin 1792
road breakers 1789
Rochelle salt 1744–5
rocks, past magnetism (paleomagnetism) 1777
rotational molding, thermoplastic 1775
RPVs (remotely piloted vehicles) 1747–8
rubber
synthetic 1771–2
ABS 1772
ruthenium 1781, 1782

S
saccharimeters 1793
saran 1771
Saturn 1757, 1758, *1760*, 1761
moons *1760*
schizophrenia 1868
screens, movie and slide projector 1855

seafloor *see* ocean floor
sea levels, varying 1780
seaplanes and amphibians, flying boats 1747
selective serotonin reuptake inhibitors (SSRIs) 1868
sewage treatment *see* wastewater treatment
sex-change operations 1765
shock lung 1791
silicon chips *see* integrated circuits
skin
galvanograph records 1807
grafts 1765, 1766
resurfacing 1767
slides, projection 1854–5
smokeless zones 1802
snakes, venom 1792
somatoform disorder 1867–8
sound mixing 1822
sou'westers 1861–2
space suits 1862
spectrum, of colors 1853
sperrylite (platinum diarsenide) 1781
spheromaks *1762*
sports equipment, clothing 1862–3
SSRIs (selective serotonin reuptake inhibitors) 1868
standard cells 1822
stapling machines 1789
stars
cannibalize their own planets 1761
T-Tauri 1758
steam digesters 1841
steel *see* iron and steel
sterilization (surgical) 1818
stomach pumps 1791
stress (on materials), photoelastic analysis 1796
styrene (phenylethene) 1770, 1771, 1772
Styrofoam 1776
subduction 1778, 1779
substations, electrical 1837
sugar refining, quality-control 1793
sulfur *1794*
Sun 1758
formation 1758
Sundra Trench 1779
switch gear 1837

T
target-augmentation techniques 1748
Teflon *see* polytetrafluoroethylene
telescopes, astronomical, polarimeters attached to 1793
temperature, transition, glass 1809
Tesla, Nikola *1834*
tetraethyl lead 1802
tetrafluoroethene (tetrafluoroethylene) 1813, 1814
tetrodotoxin 1792
Tevatron particle accelerator 1763
thermocouples 1783
thermoforming, vacuum *1773*, 1775
thermolysin *1864*
thermometers, resistance thermometers 1783
thermoplastics
pipes 1750
powder coatings 1823–4
processing of *1773*, 1774–5
thermosets 1775
for pipes 1750
for powder coatings 1824
thermostats, hot-water tank 1785
toads, poisonous 1792
tokamaks 1763
torque, control 1789
torque-controlled motor system 1789
toxicology, forensic 1792
Trans-Alaska pipeline 1753

transducers, piezoelectric materials as 1745, 1843
transformers 1835, *1838*
generator 1830
in power plants 1830
unit 1830
Trans-Mediterranean pipeline 1753
transplants
animal organs (xenotransplants) 1734
liver 1734
skin grafts 1765, 1766
trenches, ocean floor 1778
Tricel 1769
trichloroacetic acid (TCA) 1767
trichloromethane 1769
tricyclic antidepressants 1868
T-Tauri stars 1758
tubes, capillary, manufacture 1752
tungsten, for lightbulbs 1782–3
turbines
steam 1827
see also gas turbines
turbogenerators 1830

U
ultrasonics 1745
unit cells 1744
uranium, used in nuclear reactors 1831
Uranus 1757, 1758, 1761

V
vacuum forming, thermoplastic 1773, 1775
Valium (diazepam) 1791
valves, mechanical, nonreturn (check valves), for taps 1787
varnishes
on paintings 1741, 1742–3
solvents 1823
vasectomy 1818
vents, hydrothermal 1780
Venus (planet) 1757
vinyl acetate 1771
viscose 1769
VOCs (volatile organic compounds, or components) 1823
voice-stress analysis 1808
volcanoes, and plate tectonics 1778
voltage dividers 1821–2

W
wall paintings 1743
wastewater treatment (sewage treatment) 1803
water
on Earth, source 1761
hard 1786–7
softening 1787
watercolors 1743
water hyacinths 1803
water supply 1786–7
waterwheels *1825*
Watt, James 1826
web-offset printing 1850
Wegener, Alfred 1777
Weston standard cell 1822
wind power 1826
work 1825
wrenches, pneumatic *1789*

X
X-43 (aircraft) 1748
xenotransplants 1734

Y
yeast, and protein production *1866*

Z
Ziegler-Natta polymerization catalysts 1770, 1810